en allant prendre le métro ru...
Auber qu'est ce que je vois passer
une camion automobile.... a...
Puis sur le coup de 10 H les
allemands enfin les forces moto
risé allemandes sont entrés dan...
la cour de la préfecture pa...
la porte notre dame.

Quand j'ai quitté ce soi...
la cour était remplie de f...
désarmés et d'Allemands — f...

Leur tenue est vert de gris
il faut reconnaître qu'elle n...
pas mal.

Mais quelle honte pour l...
France que de voir Paris occ...
moi j'en ai pleuré et pour...
tant j'ai jusqu'à présent
été aussi courageuse que poss...
mais he... ... j'ai
flanché. ... 5

# ANDRÉE'S WAR

# ANDRÉE'S WAR

How One Young Woman
Outwitted the Nazis

FRANCELLE BRADFORD WHITE

First published 2014 by
Elliott and Thompson Limited
27 John Street
London WC1N 2BX
www.eandtbooks.com

ISBN: 978-1-78396-024-8

*Picture credits:*
Endpapers: Pages taken from one of the diaries of Andrée Griotteray, June 1940. Images in plate section reproduced courtesy of: page 4 (top) Jean Pierre Jobelot; page 4 (inset) Yves de Kermoal; page 4 (bottom) originally reproduced in Alain Gandy, *La jeunesse et la Résistance: réseau Orion, 1940–1944* (Presses de la Cité, 1992); all other images from the author's personal collection.

9 8 7 6 5 4 3 2 1

A catalogue record for this book is available from the British Library.

Typesetting: Marie Doherty
Printed in the UK by TJ International Ltd

*For Andrée*

## A NOTE ON THE TEXT

The majority of the material in this book is drawn from a variety of sources, including Andrée's diaries and notebooks, a recorded interview from 1996, written sources such as memoirs and a history of the Orion Group, and other published works. Some is based on conversations the author had with her mother, Andrée Griotteray, and with other members of Orion, including her uncle, Alain Griotteray. Occasionally, to fill an unavoidable gap in the narrative, the author has had to rely on supposition, supported by the evidence gleaned elsewhere.

# *Contents*

# Introduction

When my mother, Andrée, began to show the initial signs of the disease generally known as Alzheimer's, I was not sure how to cope with my emotions. At some stage in the past I had been told that when you are upset it can help to express your feelings on paper, so I decided to write about her. Andrée has done many interesting, wonderful things throughout her lifetime but it was what she did during the Second World War that had always caught my imagination.

In 1945 Andrée was given the Médaille de la Résistance. She was also awarded the Croix de guerre, with a citation personally made out in the name of 'le Général' (Head of the Provisional French Government) – an honour not given to all recipients. How could a woman who had shown such courage, intuition and energy (and who remained, into her seventies, so attractive, beautifully dressed and resourceful) fall prey to such a devastating and cruel disease? When she first became ill she was still at the helm of a family business with headquarters in London and subsidiaries in Paris and New York.

As my brother and I fought to cope with her prognosis, I filed my writing away and moved on to deal with the consequences of an illness we still know so little about.

In 2008, Andrée's brother and my uncle, Alain Griotteray, died aged eighty-five. In 2001 Alain had been made a Grand Officier de la Légion d'honneur by the then president, Jacques Chirac – an award held only by a limited number of Frenchmen and women at any one time. The address at his funeral, which was attended by several members of the French government, described Alain's contribution to French politics during the twentieth century before focusing on his role, at eighteen years of age, as one of the youngest leaders of a French Resistance group. As we returned to London after the funeral, I thought to myself that their story deserved a wider audience. Much has been written in French about Alain and Andrée and their Resistance colleagues, but I knew only too well that most of Andrée's six grandchildren and their descendants were unlikely to read anything about their grandmother unless it was in English. Besides, Andrée herself loved Britain and the English language from a young age, as did her mother before her: the strong links that Yvonne established in England are still evident one hundred years later. Andrée ultimately married an Englishman and raised her own family in England (always speaking English with them); it was right that her adoptive country should know a little more about her. Nine months later, I returned to Paris to begin to research the story you are about to read.

But where to start? I am not a writer nor a historian, let alone an academic. I began by walking the streets of Paris, following in Andrée's footsteps when she lived and worked there during the war. I took the *métro*, the bus and cycled, as Andrée did to her job at the Préfecture de Police (Police Headquarters), where she worked under the supervision of members of the Wehrmacht. I visited the police archives and discovered *Les policiers français sous l'Occupation*, a book by Professor Jean-Marc Berlière, who was, I believe, the first person to write in detail about the involvement of the Parisian police in the pogrom of approximately 13,000 Jews on 16/17 July 1942, and about which I knew very little. Jean-Marc had worked obstinately for several years to force the police and the Ministry of the Interior to open their archives. I visited the Musée Jean Moulin, the Musée des Invalides and the Jewish Museum; with my son I searched the archives of the Ministry of Defence at the Château de Vincennes to find the files held on the Orion Resistance Group, as Alain named his Resistance network. My story – their story – was beginning to take shape. I wrote down everything I could remember my mother telling me about what she did during the war. I spoke to relatives, including my uncle, Bernard Leclair. I had a long interview with François Clerc, deputy leader of the Orion Group and one of Alain's closest friends (and who had known me since I was a baby), and I continued to walk, passing the landmarks Andrée would have passed – the

Hôtel Meurice (headquarters of the military during the war); the Palais du Luxembourg, where the Luftwaffe were based; the Champs-Élysées, down which the Wehrmacht marched every day for four years. These landmarks were all within a few minutes' walk from where Andrée and her entire family had lived. I thought about what had happened on the streets of Paris during those dark years and then, to cheer myself up, I imagined the city on the day of its liberation, which Andrée had so often described and about which I was also able to talk with my eighty-seven-year-old friend, Jeanine Louveau.

My brother was vaguely aware of what I was doing and, on my return, he said, 'You had better have these.' In a paper bag were ten journals written by Andrée between 1934 and 1947. In them Andrée had described her thoughts about the invasion and the occupation of Paris, along with a record of daily life, her work at Police Headquarters, her friends and boyfriends. There were also several little black notebooks containing notes of appointments, reservations, train times and destinations; these were a vital source of information about Andrée's travels around France on behalf of the Resistance, especially after the Normandy landings in June 1944 when she seemed to be constantly on the move. Despite the brevity of the information, it was surprising to find she had put so much on record, given the dangers implicit in doing so.

Much of the information in the diaries, by contrast, was written in code – nothing that a professional code breaker could not have translated, but indicative that Andrée was conscious of the need for caution. As the diaries went on, and especially after the landings, the entries became increasingly emotionally charged and harder to follow, with dates jumping around and entries appearing out of order. Some pages had been torn out. Andrée was working extremely hard at this time, travelling frequently on a rail network that was being bombed regularly. She was under pressure to get the material she carried safely to its destination before travelling back to work in Paris, but the trains were hugely unreliable, not to mention dangerous.

Despite being bilingual, translating her diaries and notebooks has not been easy. Andrée spoke very good English but she always wrote in French, and I have found that often she would describe or talk about something in a way in which a native English speaker would never have done, which has been a challenge. I wanted to capture her voice, including the phrases and idioms I remember her using. My brother also gave me the letters our father wrote to Andrée between 1945 and 1947, and while I am confident these were kept for us to see, I have tried to ensure that the more personal entries will be kept within our family.

On my next research trip to France I flew to Biarritz, hired a car and drove to Orion, where I stayed at the Château d'Orion, which had been the headquarters of the Orion Group. I was warmly welcomed by the château's present owner, Frau Elke Jeanrond-Premauer from Munich, and I met Marguerite Labbé, widow of Jean Labbé and daughter-in-law of Madame Labbé, the châtelaine during the war years. She told me many stories about what happened during the 1940s and I also spent some time with the mayor of the tiny hamlet, who had helped to arrange a large memorial service and commemoration for the members of the Orion Group in September 1985. More than 1,000 people attended, including Jacques Chaban-Delmas, a former prime minister of France, and Jacques Soustelle, head of the French intelligence services in Algeria during part of the Second World War, plus several leading members of the French Resistance movement. All were there to pay tribute to the importance of the château to the Orion Group and France's wider Resistance story.

I learnt about the 'routes d'évasion', the escape routes through the Pyrenees for Frenchmen wanting to fight against the Nazis, and about the inhumane holding camps on both the French and Spanish sides of the mountains. On one side the French held Spaniards escaping Franco's Spain, while on the other the Spaniards held Frenchmen escaping Hitler's occupation. It was a beautiful place, despite the horrors of the past, and as I soaked up the stunning Basque countryside I thought about what it must have been like, back then.

To help fill the many gaps in my growing knowledge of the period, I turned to Alain Gandy's book, *La jeunesse et la Résistance: réseau Orion, 1940–1944*, published in 1992 and written with the help of several Orion members. It has been my 'bible'; without it I would not have been able to piece the whole story together and I am very grateful to the author. Similarly, two of Alain Griotteray's books, *Mémoires* and *Qui étaient les premiers résistants?*, gave me a huge amount of information about the period.

Further gaps were filled by Yves de Kermoal, an Orion member who, along with his wife Patricia, invited my husband and me to stay with them at the Domaine de Rateau, from where we visited the station in Bordeaux where Andrée had been arrested.

To the best of my knowledge and my ability, everything in this book is based on fact, although when dealing with wartime intelligence one can never be entirely certain of everything, nor always understand the way in which something has been recorded. The events described took place over seventy years ago (and several of the key accounts I've relied on were only recorded many years after the fact); they have been described in different ways by different authors, sometimes with different dates recorded. In a book recently published by the Service Historique de la Défense, *Les réseaux de résistance de la France combattante* (The Resistance Groups of the Free French), Andrée is described in the Ministry of Defence records as having been a P2 agent; an agent working solely for the Free French and in no paid employment between 1942 and 1944. Her title was recorded as Chef de Liaison (chief liaison officer). Yet she was clearly also working at Police Headquarters from October 1940 until December 1944, according to both their official records and her diaries. Why the discrepancy? There may not be an explanation for everything.

At times I have had to step away from a factual account to fill in gaps in my narrative. I have based all such accounts on conversations with my mother over the years. She told me about the time she stayed in a brothel following a trip I made to Mexico when I was twenty-two years old, and returned home shocked by the conditions of the accommodation I stayed in. On my twenty-fourth birthday she gave me a Swiss gold coin; at the time charm bracelets were in fashion and it was common to add coins to one's bracelet. This led to the story of how she came to be responsible for smuggling a number of gold coins into Paris to fund Resistance work. And then there was the day she took a German general out to lunch. I remember her telling me about it in her kitchen in London. I was in my late twenties, we were discussing a war film and I casually said it must have been impossible to bribe German soldiers. She contradicted me.

Many people who lived through the difficult years of the Second World War had no wish to talk about it afterwards. This was not the case for my mother. She often talked about their exploits, always modestly dismissing her own achievements (she told me more than once 'I was only a postman!') but emphasising her delight at any humiliation bestowed upon the Wehrmacht. Both Andrée and her mother, Yvonne (my grandmother), often spoke of the difficulties of living under the occupation: Andrée described the bombing that Paris suffered in her diary and described herself and her fellow citizens as 'prisonniers civils', though she was always insistent that it was nothing compared to what the British had to endure, especially in London and Coventry.

Yet some wounds remained raw many years after: I have no memory of either my mother or grandmother ever referring to Pétain or Vichy, or talking about what happened to the thirteen thousand Jews during the shocking Vel' d'Hiv pogrom of 1942. Andrée did, however, speak about a Jewish girl who stayed with them, described later in this book. Were there others? There is little specific in writing, though instinct tells me Yvonne was involved in helping other Jewish emigrés. Several notes in one of Andrée's black diaries show that she met up over a dozen times in 1941 with a Jewish woman who was not a known friend. And as my uncle, Bernard Leclair, pertinently said: 'Surely you don't think they recorded everything they were doing back then?'

Much of what the Orion Group did, for security reasons, went unrecorded, although official Ministry of Defence records in Vincennes show that thirty-one separate pieces of intelligence were passed on to British Intelligence by members of the group between April 1941 and October 1942. After the group began to supply the US Office of Strategic Services (OSS) with intelligence, there is no record of the number of pieces of intelligence passed on, so there is no way to be sure of how much they did ultimately, but what is certain is that, through her work as a courier, Andrée was responsible for a significant amount of documentation reaching the British and American intelligence services.

Inevitably, in an account like this there will be omissions and differing viewpoints and interpretations of history. To the best of my ability I have tried to produce an accurate record of 'Andrée's war', but I apologise in advance for any errors. I am particularly conscious that I may have made mistakes in the physical description of some members of the Orion Group; some I met only as a child and so have had to rely on those memories, while others I met when they were in their sixties or seventies and therefore trying to describe them as they would have been in the 1940s was not always easy.

# 1

# *An Acknowledgement*

It is 8 May 1995. Fifty years have passed since the end of the Second World War. Andrée White stands in the main square of Charenton-le-Pont in Paris by the memorial to the dead of the First and Second World Wars, the town church in the background. The 'Marseillaise' is playing. Some of the 'Anciens Combattants' are bearing the French flag, the Tricolore. The flags are slowly lifted. The music stops. Alain Griotteray, Mayor and Member of Parliament (and, coincidentally, Andrée's brother), moves forward. From a velvet cushion he slowly lifts the medal of the Légion d'honneur, the highest award given by the French Republic.

> 'In the name of the President of France, François Mitterrand, I award
> you the Légion d'honneur *a titre de résistants particulièrement valeureux*
> [for your exceptionally brave actions during the Second World War].'

He pins the medal onto Andrée White's jacket, smiles and kisses her on both cheeks. Her daughter and son are there to witness the event, along with three of her grandchildren and her son-in-law. The square is full of people watching this special and unusual event; many of whom have known Andrée for many years. It is not the first such award she has received, however.

Ten soldiers salute the new Légionnaire. Andrée stands to attention. She wears a midnight-blue wool suit with gold buttons that shine in the sunlight. Her blond hair is cut short. On her suit the ribbons of her other medals have already been sewn onto her jacket, as is the custom in Europe. Her new medal sits on the blue background. Shaped like a five-sided double-pointed star, it is made of white enamel. It is encircled by a green wreath of oak and laurel leaves and surmounted by a smaller similar wreath. The head of Marianne, the symbolic figure of the Republic, appears on the front of the medal, the tri-coloured flags on the back. The inscription on the front reads: 'République Française' (French Republic) and on the back: 'Honneur et Patrie' (Honour and Motherland). The Légion d'honneur was created in 1802 by Napoleon Bonaparte. It is the highest award given by the French Republic for outstanding service to France and is given regardless of the social status or the nationality of the recipient.

The 'Marseillaise' is played again. The band stops. Andrée and her family leave the square. The soldiers and war veterans march away. The crowd disperses. That night there will be fireworks in Charenton-le-Pont. France is celebrating fifty years since the end of the war. She is also celebrating the victory of a new Gaullist president, Jacques Chirac. It is a warm evening and the streets of Paris are alive with people. The Champs-Élysées had been brought to a standstill that afternoon. Just before the fireworks begin, a special speech is to be made before a crowd of more than a thousand people.

In that speech, Alain Griotteray will recall the dark days of the war and the suffering endured by millions. He will describe the Resistance group he established, and the dangers he and his colleagues faced during the four years of German occupation – four years in which so many Frenchmen and women were deported to Nazi concentration camps in Germany and Poland, never to return. He will recall a time when citizens were often starving; when German soldiers patrolled the streets of Paris; when French signs were replaced by their German equivalents; and when the French flag had to be hidden away.

Above all, he will talk about the contribution his sister made to France's ultimate liberation – a contribution so great that he will say it is 'impossible to measure its true value'. He will pay tribute to her bravery at a very young age, to her unassuming modesty and energy, and to the inner strength that enabled her to risk her life repeatedly in service to the Resistance. He will praise her as 'a true patriot, French through and through', and one who expected no reward or recognition for her actions. He will end his tribute with the following words:

Today, as we celebrate the fiftieth anniversary since the end of that war, I think back to the enormous risks I asked my sister to take on behalf of me and our group, risks which could so easily have led to her death many times at the hands of the Gestapo and the Nazis.

## 2

# The Making of a Resistance Fighter

What made Andrée and her brother Alain into the kind of youngsters they were? What was it that encouraged them to join the French Resistance and risk their lives? How did their involvement with British Intelligence, the Office of Strategic Services and the French intelligence network come about?

The question of what makes us who we are is endlessly fascinating. Is it your genetic make-up that determines your personality? Do the lives and characteristics of our parents, grandparents and ancestors mould us into the people we are? Can language skills and exposure to other cultures and ways of living shape our destiny? Does personal grief or pain alter the way that we choose to live our lives?

Descending from a line of proud and patriotic French and Belgian families, both the Griotterays and the Stocquarts were renowned for their fierce independence, presence of mind, confidence, eccentricity and initiative. At the outbreak of the Second World War, Andrée and Alain would not be slow to display these characteristics.

Edmond Griotteray, Andrée and Alain's father, was a small, plumpish, energetic man with an authoritarian yet fun-loving nature, fiercely loyal to his country. His father raised him that way: a few years before his birth, Alsace-Lorraine had been annexed by Germany in 1871 following France's defeat in the Franco-Prussian war. It was a bitter blow for Edmond's family and their fellow patriots. Neither he nor his father were ever to acknowledge Alsace's changed legal status, and there was much rejoicing when the area was joined once more to France under the 1918 Treaty of Versailles (though the Second World War would bring further upheaval when Alsace again fell under the rule of the Germans after France was defeated in 1940).

Edmond traced his Savoie ancestors back to Jean Baptiste Griotteray, whose French naturalisation papers had been signed by Louis XV, 'Roi de France et de Navarre' and by the French regent, le Duc d'Orléans, in 1716. Jean Baptiste was recorded as having been a merchant of Catholic faith, living in Montvalezan in 1680 with his parents, Jean Antoine and Pantaléonne Brun. During the seventeenth and eighteenth centuries the Griotterays prospered, serving as lawyers, judges, mayors and merchants in the small alpine community. In 1832 Edmond's father, Thelcide Constantin, moved to Paris, looking for a more interesting lifestyle. In 1848 Thelcide is recorded as working as a chemical engineering merchant in Paris, then a highly unusual professional occupation. It was around this time that he fell in love with Rosalie Weiler, the Swiss-born daughter of a Geneva banker whose beauty and energetic, enterprising personality endeared her to everyone she met. Thelcide and Rosalie went on to marry and have three children. The eldest, Julie, worked alongside her brother in his chemical engineering company (most unusual for a married woman). Her husband Paul was a cousin of Fernand Labori,* the lawyer who defended Émile Zola in the infamous 'J'accuse' trial of 1898.† Edmond and Julie had regularly attended private soirées and dinners in Paris in the presence of Zola, at which the Dreyfus affair was discussed, and the Griotteray children often heard their parents talk about the case with anger, many years after the event.

Thelcide's and Rosalie's oldest son, Marcel, served in the First World War and was killed at Verdun in 1916. Like so many others, the family

---

* According to Griotteray family documents, including Andrée's birth certificate, Labori was always spelled with an 'e' at the end, though this does not correspond with what has been written about the Dreyfus affair.
† On 13 January 1898, Zola published an article in the newspaper *L'Aurore*, accusing the French government of anti-Semitism in their campaign against Dreyfus, a Jewish army officer who was infamously accused and convicted of treason, stripped of his rank and service medals and sent to Devil's Island to serve out his sentence. Zola, meanwhile, was prosecuted for criminal libel. The Dreyfus Affair ultimately resulted in the resignation of the Home Secretary (the Minister of the Interior) and almost brought down the French government.

mourned his death deeply, searching to make sense of the futility of the events unfolding around them.

Edmond, their second son, who had been born several years after the Franco–Prussian War, in 1874, had chosen to study architectural interior design at the École Boulles in Paris, where – according to his son Alain – he met Auguste Rodin. Rodin's generosity towards his students and friends was legendary and he once gave Edmond a marble bust, which has been passed down to subsequent generations.*

Graduating from the École Boulles, Edmond soon started up an archi-tectural interior decorating business on the rue Auber near the Place de l'Opéra, opening an antique shop to help his clients furnish their houses. At some point during the autumn of 1919 he was introduced to a fair-haired and blue-eyed young woman by the name of Yvonne Stocquart, who at twenty-seven was nineteen years his junior. The couple were married within six weeks of meeting.

Yvonne Stocquart was a confident, attractive young woman who was descended from an established family of Belgian lawyers. In the mid eight-eenth century her great-grandparents lived in a house on La Grande Place in the centre of Grammont (Geraardsbergen) in central Flanders, whose town square is a mini replica of the Grande Place in Brussels. During the seventeenth and eighteenth centuries the area known today as Belgium came under Spanish rule and it was from here in 1835 that Yvonne's grandfather, Charles Josephus Stocquart, left Grammont for Ixelles in Brussels, where he joined his uncle's law firm and helped draw up Belgium's new constitution. Yvonne often referred with grandeur to 'les oncles' and their family home in Grammont stands to this day, having benefited from huge government investment due to its architectural heritage.

Yvonne's father, Arthur, a sophisticated, aristocratic-looking and impeccably dressed man, who at 1.9 m tall towered over his friends, had been appointed Professor of Law at Louvain University when he was just

---

* I still remember to this day the warm smile on the model's face looking down at me when I stayed at my grandparents' flat near the Quai d'Orsay as a small child. The colour and texture of the marble stood out against the dark decor, and seemed almost to glow at night.

twenty-eight. His opinionated and unconventional behaviour led to many deep arguments with the university authorities, which did not help his career.

Arthur and his wife Marie Françoise had decided their children should be brought up by a young Scottish governess, Mary Murphy, whose duties were to open her young charges' minds to the British way of life and teach them to speak English. Madame Stocquart was renowned in the vicinity for reprimanding young German soldiers when their behaviour was not up to the standard she expected, threatening to report them to their commanding officer. Marie Françoise's heavy build and stern, unsmiling face belied her inner warmth and kindness, reserved for her family and friends, but it was her commanding personality that would help her daughters develop their self-reliance during the First World War. Yvonne and Léa's brother, Émile, had been shot as a spy by a German firing squad in 1916 and the sisters (then aged twenty-two and twenty-four) were desperate to do anything they could to fight the occupying forces.

Courage, sangfroid and confidence were passed on from grandmother to mother to daughter, and on 29 August 1920 Yvonne gave birth to Andrée, in Ville d'Avray near Versailles. Present at her birth was Mary Murphy, her mother's Scottish governess and a British citizen.

Andrée enjoyed a happy and carefree childhood; at two years old she was introduced to her brother, Alain, and five years later to her sister, Yvette, followed shortly after by another sister, Claude.

In 1930, in search of the sun, the Griotterays left Paris for the south of France. In Cannes, Edmond launched a new antique shop and an interior decorating business, along with a company specialising in the production of Provençal furniture. A year later the family moved to Nice and bought a house on the seafront on the Promenade des Anglais – to this day one of a few private houses still standing among the high-rise hotels and apartment blocks. In the 1930s, when the Côte d'Azur was still an exclusive destination, there was no road between the Griotterays' house and the beach and Andrée often described how her father 'encouraged' her and her brother to walk straight out of their house onto the beach at 6.30 a.m. every day between May and October to swim in the sea.

At eleven, Andrée was registered as a pupil at the Lycée de Nice pour Filles where, over the next three years, she was to study German, among other subjects, English not being available on the curriculum. So important was the study and knowledge of German in her parents' eyes that extra private lessons were conducted after school and in the school holidays. After the invasion of France in 1939, Andrée never acknowledged knowing the language and it was only when reading her childhood diaries that I became aware of my mother's command of the language.

For the Griotteray children, life in the south of France centred around family. When the heavy, dry heat of summer arrived, they would move up to the Belgian coast for the summer months, stopping in Paris on the way, where Edmond conducted intense architectural and history of art lessons. The influence of their Belgian grandparents was very strong and through them the children gained an in-depth knowledge of Brussels and the Belgian coastline.

It was around this time that Andrée started to write a diary, which she kept right through the 1930s and 40s.

In 1936 the Griotteray family moved back to Paris and then, three weeks after her sixteenth birthday, Andrée left for England, where she stayed for over a year to learn English, living in Bournemouth with friends her mother had made on her visits to England during the First World War. As a young sixteen-year-old, nothing could have prepared her for how different English country living was from what she had been used to in the south of France, Paris and Belgium, but she soon amassed a group of English friends who invited her to stay with their families around the country. As her language skills developed, her confidence and independence grew and she found herself working in a pre-preparatory school as a French assistant, shocked by how the British could send their children away at such a young age.

Before her departure for England, Edmond and Yvonne gave Andrée a special handmade suitcase as a birthday gift. The case was made of soft brown kid leather with thick, dark stitching on every side. A thick leather handle was attached by a pair of tiny silver plates screwed into the leather. At the centre of the plates a silver lock had been carefully fixed. It had a thick silk lining, made from silk which had belonged to her Swiss grand-mother. That lining was to prove invaluable.

While Andrée spent a year in England, gradually falling in love with the country, her fourteen-year-old brother Alain had been sent to Germany for three months during his school holidays to perfect his German. His Hitler Youth host greeted him by saying, 'Have no doubt about this. In time we will invade and conquer France.'

In 1938, with the hostilities between England, France and Germany gathering pace, Edmond and Yvonne decided their daughter should return home. Not quite eighteen years old and back in Paris, Andrée began her career as a sales assistant in a small antique shop. In the evenings she attended a secretarial course. Shortly before Germany's invasion of Czechoslovakia, her Belgian uncle and aunt, Auguste and Léa, invited their niece on a two-week touring holiday of Germany. Andrée's diaries include extensive descriptions of the country and its people, and an awareness of the Nazi Party's dominance over the German population. The experience left a lasting impression on Andrée and her cousin.

Reggie Harland (one of Andrée's English friends, later to become Air Marshal Sir Reginald Harland KBE, CB) visited Andrée in Paris with his aunt, Toddy. Just as Reggie and his family had introduced Andrée to hunt balls, meets, the English countryside and cocktail parties, Andrée showed Reggie the sights of Paris – elegant living, beautiful clothes and good food. Reggie's visit would be her last contact with any of her English friends for the next five years. She was to be cut off from an important and influential part of her youth and in her diary she later describes with sadness both her English and French friends being called up to go to war.

The Griotteray children retained close lifelong ties to Belgium, the land of their grandparents, as well as their native France. But Andrée's travels as a teenager had sparked a deep love of another country: Britain.

## 3
# *War!*

As tensions in the run-up to the Second World War began to heighten, day-to-day living in Paris continued relatively unchanged for families such as the Griotterays, living in the centre of the city, but heated political debates and chatter in the cafés, in the bars and on the streets of the capital were ever present among a population keen to discuss French rearmament, the strength of the military, the Nazi persecution of the Jews and the 'Anschluss' (occupation) of Austria.

On 14 January 1939, Andrée describes in her diary attending *le bal du cercle militaire*:

> *Papa invited me to join him at the officers' ball at the Colisée. The President, Monsieur Lebrun, attended as did Monsieur Campinchi, the Naval Minister. The Bigards joined us and some excellent champagne and canapés were served. I wore a pale-blue silk dress which Maman had just had made for me.*

In September 1938, Andrée was back in Paris and working in an antiques shop close to her home in the rue Godot de Mauray near the Place de l'Opéra. The owners, friends of her parents, had an interesting collection of antique French furniture which was exhibited in their ground-floor gallery and Andrée was responsible for helping to run the shop and deal with clients showing an interest in the collection.

As an attractive, outgoing eighteen-year-old, Andrée soon developed a circle of friends with whom she could easily meet up and have fun. Her brother Alain, despite being two years younger, had always been a soulmate and their group also included Margit Ehrart and Jean Barbier, whom they had met in a café on the boulevard des Capucines. Serge Bigard, the Jewish son of two of Andrée and Alain's parents' closest friends, was another. Engaging and fun-loving, Serge was as generous as anyone could be and, to everyone's amusement, every year on his birthday he gave his mother an enormous bouquet of flowers to thank her for giving birth to him. His easy-going personality and great charm led him to forge close friendships with all those he met, but in 1942, after escaping the Nazi persecution in Paris, he moved into the Free Zone and no one heard from him or his parents again.

Andrée's glamorous half-sister, Renée, had a huge influence on her early life. She was Edmond's illegitimate daughter from a previous relationship, and was fifteen years older than Andrée. Edmond had recognised her as his child and she regularly visited the Griotteray family. As a leading actress on the French stage, she was greeted enthusiastically wherever she went and chaperoned her younger half-sister through the artistic society of Paris, inviting her for tea, cocktails and dinner at the capital's leading hotels, res-taurants and bars. Her husband Steve Passeur (whose real name was Étienne Morin; Steve Passeur was his professional name) was one of France's leading playwrights, and through the couple Andrée and her family attended many of the major plays of the period, often meeting the authors, producers and playwrights as well.

### 15 January 1939

*Steve and Renée invited us to l'Opéra Comique. Fanny Heldy was playing Louise. She was 'très chic'.*

Renée was then one of the most stunningly attractive and beautifully dressed women in Paris, renowned for her vivacious personality. In 2012, seventy years after last meeting Renée, one of Andrée's friends still remembered her as 'quite stunning, so beautifully dressed, so immaculate in every way'.

In 1939, Steve Passeur's most successful play, *Je vivrai un grand amour*, was staged in Paris for the first time. Renée played the lead role and per-formances were selling out each night. It was during the preparations for the staging of this play that Alain, then nearly seventeen, became friendly with François Clerc, a young man from the Bordeaux region of France, who at nineteen already held a pilot's licence and had started a small removal business moving theatre props around the capital. He moved with such speed that one moment he was there and seconds later he had disappeared from sight. His political views dovetailed with Alain's and the boys became close friends. Later he was recruited into the Resistance and would take over the leadership of the group when Alain escaped France and headed for Morocco in 1943.*

Andrée was looking for a challenging, well-paid job and on 19 May 1939 recorded in her diary:

*Today I am having lunch with Renée. She might be able to help find me an interesting job.*

On 20 May she noted her conversation with Renée:

*Renée came around to tea this afternoon and told me that she had arranged for us to meet a close friend of hers, Roger Langeron, who is the Head of Police at Police Headquarters in Paris. She told me we were to meet him tomorrow and that I was to make sure I looked attractive and that I was elegantly dressed. She said that Langeron wanted to meet me and described him as a thoroughly decent, straightforward chap who has an aristocratic manner about him, thoroughly charming and not too old! I wonder?!*

On the day of the interview, Renée invited her younger sister to lunch Stepping from the Place Vendôme into The Ritz, Andrée felt buoyed up with confidence as she and Renée made their way into one of the most elegant dining rooms in Paris. Renée complimented Andrée on what she was wearing and the way she had done her hair, although she could not resist having a dig at the British sense of dress by saying: 'I was seriously worried you might have lost your dress sense while you were living in England, but no,

---

* François was later awarded the Légion d'honneur and at ninety years of age was still piloting his own plane. Having met him again at that age, I confess he remains one of the most attractive Frenchmen I have ever encountered.

you are as elegant as you ever were and being eighteen months older you have developed a quiet yet sophisticated air which will be noticed by all those you meet.'

They enjoyed an excellent lunch, during which Renée continued to build up her sister's confidence with a stream of compliments, before leaving The Ritz to make their way to Police Headquarters, an imposing grey building lying alongside the Seine on the Left Bank, near Notre Dame. As they approached the building, Andrée found it difficult to dismiss her thoughts about the procedures and events which took place within the confines of the building, a venue which over the years had housed some of the most notorious criminals in France. It was an austere, soulless government building with long, endless corridors, police cells and police interview rooms, and crowded with large numbers of uniformed police officers with loaded guns attached to their hips.

They smiled at the duty officer by the gate, who immediately recognised Renée, and minutes later the two young women were sitting in the office of one of the most powerful men in Paris.

Préfet Langeron was a tall, imposing man in his forties with the forceful personality that often accompanies great power and authority. As Renée knew, he was looking for people he could trust. He spoke kindly to Andrée: 'I understand from Renée you are interested in working at Police Headquarters. We need someone to help out in the Passport and ID Department and I like to take on people I know personally. I will follow your career carefully and do anything I can to help its progress. I hope you will decide to come and join us.'

Andrée, whose initial shyness and quiet behaviour had now disappeared, eagerly and graciously accepted her new appointment.* As the two women left the building, walking through the flower market and making their way home, Renée told Andrée how pleased she was with the outcome of the meeting. She knew that Langeron would like her younger sister, and she felt confident that Andrée would prove herself to be a loyal member of staff.

---

* Although she did not know it then, as one of the first women to be employed at Police Headquarters, Andrée was something of a pioneer.

But she also wanted Andrée to be fully aware of what she was doing, and warned her that Langeron was not universally popular. 'As you may know, he is renowned for searching and rounding up many active members of the Communist Party and his zeal for this has earned him many political enemies.'

Andrée, though, was not to be dissuaded. Her diary entry for 20 May 1939 says simply:

*I had a meeting with Roger Langeron, the head of the Paris police force and he has offered me a job.*

In the six months following her return to Paris, Andrée enjoyed herself enormously, living and working in one of Europe's most exciting cities. She regularly went to the cinema and her diary records her enjoyment at seeing films starring Moira Shearer and Clark Gable. Family outings to some of the best restaurants in town were the norm, as were regular trips to the theatre. For her nineteenth birthday she was given a bicycle and, with her first boyfriend, Raymond, and a circle of friends, she began cycling along the banks of the Seine and spending weekends camping outside Paris.

These carefree days were, of course, to come abruptly to an end. Following the invasion of Poland, a dark cloud fell over the world; the United Kingdom declared war on Germany on 3 September 1939, followed within the hour by France. That day Andrée wrote simply:

*That's it – war has been declared.*

It was the beginning of a great change; the scene was being set for how they would live over the next four years. Balls, staying out late, good food, travelling freely around Europe – all the things Andrée enjoyed – were no longer an option and as curfew, travel restrictions and food shortages came into force, life would become seriously difficult. Shopping, a choice of reasonably elegant clothes, a choice of books, non-censored press, attending university, things which today are taken for granted and which should have been theirs, were no longer possible.

At nineteen and seventeen respectively, Andrée and Alain had to grow up fast. On 15 September 1939, Andrée wrote:

*Dear little diary,*

*I think that during the difficult times in which we are living you will be so much a part of my life. I am nineteen and I want to have fun but we are at war! Yes, once again several countries who should be at peace have declared war on each other. The Germans, under their Führer Adolf Hitler, invaded Poland on Friday, 1st September. They did not declare war on Poland, they simply marched in. Traitors is the only way of describing them. Since the fighting started in Poland, they have invaded half of the country and are committing the most awful crimes, relentlessly bombing so many of the Polish cities.*

*As for the French, we are now fighting the Germans in the Sarre between the Maginot and the Siegfried Lines.*

*The other day Maman saw a train full of wounded soldiers at La Gare St Lazare. It is so awful I can hardly take it all in. Every man up to the age of fifty-two has been called up, but there is no option: we must fight on. Hitler has to be stopped.*

*We have to think of victory and shout 'Vive la France'.*

### Sunday, 8 October 1939

*I am alone at home in Paris. Tomorrow I start a new job at Police Headquarters, reporting directly to Monsieur Langeron, the head of the Parisian police force.*

### 11 October 1939

*Dear Diary, you have actually made your way into Police Headquarters! I have been assigned to the Tourist Office, 'the Foreigners' Office'. 'Affectée au bureau des touristes service des étrangers.' It is a small office separate from the main stream of Police Headquarters. Our job is to check the passports and documents of any foreigner who wants to stay in France for more than three months. It is an interesting job because one meets a lot of people, but you have to be very careful about the small details in the documents and we have to work very quickly.*

As Andrée walked through the gates of Police Headquarters for the first time in October 1939, she felt excited and nervous. She had, of course, no idea that the building would come under the control of the Wehrmacht following the Nazis' entry into Paris, nor the extent to which the French police would collaborate with the German army of occupation.

As her work in the 'Touriste' department began to unfold, Andrée took stock of her work colleagues, later describing them in some detail:

*Firstly there is our department head, M. Kervella, a wounded veteran of the Great War who comes from Brittany and who with his very fair complexion looks like a Viking, then there is Madame Chantebout, a very charming woman who keeps me in touch with all the gossip. She is fair, rather overweight and in her forties. She has been very helpful and kind to me. Monsieur Plagnard is about my age. He is rather dull, badly dressed and his mouse-coloured hair is always untidy. Finally there is our orderly, Monsieur Perny, who is so helpful and efficient.*

### 26 October 1939

*We have a lot of work in the office at the moment because all the foreigners living in France who have not registered their presence are coming to have their documents updated.*

### 3 January 1940

*I witnessed and recorded the details of fourteen people who came to have their ID cards updated.*

*Maman had been sent a Christmas pudding by her friends in Bournemouth, so we put some brandy on it and lit it up with a match as they do in England, and had it for dinner.*

## 23 January 1940

*We are living through such sad times and I am not having any fun. War is such a disgusting state of affairs. Because there are different nations who are unable to sort out their differences, we youngsters have to suffer the consequences. It sickens me.*

*We had dinner last night at Le Cabaret and then went to see* Mr Smith Goes to Washington. *It was the best film I have ever seen.*

*Everyone is depressed.*

## 5 February 1940

*On Saturday night I went to the one hundredth performance of* Je vivrai un grand amour.

*After the show I was invited to attend the reception. Steve arrived around nine o'clock, looking so smart in his beautifully cut suit and, with his sophisticated, cool, rather distant manner, reminds me so much of some of my English friends. Renée was wearing black from top to toe and had the most gorgeous long and very full dress. She looked amazing. Monsieur Langeron attended the performance and shook me by the hand; I offered him a glass of champagne.*

*Harry Baun, André Luguet, Lucienne Bogart, Alice Locca and many other celebrities joined our party.*

*We talked to the Bernsteins, the Rubinsteins and André Hesse. Steve invited several British officers. One of them was looking at me in such an admiring way. Jean Barbier and Alain were there along with Fescourt, France's most famous theatre producer.*

## 8 March 1940

*There is a lot of work at Police Headquarters. I have been to the theatre twice with Renée. We went to see* School for Scandal, *a satire by Sheridan – the sets were amazing and the costumes all quite lovely – and another evening we went to see* Richard III *at the Atelier Theatre. It is a play by William Shakespeare.*

In April 1940, Hitler invaded Denmark and Norway, followed by Belgium and Holland on 10 May, when Rotterdam was bombed almost to extinction. That day Andrée wrote:

*Last night there was an air raid. From 05.40 until 06.30 the DCA was working non-stop and what a noise. And this morning, coup de foudre. The Germans invaded Luxembourg. At 03.00 in the morning they bombed Antwerp and Brussels. It was all so sudden I can't get over it. They have also bombed several French towns: Nancy, Lyon, Luxeuil, Pontoire and Colmar. I came home for lunch and Alain, who was also at home, kept repeating to himself 'bastards, bastards'. I was heartbroken and then later in the day learnt that our Whitsun holiday has been cancelled. No point in complaining. We are at war and life is certainly going to change. C'est la guerre.*

It was also the day that Germany attacked France, coming over the border in the Ardennes. Within six weeks the whole country had been defeated and occupied.

### 1 May 1940

*I now work in the Information Department.*

*It is May 1st [la Fête du Muguet] so I bought a bunch of lily of the valley for Madame Chantebout, Madame Joly and Madame Yoanoff.*

*Today after work I am having cocktails with Jean Barbier, Alain and Margit. We all have such fun together. Tomorrow Margit and I are planning to go to Maxwell on the Boulevards to have an ice cream. There is always an orchestra. I must stop writing and I will say au revoir to you, dear diary, in English, 'Goodbye'.*

### 14 May 1940

*There was an air-raid alert at 02.30 and we went down into the cellars. I was surprised because it was rather comfortable.*

*On Sunday night there were two air raids. One was between midnight and one o'clock and the other from half past six until ten minutes past seven.*

*It seems they had dropped bombs around Choisy-le-Roi and Villacoublay. Madame Chantebout arrived at work saying how frightened she had been.*

*Luckily I had gone to bed early. On Friday evening I went to Renée's and we went to see a play at the Odeon called* 1939. *It is by Denys Amiel and could not have been more boring.*

*The play is about day-to-day living in France and Germany in the days leading up to war. The first act takes place in Germany and shows a secret meeting between Hitler and the Russian Ambassador to Germany. They are discussing the partition of Poland between the two tyrants. The second act takes place in France and shows a French family who live in the Périgueux quietly having lunch and talking about the war. They are shown as not wanting to come to terms with what is happening around them.*

*It just goes to show how weak the French are and how we are not facing up to reality. The play was long and it was very boring. I was home by eleven, but at six o'clock there was again another air raid.*

*The next day Margit came round with Alain and Jean Barbier. We had a supper of cheese, saucisson, grilled bread and milky coffee.*

On 15 May, Winston Churchill became head of Britain's new wartime coalition government, with Clement Attlee – leader of the Labour party – as Deputy Prime Minister. Andrée told me that when she and her mother learnt of Churchill's appointment, they felt relieved that Britain now had a forceful leader who would, as she phrased it, 'put the Germans squarely in their place'.

### 15 May 1940

*I am at work and one of my colleagues, Madame Chantebout, has been discussing the political situation. She talks absolute rubbish and has no understanding whatsoever of the events unfolding around us. She is a defeatist and should be arrested for her unpatriotic views. She really upsets me and I look at her with contempt. One of these days I will tell her exactly what I think of her. There was another air raid at 2.30 p.m. We went into air-raid shelters. It was very comfortable.*

### Sunday, 19 May 1940

*It is eleven o'clock in the morning. I should be at Maison Laffite with my family but I am at Police Headquarters where we now have to work on Sundays until we receive our new schedule. We are not being paid any extra for working on Sundays.*

*I went home for lunch today and wore my beautiful new hat. The designer is American and it is very large and a stunning navy-blue colour. I also bought myself a pair of navy-blue shoes which still hurt even though I have been wearing them for two weeks and my hair is worn in curls (un rouleau interclair).*

*I had another argument with 'La Mère' Chantebout about the political situation and because of this have not spoken to her for three days.*

*Dear little diary, I am now going to stop writing. It is so very special that I can confide in you in this way.*

# 4

# *The Evacuation of Paris*

## June 1940

On the eve of the invasion, according to Jean-Marc Berlière, there were approximately half a million foreigners registered in Paris and the surrounding region. They included central European Jews who had escaped persecution by the Nazis in their homelands, anti-Nazi Germans, anti-fascist Italians, Spanish republicans, Hungarians and gypsies. Throughout the 1930s it had been a legal requirement for every foreigner living in France to register their presence at the local police station. In Paris, detailed records of these people were passed on to Police Headquarters with the date of their arrival, their name, age, profession and address all noted.

In the days running up to the arrival of the Nazis in Paris, large queues of people started to form at Police Headquarters; at times the queues were so long they ran all the way around the building. Those who wanted to stay in France needed to make sure their ID cards and documents were up to date.

On 3 June 1940, '300 German aircraft bombed the Citroën and Renault factories on the south-western edge of Paris, killing 254 people, including 195 civilians.'[1] Andrée wrote in her diary:

> *On 3 June, Paris was bombed. At 1.15, just as I was going back to work after lunch, I heard an air-raid alert. I was at home so I took my coat off and stayed in the flat. I heard a few planes circling overhead but nothing else. I was back at work within the hour and so when Monsieur Kervella walked into my office and said, 'Well they have certainly dropped a lot of bombs, the Citroën and Renault factories are on fire,' I replied, 'You must be joking.'*

*'I most certainly am not, the whole of the 15th arrondissement has been bombed.'*

*Once again there are plans to evacuate Paris. We are all very frightened. The state schools have been closed. The classes of '39 and '40 have been called up. André Hesse and Jean Barbier have left. Maman, Alain and the girls are planning to leave Paris tomorrow. They are heading for Nantes. Papa is hesitating. He says it is too early to leave. Yvette has just passed her brevet and Alain is due to take his baccalaureate on Monday. Poor chap. What a life.*

On 9 June, she wrote the following entry:

*There was an air raid last night and Maman made us all get up and go down to the cellar. It was very frightening…*

*It is Sunday and I am again at work. I am so depressed. France is in the most desperate position. The Germans crossed the Aisne this morning and are overrunning the country. The King of Belgium is guilty of treason. The Flanders army withdrew at Dunkirk but thank goodness they have been saved. Many major battles are being fought. There must be thousands of dead soldiers. It is just too awful for words.*

The evening of 10 June was a warm one and before going to bed Andrée had left the shutters of her bedroom window ajar. She awoke early the following morning to strong light filtering through her bedroom window. The days were now much longer and she liked to get up early. Despite living in central Paris, she could still hear a few birds twittering at daybreak and their chatter helped her wake up. She threw the sheets off her bed and went to the window. She opened the shutters and looked down on the street below. It was totally deserted. In the kitchen, she boiled some water and poured it onto the freshly ground coffee Mémé (the family's housekeeper) had recently brought back from Brussels. From the Normandy-style wooden bread cabinet in the dining room she helped herself to a piece of bread, warming it up in the oven before spreading it with some of Mémé's greengage jam.

As she ate her breakfast at the dining room table, Andrée thought long and hard about the day ahead. Monsieur Langeron had asked her to come to his office at 7.00 a.m. for an important meeting, to which he told her he had also invited three of her colleagues whom she might not know but in whom she could have total confidence. She knew nothing more about why this meeting had been called. Initially she feared she might be in trouble for not doing her work properly, but she had not been reprimanded about anything and she seemed popular with her colleagues. It was true she kept herself to herself at work and never mixed with her fellow employees outside office hours, but no one would have described her as unfriendly. She was always hard-working, approachable and certainly had no airs and graces.

Having finished her meal, she dressed in a simple navy-blue polka dot dress and flat cream-coloured shoes, and left the flat. On this fresh, warm morning she decided to walk to the Place de la Concorde, where she could catch a bus over to the Assemblée Nationale and then walk along the Quai d'Orsay. As she arrived at Police Headquarters and walked through the main entrance, a policeman saluted her. 'Bonjour, Mademoiselle, you are very early this morning.'

Andrée returned the greeting and quickly made her way up to her office where, as yet, no one else had arrived. She placed her handbag neatly in her drawer and with a pad and pen made her way to Monsieur Langeron's office. Her best assumption was that he might want her to type some personal and confidential letters and, because of his close friendship with Renée, he knew she would be discreet.

As she knocked at Monsieur Langeron's door, she could hear the bells of Notre Dame chime seven o'clock. She waited for his acknowledgement and, as she did so, a dark-haired, slim man about her age came up beside her and said hello. Andrée wondered who he was but then the call came to enter. Inside there were two other people, both sitting opposite his desk: a young woman, a little older than Andrée, with auburn hair and a lot of make-up, and a small man who appeared to be in his late thirties but whose hair was already going grey.

Monsieur Langeron stood up and formally shook the hands of Andrée and the young man next to her before introducing them to the other people in the room.

'Monsieur Dupont, Mademoiselle Grisson, this is Mademoiselle Griotteray and Monsieur Paul.'

Langeron came straight to the point. 'You may be wondering why I have asked you to come to my office so early in the morning.'

'As you are well aware, we have always closely monitored the number of foreigners living in and around Paris. You, Mademoiselle Griotteray, have carefully checked their ID cards and recorded them on our central filing system. Monsieur Paul, Monsieur Dupont, Mademoiselle Grisson, you have all worked on the same project at different times. The Germans could reach Paris within days and I do not want this information to fall into their hands. They may take over Police Headquarters within the next few days, but it is my intention to remain as head of police. I will take full responsibility for the decisions I make.'

As he spoke, the little group were all aware of the seriousness of what he was proposing, and each felt a little frightened.

'On 12 June, all the records on the foreigners will be boxed up and taken down into the main yard where they will be loaded onto vans. Many of my trusted officers will have packed up the files and brought the boxes up from the cellars. They will be very tired as they will have been working for almost forty-eight hours non-stop. At 6.00 a.m., the vans will be ready for loading. The officers assigned to the task are well aware of their duty. Your job, Mesdemoiselles, Messieurs, will be to make yourselves available should your assistance be needed and you will report immediately and directly back to me if there are any problems. I know the officers assigned to the operation well and they are all loyal, but it is possible that there are some people among my staff who would like the Germans to know where these foreigners live, especially the Jews. We will be moving the files as quickly as possible and I aim to have them all out by late morning. They will then be taken out through the yard onto the Quai du Marché Neuf and straight to the Quai des Orfèvres, where they will be loaded on to two waiting trawlers. The trawlers must leave at 2.00 p.m. at the latest.'

Andrée quietly watched her colleagues' reactions as Monsieur Langeron finished speaking. She saw their sense of excitement mixed with apprehension as the importance of the task ahead began to sink in.

'Please return to your offices and carry out your work today as you normally would. The designated officers know exactly what they have to do. I want you to work in pairs and watch what is happening. If there are any problems, you are to report back to me immediately. Now, we all need to get on with today's work. I will see you tomorrow at 5.30 a.m. in la Cour Vaubert.'

Andrée walked back to her office and thought about the day ahead. She knew she would be busy updating the records of the many foreigners living in Paris who would be visiting her office, but she also wanted to make sure she knew exactly where the trawlers would be moored and decided to walk down to the Quai des Orfèvres during her lunch break.

Whenever Andrée was upset or anxious, she found comfort in food and that day was no exception. The morning went by quickly and on hearing the clock chime twelve, she made her way to the Brasserie les Deux Palais, where she knew the owner and was confident she would have a good lunch. It was her treat to herself after a tiring morning. She chose a table at the back of the restaurant, sat down and looked at the menu. After ordering she looked around the restaurant, which had first opened around 1900 and still had many of the period's original features: the colourful mosaic floor, the high mirrors covering all the walls and the long red leather bench with a series of small tables facing it. Andrée considered her fellow diners, many of whom were no doubt also aware that this might be their last good meal before the arrival of the Germans.

She ate an egg mayonnaise to start with, followed by the plat du jour – osso buco (a rich, thick meat dish cooked in a tomato, onion and garlic sauce). While she ate, she thought about how difficult life would be over the weeks and months ahead. As a young nineteen-year-old, she was not totally in tune with Langeron's political beliefs and activities, but she was determined to help him – not least because of her sister's admiration for him. She drank her coffee and, having paid the bill, walked down to the Quai des Orfèvres. From the main road outside the Préfecture de Police, which lay along the Seine, a slip road went down to the river. Large cobblestones had been laid along the road's surface back in the nineteenth century and at the bottom of the road she noticed several iron rings on the quayside to which trawlers could be moored. Happy about the logistics and hearing the bells of Notre Dame chime two o'clock, she hurried back to the office. She felt confident the archives could be moved onto the trawlers, but organisational speed would be vital.

On 12 June 1940, Andrée wrote:

> *As I arrived at work today the courtyard was full of trucks. It was an important day. All the archives were being moved out of Police Headquarters. Many of my colleagues were early at work to help out.*

Andrée was standing in la Cour Vaubert at 5.30 a.m. Despite the early hour she could see from the clear sky that it was going to be a hot day. Minutes after her arrival, the heavy gates of Police Headquarters were opened and several more large trucks drove into the yard. During the night the boxes of files had been brought up from the cellars to the ground floor by Langeron's loyal team of officers. They loaded the vans quickly and, as soon as they were full, each made their way out to the Quai d'Orfèvres, towards the waiting trawlers. As the first truck arrived on the quayside and the boxes were being loaded, the captain of the vessel greeted the driver. 'Bonjour, Monsieur, we have no time to lose. We must load the boats as quickly as possible. My permit allows me to leave the Quai d'Orfèvres at 2.00 p.m. and, whether my cargo is loaded or not, I will be leaving on time.'

For the next eight hours, police officers and van drivers worked tirelessly to load the trawlers.

'Where are you heading for?' asked one of the drivers as the cargo was being loaded.

'Not sure exactly, but we are heading for the South of France. I will receive further instructions when I reach Vienne, but I know from my patron that these boxes will be well and truly hidden; the Germans will not be able to get their hands on them.'

By mid morning, rumours had spread about this extraordinary operation. Many of the staff had not realised the importance of what was going on around them, but as Andrée and her colleagues watched the trawlers move out of the quay, she acknowledged to herself that this was the beginning of her own personal fight against the invasion. She promised herself that she would use whatever opportunity she had at Police Headquarters to resist the Germans.

As planned, the files left the Quai d'Orfèvres at two o'clock in the afternoon on 12 June 1940, two days before the Wehrmacht's entry into the capital. Sadly, events did not go smoothly from that point onwards.

On 13 June 1940, Andrée recorded in her diary:

> *This morning Monsieur Langeron called a meeting of the administrative staff and gave a really good speech telling us that if the city was to be occupied, the police and the Head of Police would all stay in their jobs.*

Paris waited anxiously, nervously, for the Nazi arrival. Langeron did everything he could to maintain order, but there was panic in the air. Several days earlier, on 9 June 1940 Andrée had written:

> *This evening I packed my suitcase just in case I suddenly have to leave Paris. I had better take Souki [the family dog] with me. Maman and the girls are leaving tomorrow for Nantes. Papa is hesitating. He thinks it is still too early to leave. He is simply ridiculous and besides which, if anything were to happen, he would be evacuated by car.*
>
> *Thursday night we had a small get-together at Barbier's flat with Margit and Alain. We had sandwiches and a lot to drink. We did not get to bed until 4.30 in the morning and at 5.30 there was an air raid. The latest news is the Germans are still advancing. Bastards. Well, maybe I should not say too much. If my diary were to fall into their hands, it would not help my career prospects at Police Headquarters.*

*Yesterday I went to the dressmaker with Maman and afterwards we had dinner at Garnier's. We had a lobster mayonnaise, a strawberry tart and an ice cream. This may well be my last good meal. Maman leaves tomorrow and I have no idea what will happen to me.*

Her entry for 13 June continued:

*Paris is still a free city but what will tomorrow bring? The Germans are so near. It is unbelievable. Hitler said he would reach Paris by 15 June and* ma foi, *he is almost here. We should not have been so careless and made such fun of them. This is going to teach us a lesson. It so ironic to think that when Maman was exactly my age, the same thing happened to her. It was 1914, she was twenty-one and she was living in Brussels. It is 1940, I am nineteen and I am living in Paris. I am not frightened, nor am I worried, which does help, but everyone else at the office is terrified. I am so pleased that Maman, Alain and the girls were able to leave Paris.\* They were lucky. They finally left Monday night on a train going to Nantes* [from where they hoped to board a ship which would take them to England]. *I saw them off at the station. Papa is due to join them but, thank goodness, he is still here. I would not have liked being all alone in Paris. Renée has left with her mother, at least I hope she has. Margit left me a note to say that she was leaving with her family. All my friends have gone. We are alone and it is very scary, but hopefully it won't be too awful.*

*Another thing which is worrying me is the mail. The post is just not getting through and so we have no letters.*

*Tomorrow we may wake up under the German occupation of Paris. I am eating as many cakes as I can, especially while there are still some left in the shops.*

*Bonsoir, I am going to have to start learning German again. What a pity I gave it up when I was fourteen. It could be very useful now.*

---

\* Following the invasion, civil servants were forbidden from resigning and so Andrée did not have the option of leaving Paris with her family.

### Friday, 14 June 1940

*A day I will remember for the rest of my life, whether it be long or short. I will never forget 14 June 1940.*

*Firstly, and what a stab in the back, as I was walking up the rue Auber to catch the métro, what did I see coming down the road? A truck, a truck full of German soldiers.*

*Then, at ten o'clock on the dot, the Germans marched into Police Headquarters through the gates of Notre Dame. I looked out of my office window and there they were. When I left in the evening the yard was full of disarmed policemen and German soldiers. The German soldiers' uniform is a sort of green/greyish colour and I have to admit it does look rather good on them.*

*But what a loss of face for France. What a tragedy. Paris occupied by a foreign power. I cried and cried and cried. Until now I had been so brave, but at lunchtime I just completely fell apart. I cried solidly for ten minutes. I am unable to write any more. Some of my colleagues have literally disappeared, not wanting to have Germans anywhere near them. Tonight I will go to bed and go to sleep under the German occupation of my city. For how long will we be civilian prisoners? What is going to happen next?*

Andrée was well aware of the exodus currently taking place from Paris. She and her father discussed the plight of the refugees on the roads, many killed as low-flying Luftwaffe bombed the roads out of larger cities. She felt desperately sorry for anyone escaping, but also a little fearful for her own safety in Paris. Not as worried as her father, however: Edmond insisted on accompanying Andrée to work on 15 June, which she regarded as a ridiculous overreaction. She explained his reasoning to Alain Gandy after the war, with a hefty dose of sarcasm: 'My father was worried I might meet the wrong sort of men out on the streets of Paris after the Germans arrived.'

### 16 June 1940

*Our Prime Minister, Paul Reynaud, has fled to Bordeaux and has tried to bring about a sort of coalition government between France and Britain*

*at the initiative and invitation of Winston Churchill, but the plan has*
*failed.*

*I miss Maman enormously. There are Germans everywhere and there*
*are German cars on every street corner. It breaks my heart and the worst*
*of it is I have no idea where anyone is. Where are Maman, Yvette, Claude,*
*Alain? What is going to happen to us all? Thank God Papa decided not to*
*leave. He did not want to leave me alone. How would I feel if he had left*
*with Maman? All my friends have gone. The 9th arrondissement where*
*we live is completely deserted. Everyone has left. There is simply no one*
*around. Curfew is at 11 p.m. and all the buses, cars and taxis have been*
*requisitioned by the German army.*

*I have been looking back through my diaries and forgot to say that on*
*the evening of 10 June the Italians declared war on France. A real stab in*
*the back which does not surprise me in the least because the Italians have*
*always been something else.* *

On 15 June 1940, the *Manchester Guardian* published an eyewitness
account of the invasion: 'The main German forces entered the city at noon
yesterday. They came from the north-west and by the Aubervilliers Gate
from the north-east. From the north-western suburbs they marched through
the west end down the Champs-Élysées – tanks, armoured reconnaissance
cars, anti-tank units, and motorized infantry. Machine gun posts were set up
at important points, and the wireless stations were seized. The people left in
Paris watched the entry in silence, reports the Associated Press correspond-
ent. Small groups of people still sat along the terraces and boulevards and
in the cafés. Shops were boarded up. In the Place de l'Opéra stood a solitary
motor car with a large "for sale" sign. The Paris police still patrolled the
streets. Occasionally could be heard the drone of an unmolested plane.'[2]

---

* Andrée's view of the Italian declaration was borne out by subsequent
historians. In *All Hell Let Loose*, Max Hastings commented: 'Italy entered the
war alongside Hitler on 10 June 1940 in a shameless, undignified scramble for
a share of the spoils. Mussolini feared Hitler and disliked the Germans, but he
was unable to resist the temptation to secure cheap grain in Europe and the
allied African empires.'

Andrée was disgusted at the thought of the German army marching down the iconic Champs-Élysées, accompanied by a military band. In a statement to the Minister of the Interior, Monsieur Peyrouton, Langeron was quoted as saying: 'The whole of the police force is in place. The force has watched over Paris and I will continue to protect the city and help in the difficult times ahead. We will collaborate fully with the orders of the occupying forces to maintain public order and safety.'

Meanwhile, news had arrived about the trawlers, little of it good. Jean-Marc Berlière records that as the vessels headed south down the river they came across a munitions boat, which had exploded at Bagneaux-sur-Loing in the Seine-et-Marne just to the south of Fontainebleau. One trawler, carrying political archives and general information, was able to get through, but amidst the general chaos the other, carrying individuals' files, did not. Many boxes of those files ended up in the river. The full details of what happened were not recorded, but it is clear that the hold-up proved fatal to Langeron's original mission.

Once in Paris, the Germans quickly learnt of the operation and ordered the return of all files. Damaged sheets of paper were dried and then copied, in an attempt to rescue as much information as possible. By mid July, the boxes had been returned to Police Headquarters and, as the war progressed, the contents were used to persecute some of the people recorded therein. At this time an ID card did not record the bearer's ethnicity, but some names would have been identifiable as Jewish. Langeron's daring attempt to shield so many immigrants at risk from Nazi persecution had failed.

Langeron was arrested on 23 June on an unrelated offence regarding his objection to the dismissal of four police commissioners, in violation of the armistice agreements; he was released a month later and permitted to return to his official duties. In January 1941, however, he would be arrested once again and he was subsequently removed from office by the Vichy government. He remains a controversial figure, claimed by many as a hero of the Resistance, but denounced by others as a collaborator.

## 5

# *Life Under Occupation*

From June to November 1940, Andrée's diary tells a story of ordinary life continuing during the occupation. In some ways, things continued much the same as usual – her preoccupations might be those of any nineteen-year-old: food, shopping, annoying colleagues at work, clothes. But this was only one part of her life at that time. What was happening in the other part could not be written down.

### 21 June 1940

*I am at work again at Police Headquarters. M. Kervella never stops drinking. I suppose it is his way of ignoring what is going on around him, which makes him even stupider than usual! There is still no news from Maman and there is still no mail.*

*I now see Germans on the streets of Paris every day. They walk around as if they own the place. They are continually to be found in our cafés and our bars, where they sing and drink. In other words, they are just having a ball. I am so very proud of myself because so far I have managed not to talk to a single one of them and when I see them on the streets on my way home I cross the road and pretend they do not exist. As for the airspace above Paris, the pilots are having the most wonderful time flying their planes so low they almost scrape the roofs of the houses. They travel around in the most amazing cars, which I am sure they have stolen in Holland, Belgium and Northern France. The whole thing disgusts me beyond belief, but at least I have my books and I can read, read, read. It helps pass the time since I have nothing better to do.*

*Oh, let's write about something else. I have just bought a pair of shoes from Berthelot. They are very comfortable. My two hats are finished, but I do not feel like wearing them. On Monday I am due a day's leave, that is if we are not all dead. I have not had a day off in three weeks. Incidentally, M. Bear from the Information Department has disappeared. He was not prepared to stay and work here at Police Headquarters with the Germans around. I go and see Madame Yoanoff from time to time. She is interesting and intelligent. It is quarter past nine in the evening French time, but I am going to have to go to bed because the Germans have put the clocks forward by an hour. 'La Mère' Chantebout has escaped, or at least that is what I think she has done, because she has not been seen since 13 June. At least we will have some peace.*

## 22 June 1940

*I am sitting at home alone looking out of the window. It is pouring. Thunder and lightning are raging all over Paris and I am depressed. Why must I feel so broken-hearted every time I walk past a German soldier or when I see one of them sitting on the terrace of one of our cafés?*

## 23 June 1940

*Hitler is in Paris. I feel sick.*

## 24 June 1940

*I must go to the hairdresser and have a perm, but I have just bought another pair of shoes so I have no money. Today Papa and I went cycling.*

*There are German planes constantly flying over Paris. They fly so low that one day one of them will fly into a chimney.*

*To think that some of these pilots have only had nine hours' training, which is what I overheard being said at Police Headquarters yesterday. I admit they certainly know how to fly. We have no fuel but they are using it recklessly. Still, it is nothing to do with me. I am a totally insignificant person wanting only to live in peace and this is not the way of the world at the moment.*

*Tonight there is something else worrying me. Monsieur Langeron has been relieved of his duties as head of police and this concerns me because my 'Piston' [mentor] will no longer be around to help if I get myself into trouble. Hopefully Monsieur Blanc, his number two, is still at Police Headquarters.*

*Still no news from Maman and the children.*

## 26 June 1940

*It is 1.15 German time. I wonder how long this nightmare is going to last. I am feeling depressed in a way I have never felt before. I now go to Police Headquarters by bike, it is quicker and it costs less.*

## 28 June 1940

*19.05 French time. I have a migraine. I am so depressed. I am continually depressed.*

*Today we were given some slightly more encouraging news. The French postal service is to be resumed at the end of the week.*

*I have no more to say to you, little diary, my heart is full of pain.*

## 2 July 1940

*Today I went cycling with Papa to Maison Lafitte. We went the long way round because so many of the bridges had been bombed. As we cycled, we saw large numbers of people walking back into Paris, refugees making their way back home. It was so unbelievably sad. We bought some food, but there is almost nothing to buy.*

*At lunchtime Papa made a 'jardinière' [a dish made of garden vegetables] and for pudding he had prepared a dish of gooseberries. It was so delicious I was over the moon.*

*Later I went to see the Ullmans, but they upset me so much. Madame*

*Ullman has no news of her son Leo and she did not stop talking about it. I told her I had had no news from my family or any of my friends. No news from my mother, my brother, my sisters, my best friend Margit, my boyfriend André, let alone Jean Barbier. But she can barely hear because she is deaf and she is not in the least bit interested. Then in the afternoon I went to see Jacqueline Remy. She is the only one still around.*

## 5 July 1940

*There are still so many Germans on the streets of Paris, even more so than when they first arrived. I simply cannot get over seeing them walking around as if they owned the place. Now some of them even walk around in civilian dress.*

*At two o'clock this afternoon I saw four soldiers who, because they were meeting an officer, saluted each other with the 'Heil Hitler'. Then a little further along at the Place du Théâtre Français, I saw four officers and two young men dressed as civilians. As the two civilians were introduced to the officers they thumped their heels, did the 'Heil Hitler' and finally shook each other by the hand. As for me, I was crossing the road so as to avoid them but I must have had such a disgusted look on my face because the older officer looked at me and made a comment to the others. What he said I will never know, but I heard him saying 'Frau', which means he was talking about me.*

*The class of '40 and the last group of '39 are about to be released* [from service in the French army]. *It is just as well for André and Jean Barbier* [friends of the Griotteray siblings]. *Well there is a bit of good news. If only there was a letter from Maman.*

## 7 July 1940

*Finally a card from Maman. She is in the Sables-d'Olonne but the card was written on 15 June.*

*It is midnight German time but I must write today's wonderful news in my diary.*

## 8 July, 1940

*Maman came home today, late evening, with Alain and the children. They are so brown and the adventures they have had are just amazing. Alain tried three times to get onto a British frigate but he was turned away each time.*

## 14 July 1940

*Bastille Day, the Germans in Paris. What a nightmare. Last year we were camping in the Bois-le-Roi. The weather was wonderful. We were so happy.*

*Today I went to check Renée's flat because she is still in Arcachon. On the way back Maman and I had a drink at the Viel and it was full of Germans and Italians. It is so sad.*

*The whole family is together again but I am arguing a lot with Papa. I think that since the Germans arrived in Paris, he has become slightly unhinged. He is so upset. He lived through the occupation of Paris during the Great War and he grew up with his parents, who had lived through the Prussian occupation of Paris.*

*Well, I am going to bed. I am getting through loads of books. I am lucky, it is a means of escape.*

## 5 August 1940

*It is unbearably hot at the moment. We are leading the most awful life.*

## 12 August 1940

*Last Saturday at three in the afternoon, we left Paris and went to Rochefort by bike. We had a difficult journey because we had Yvette with us* [Andrée's sister was only 13 at the time, and not used to cycling] *and it was seriously hot. We finally got to Rochefort in time for supper. Mémé had prepared a pot-au-feu and an absolutely delicious prune compote. We slept at Papa's house and in the morning Mémé brought us breakfast in bed: café au lait, bread, baguette and two different types of jam, prune and a gooseberry one. After breakfast we went for a walk around the village, we swam in the lake and then visited the old church, which dominates the village. We returned to Papa's house where the most amazing lunch was waiting for us, mackerel, olive oil, a steak with potatoes sautéed in butter and a fresh lettuce salad. There was the most delicious chocolate mousse and finally a small coffee. It was then time to return home, leaving Yvette with her dear Mémé.*

*We left at 13.30 and initially it seemed quite an easy road, but then we took a wrong turning and cycled an extra six kilometres. At 15.30 we were on the Quai d'Orsay, where we were very greedy and had a mirabelle tart. We then travelled along the Quai d'Orsay and my brakes gave in. It was so annoying. Having repaired them, we managed to get to the Pont de Sèvres and then along the Seine to the Place de la Concorde. After that we had a quick stop and a coffee at the Eiffel Tower. We had cycled 114 kilometres.*

## 13 August 1940

*There was an article in the newspaper today that talks about couriers travelling between Paris and Brussels, and so I decided to give one of them a letter for Tante Léa, asking her whether I could go and stay with her and l'Oncle Auguste. It won't be easy. Firstly I will have to get permission from Police Headquarters and then from the Kommandantur* [the Nazi headquarters in Paris]. *I wonder which will be more difficult. Then I will have to buy a railway ticket. Well, one rarely has fun without working hard at it.*

*On Saturday Papa brought half the furniture from our house in Mesnil-le-Roi back to Paris. Why on earth did he have to do that? It is impossible to find milk, cheese, oil or soap in Paris at the moment. There is no coffee and one hardly ever finds rice or pasta.*

*Well, no point in complaining.*

*Germany is preparing for her big battle with England. We are all very worried and awaiting the outcome. Hitler told us he would be in London by the middle of August. It is already the 13th, so he had better get a move on. On the BBC they are saying, 'Hurry up, you only have two days left.'*

*At the office, M. Kervella is ill, probably drunk because it is his way of hiding his worries. Madame Chantebout has caused absolute uproar here at the office because she has managed to get her husband released from a prisoner-of-war camp and Madame Joly is divorcing her husband.*

## 21 August 1940

*In eight days' time I will be twenty. I am trying to decide whether or not to go to Brussels. It would all be rather complicated. Tante Léa would love to have me to stay, but I need the permission of M. Blanc, the Acting Head of Police. Renée will hopefully help me with this and then I will ask Margit to help me obtain the permit from the Kommandantur. Is it worth it? It will be so expensive.*

*Last Sunday Margit and I went cycling along the Marne. We left via the Bois de Vincennes. We found an abandoned railway track and cycled along it and found we were on the Eastern railway track of France. We eventually reached Gournay and we got rather sunburnt. I am as brown as a berry. I look great.*

…

*My trip to Brussels is not going to happen. It would have been unbelievably expensive. M. Blanc told Renée that I would first need the permission of the commandant and that he would be surprised if permission was granted. I think it would be easier if I spent my holidays in Fontainebleau. We thought Alain had typhoid, but luckily the doctor has just told us that it was only a stomach infection. Yvette is coming home from Rochefort tomorrow.*

## 22 August 1940

*Dear diary, it is almost a whole year since I started writing in this little booklet. We are no longer at war. We have been defeated. As a nation we are worthless.*

*Germany is planning her invasion of England, but we are still waiting for it to happen. They may not have reached London, but they are bombing the whole of England and the British are bombing the German towns. There are thousands of civilians being killed. War is just so awful. What a wonderful day it will be when the people of the world can get on together. Meanwhile, communication between the Free Zone and the Occupied Zone has been cut.*

*As for life in Paris, we have to queue for everything. It is absolutely awful. We queue for butter, milk, coffee, cheese, meat, if we can find it, and oil.*

## 23 August 1940

*I now have a little blue diary. I love anything blue.*

*Life is so sad. It is impossible for a young French girl to be carefree and happy because the Germans are occupying most of my country. Maybe it does not upset everyone in the same way, but for me to walk around Paris, my home town, to see Germans travelling around in cars and admiring the sights, is heart-breaking. I do understand the government's position in allowing them to march in, not wanting Paris to be bombed and destroyed, but it is very hard. In Paris the occupying forces are behaving themselves, but in the country we hear they are despicable and looting whatever they can find. I am living in the hope that the British will get them and it will not be too soon. Even the German soldiers have had enough. They are always at war and their victory has been too quick.* \*

---

\* Andrée was aware of the Battle of Britain currently taking place and, like many of her compatriots, hoped that the RAF would win. Working at Police Headquarters, she may have heard some of the Germans talking about the war. Her entry here may refer to the cynical position adopted by some that the Germans felt they had won too quickly, and would have preferred a more challenging fight. Not all Wehrmacht soldiers were Nazis, of course, and many may not have wanted to wage war in the first place.

### 24 August 1940

*I am now working in the north-eastern part of the building. It is awful. I work with the most dreadful group of people. I have decided to ask the Head of Police to find me another job, that is if I am not made to return to the Tourist Department. I am now in the Passport Department.*

### 30 August 1940

*Madame Chantebout and I spend most of our time going between coop-eratives and Police Headquarters. In the morning we went to the rue Lagrange looking for lard and butter and in the afternoon we went to the rue Chanoinesse to see what we could find. Yesterday I found some chocolate and noodles.*

### 31 August 1940

*The night before going on holiday I had to go to Monsieur Blanc, the Acting Head of Police, for my ID card. He told me to write it out myself. I did think this was rather odd. He told me to bring it back for him to sign and he just signed it without checking or even looking at it.*

For the next couple of months, Andrée did not write anything in her diary. She began again on 11 November, including in one volume the brief line: 'Bagarre à l'Étoile' (fighting at L'Étoile). That is her only written refer-ence to the student protests – she was presumably aware of the dangers of incriminating herself by including details, should her diaries ever be found by the authorities.

### 11 November 1940

*I am now working for Monsieur Pouillet on the first floor of the build-ing. Here we organise and keep up-to-date information on the foreigners living in Paris. It has to be carefully kept in files and easily accessible to the Germans.*

6

# *A First Rebellion*

To understand why a young, fairly sheltered and otherwise carefree woman of Andrée's upbringing would decide to join the French Resistance, it helps to read her reaction following the German invasion of France in 1939 and the Wehrmacht's entry into Paris in 1940.

On 15 September 1939 Andrée wrote:

*We are now at war and we will have to live with it. Hitler has to be stopped. We must believe in France's victory and shout from the rooftops of Paris* 'Vive la France'.

Ten days later, she added:

*Alain just keeps repeating 'what bastards they all are'. As for me, I am totally heartbroken.*

By the early autumn of 1940, daily life in Paris was beginning to return to something approaching normality, if such a situation could be described as normal. Following one of the hottest summers on record, when 95°F had been recorded on the streets of Paris, those Parisians who had escaped the Nazis and the city for the hot summer months began slowly to return. Yvonne, Alain, Yvette and Claude had attempted without success to board a British frigate in Nantes destined for Portsmouth. There were too many people trying to leave France and they reached Nantes too late to get on. Alain tried to get on a ship on his own, but was told by a British sailor to return to his 'Mummy'. He never quite forgave the British for the slight. The family went instead to stay with friends in the Sables-d'Olonne, eventually returning to Paris about six weeks later. Despite hoping that they had managed to make it safely to Britain, Andrée was beside herself with joy to hear her mother's voice greeting the concierge on their return. Yvette and Claude, at twelve and ten years old respectively, were due to start school, while Alain was about to start university.

Returning to Paris would prove challenging. Tall, with strong Flemish characteristics and an aristocratic presence, no one could miss Yvonne. Holding her two daughters by the hand, she made her way towards the Place de l'Opéra for the first day of school. As she walked towards the Café de la Paix, Yvonne saw that the road signs had been renamed in German; the swastika flag was flying from several rooftops; and everywhere she looked she saw German soldiers walking along the streets. Hurrying on, her daughters listened as she promised: 'We got rid of them in 1918 and we will get rid of them again.'

Emerging from the *métro* station one morning, on his way to register at the Sorbonne, Alain picked up a copy of that morning's *Figaro*.* As the young newspaper vendor gave him his change, Alain made a sarcastic comment about the accuracy of news reports now that the invading forces were in control of the press. As he stood in line to register at la Faculté de Droit, he looked through the paper and realised how heavily the morning's press must have been censored. Alain was not slow in taking a decision; before he had even registered as a student, he made up his mind to publish an underground weekly pamphlet or news-sheet. He would name it *La France*, and its role would be to inform Parisians of what was going on in the world, alongside articles enticing readers to resist the occupation.

Freshers' Week 1940 at the Sorbonne was different from previous years. Being a student in 1940 would not be about working hard and having fun. France was at war. As the corridors of the university filled with youngsters registering for their chosen courses, conversations bubbled up about the

---

* In 1978 Alain Griotteray co-founded *Le Figaro* magazine and went on to be the first foreign journalist to interview President Reagan in the Oval Office.

German invasion of France and the Wehrmacht entry into Paris, and how they had been betrayed.

The atmosphere was one of bitterness and resentment as the students tried to come to terms with the speed of their country's defeat. They felt let down by their army and by a group of politicians whose management of the political situation and handling of its armed forces had been so disastrous.

One new student at the Sorbonne in 1940 was Noël Le Clercq, a young twenty-year-old who had given up officer training at Saint-Cyr to enrol as a law student. His thick, wavy blond hair and blue eyes lent him a somewhat Nordic appearance and, being a little older than his fellow students, his confident and authoritative manner endeared him to many of his contemporaries. Noël gathered his new friends around him and rallied them to resist the occupation. It was not long before Alain was attending his impromptu lectures, followed by many hours of heavy drinking in the smoky atmosphere of the Café Harcourt (whose previous patrons included Oscar Wilde) on the boulevard Saint-Michel. The two students became firm friends and Alain's plan for his underground news-sheet evolved into a joint venture.

With a heavily censored press and no broadcast media, news travelled very slowly. Listening to the BBC, a lifeline to the outside world, was forbidden and owning a radio could lead to immediate arrest; despite this, Edmond owned a radio, which he kept in the cellar but brought up regularly to listen to BBC broadcasts. In search of assistance, Alain asked his brother-in-law to introduce him to Henri Jeanson, the editor of *Aujourd'hui* – later to become one of France's most prominent newspapers. Jeanson, now in his early forties, had become friendly with Steve Passeur back in the 1920s when working as a film critic. In December 1939, Jeanson had been sentenced to five years' imprisonment for his published pacifist reports but was later released by the Minister of the Interior, Monsieur Campinchi. He had been appointed editor of *Aujourd'hui* in August 1940 and the first issue was released in September.* Alain and Noël were allowed to make regular

---

* In November 1940, after he refused to follow a German directive and take a public stand in the paper against the Jews and in support of France's collaboration with Germany, Jeanson was forced to resign as editor and sentenced to imprisonment. He was released several months later. (*continued*)

visits to Jeanson's office, listening out for any scraps of information that might be helpful in compiling *La France*. On one occasion, pushed for time, the pair met at the Café Harcourt to draft a forthcoming article. Just as they finished writing, a group of Nazi soldiers walked into the café and began a search of the customers, demanding to see their ID cards. Alain and Noël managed to move to the back of the café and escape through a window, but they vowed to be more cautious in future.*

By September 1940, Andrée had been working at Police Headquarters for just under a year. Efficient, hard-working and unassuming, she was popular among her colleagues, had made several friends and moved along the corridors of her office easily without attracting attention. Indeed, her discreet personality was one of her most important assets as a member of the Resistance.

As plans for the first edition of *La France* continued, Alain and Noël recruited two more students from the Sorbonne: Yves de Kermoal, a fun-loving, tall, fair aristocrat (whose father, a retired marine superintendent, would later record and pass on details of the German police watch along the 'forbidden zone' of Brittany's coastline), and Pascal Arrighi, an intensely intellectual law student.†

The close friendship these four men developed would last well over sixty years and their respective skillsets created the basis on which Alain's Resistance network could move forward. Eager to ensure the first edition was a success, Alain invited his sister out to dinner to discuss how best to go about printing and copying the paper in the quantities they needed. Walking into a restaurant near the Champs-Élysées, brother and sister sat down and Alain watched his sister look at the menu as he thought about the enormous risks he was about to ask her to undertake.

---

After the war he became a regular writer on *Le Canard Enchaîné*, one of France's most successful weekly political satirical newspapers today. The publication had been forced to suspend publication during the Second World War.

* After its closure in November 1940 by the Germans, the café became a German library.

† Both Yves and Pascal later received the Légion d'honneur. Pascal entered politics and further served his country as a Deputé (Member of the French Parliament).

The restaurant owner, who knew Andrée and Alain's family well, smiled sadly as he approached their table and began explaining the difficulties he had had since the occupation of Paris. Only yesterday several German officers in uniform had walked into his restaurant and asked for a table; their behaviour had been impeccable and they showed great appreciation for their meal, but as he took their order he saw with shock that the Bernsteins, some of his oldest Jewish clients and close friends of the Griotterays, had entered the restaurant and were waiting to be seated.

Alain sympathised with the restaurateur's dilemma, while noting to himself the irony of planning to discuss his underground news-sheet in a place that German soldiers chose to frequent. Discreetly he outlined his plans to Andrée as they ate; as he suspected, she was keen to proceed as soon as the first bulletin was ready for typing, and to investigate the office's printing arrangements.

The next day, Andrée arrived at work early. She knew there was a printing room with a Roneo duplicator machine on the same floor as her office, but had never been inside it as the machine was operated by the office orderly. Taking a deep breath, she walked confidently into the print-room, examined the machine, worked out how to operate it and checked the paper and ink supplies, which were stored in the cupboard. Her one concern was whether someone might notice the increase in the use of paper and ink, but this was unavoidable.

Alain gave her the copy for the first *La France* pamphlet in the Griotteray family flat at the beginning of September 1940. It contained censored news items and provocative statements encouraging the reader to defy the occupying forces in any way they thought plausible. Andrée took the material into work, typed it and made a few copies using the Roneo. She took the pages back to her office, put them carefully away in her satchel and delivered them to Noël's flat during her lunch break. Everything went smoothly.

After that, she was given a new draft to type out each week and as the group became more confident and *La France*'s circulation increased, so did the number of copies she made. No one seemed to notice what she was doing in her office or in the Roneo machine room and if they did, no questions were asked.

Early one morning, while she was typing out the latest transcript of *La France*, there was a quiet knock at her door. Absorbed in her work, Andrée did not hear the knock over the sound of her typewriter, nor did she hear the German officer enter her office until he stood in front of her desk.

Starting, she stared up blankly before recognising him as a young officer she had crossed paths with several times in the corridor and with whom she had exchanged a couple of greetings. Pushing down her initial instinct to panic, she regained her composure, smiled and asked whether there was anything she could do to help. As the captain smiled back, she invited him to sit down and as she did so she slowly withdrew from the typewriter the paper on which she had just typed the first paragraph of that week's copy of *La France*, placing it away from him on the left-hand side of her desk. Sitting down on the opposite side of her desk, he introduced himself as Captain Schurr from the Press and Information Department. Andrée wondered what he wanted, as she had nothing to do with his department, but she waited to see what would happen.

Schurr appeared simply to want to engage in polite conversation and began to tell her about a restaurant he had been to a few nights previously on the Champs-Élysées. He then asked whether he could pick up the five passports being prepared for his department head. Andrée thought it strange that he had not sent an orderly to pick them up, and was still trying to work out why he was in her office so early in the morning, but she stood up, found the passports on an adjoining table and handed them over. He began pacing up and down the room with an apprehensive look on his face.

Finally he came to the point and shyly asked, 'Mademoiselle, I would very much like to invite you out to dinner.'

Trying to hide her total relief, Andrée politely responded, 'How very kind of you. I would love to have dinner with you but it is simply not possible.'

Schurr was not to be so easily rejected. 'Is it because I am a German officer that you are declining to accept my invitation?'

Andrée bore no ill-feeling towards a man she did not know but whom she found to be charming and yet whom she was desperately trying to get out of her office. 'Oh no, Captain, it is most certainly not because you are a

German officer that I feel it would be inappropriate for us to enjoy dinner together; it is because I am French.'

As she spoke, Andrée could hear Madame Chantebout walk into the adjoining office. In a rush of relief, she explained to the captain that it must be 8.30 a.m., that within minutes there would be several clients waiting outside for the renewal of their passports and that she must get on with her work. Schurr smiled and, holding the passports in his hand, walked towards the door saying, '*Au revoir, Mademoiselle.*' Andrée leaned back and breathed deeply; only once he had left the room did she realise how shaken she felt.

As the morning progressed, Andrée found herself nervously trying to work out how she would be able to duplicate the copies of *La France* Noël needed after Schurr's visit had wasted so much time. She decided to take the draft home at lunchtime and advise Noël overnight of the delay. She would then come in early to make the copies the following morning. It was risky – she might draw attention to herself and it was always possible that she might be the subject of an ad hoc search on the streets between Police Headquarters and home. Schurr had not done her any favours but, on the plus side, neither had he noticed what she had been working on.

For several weeks, Andrée typed up and made clandestine copies of *La France.* The extra paper and ink she used appeared to go unnoticed. Andrée's natural confidence and fearlessness was the perfect cover. She had no idea whether her colleagues were members of the French Resistance, though it was probably reasonable to assume they were passive supporters, people who might turn a blind eye to what their friends, colleagues and acquaintances were doing to fight the enemy. But even so, it was dangerous to be printing and distributing anti-German material. As Armistice Day (11 November) approached, the most important edition of *La France* was about to appear.

## 7

# *A Life Lived Well*

It is July 2000. Three elderly Resistance heroes stand respectfully in front of the tomb of the unknown soldier, observing the eternal flame under the Arc de Triomphe. The traffic circulating the monument has been brought to a standstill.

Alain Griotteray, leader of the Orion Resistance Group, is grey-haired, dignified and focused. Yves de Kermoal stands beside him, thoughtful but relaxed. Beside him is Jacques Sauvage, serious and intent on the day's events. Representing Andrée Griotteray White is her daughter, proud but sad her mother is not in her rightful place.

The four stand to attention as the 'Marseillaise' is played and two soldiers lift the Tricolore. Watched by the crowd of dignitaries, Alain moves forward and places on the tomb a wreath of blue, white and red flowers.

'À la mémoire de nos amis mort pour la France, signé Orion.'
*In memory of our friends who died for France, Orion.*

The Arc de Triomphe was intended to symbolise French military victory. It was commissioned by Napoleon in 1806 as a tribute to French soldiers who lost their lives fighting for their country in the French Revolutionary and Napoleonic wars. Beneath it lies the tomb of the unknown soldier, interred on Armistice Day in 1920. The tomb's eternal flame is dedicated to those who died without identification in the First and Second World Wars. The coffin bears the French inscription: 'Here lies a French soldier who died for the motherland ['*mort pour la patrie*'] 1914–1918.'

It was here that several thousand young Parisians, university and school students among them, demonstrated on 11 November 1940 against the German occupation of France.

Every year since 1918, the French had marked the legacy of the First World War by gathering at the Place de l'Étoile on Armistice Day. In his book *The Resistance*, Matthew Cobb records that more than a million and a half French people had lost their lives in that war, of which 300,000 were civilians, and 3.5 million soldiers had been injured in some way. In 1940 the German military commander of France, concerned at impending rumours about a possible anti-Nazi protest, announced that any such commemorations were forbidden.[3]

As 11 November approached, talk spread among the students in Paris that a demonstration was being planned for the afternoon of Armistice Day. Alain and Noël Le Clercq were keen to be involved and ultimately became some of the principal organisers of the event. Together they planned to get as many of their university friends, fellow students and acquaintances onto the streets of the Champs-Élysées as they possibly could. In the days leading up to the 11th, they carefully worked out the next edition of *La France*. It would be simple, along the lines of:

> 'Resistez l'envahisseur
> L'Étoile
> vers 16 heures'*

It would also be potentially perilous; anyone caught inciting a demonstration or openly criticising the Wehrmacht could be arrested and instantly put before a firing squad.

As the date approached, and despite the danger, Alain and Noël became increasingly excited by the challenge of publicly resisting the occupation of France. Andrée had agreed to design and Roneo their latest news pamphlet using the ink, paper and machine available to her at Police Headquarters. She needed to be alone in her office to work on the leaflets safely, without anyone

---

* 'Resist the invader. The Étoile around 4 p.m.'

watching what she was doing. She knew her colleagues were less likely to be in very early in the day so, carrying her brown satchel, she walked into Police Headquarters one morning before 7.00 a.m., to the surprise of the main gate's duty sergeant. Wasting no time, she checked the ink and paper supplies and started to work on the pamphlets. It was safer to have the finished leaflets in her bag rather than attempt to work on them later in the day when there were more people around.

That morning she copied a batch of leaflets, another the following morning and the same again over the next two days. No one noticed what she was doing, and no one searched her bag. But on the fourth day one of her colleagues asked why she was always so early at work and Andrée realised she needed to stop. She took her responsibilities seriously and if anyone at work happened to find one of the pamphlets, the demonstration would be jeopardised, not to mention her own safety.

Over the next four days Andrée took the leaflets out of Police Headquarters each day during her lunch break. Travelling by *métro*, she delivered them to prearranged addresses. The first batch went directly to Noël Le Clercq's flat on the Left Bank, where Noël, known among his friends to be encouraging his fellow students to defy the occupation, did not invite Andrée in. It was vital that she leave quickly, given the high stakes. With her characteristic coolness she turned around and headed straight back to the *métro* and into a restaurant near Police Headquarters. Next she delivered copies to Alain in a fellow student's flat near the Sorbonne. Alain started to hand out the leaflets to a number of friends with whom he had discussed his plans. He instructed everyone to drop copies in the letterboxes of student flats, into the pockets of overcoats (sometimes without the wearer being aware this was being done) and at other times directly into people's hands – anyone who looked patriotic and able to move quickly through the narrow streets of the Quartier Latin if someone might be watching them. Carrying or handling incriminating evidence was one of the most dangerous forms of resistance; the evidence was on the bearer and so they needed to pass it on as fast as they could – either to someone else or safely disposed of. The third and fourth batches were delivered to Jean Barbier and François Clerc, both young men working in central Paris near the Champs-Élysées, who distributed them among friends and acquaintances whom they knew would be eager to 'resist'.

On the morning of the 11th, a small number of Parisians ignored the German directive and made their way to the Arc de Triomphe to pay tribute to their war dead. Others made their way to the statue of Clemenceau halfway up the Champs-Élysées. As Cobb has noted, 'Clemenceau had been Prime Minister of France at the end of the First World War, and for many was a symbol of France's victory over Germany.' Edmond and Yvonne had both lost siblings in the war and the two rose early, dressed deliberately in English tweed and walked down from their flat to the Place de la Concorde and up the Champs-Élysées to pay their respects to Clemenceau, ignoring the German presence around them.

Andrée had been busy the previous day, searching for food:

> Last night I went to Rochefort. Mother wanted me to go and get some food. Everyone there was delighted to see me. I brought back a chicken, some butter, some eggs and a Camembert. I was so pleased with myself because we cannot find anything to eat in Paris. I got home this morning and there was no one around.

The whole Griotteray family had arranged to sit down together for lunch on the 11th, knowing that Andrée had returned to Paris with some food the previous evening. Over lunch, Andrée and Alain told their parents about their plans for the afternoon. Despite his own act of defiance earlier that morning, Edmond was initially angry, saying that he was not at all happy about his son and daughter joining in the demonstration as it could turn very nasty and dangerous. Alain explained that his friends would be already making their way to their meeting-place and he could not let them down; Andrée similarly had rallied several of her friends to the cause, among them her close friend Margit.

Yvonne was quiet, resigned to the dangers both her daughter and son would be facing. Edmond realised there was not much more to be said.

They finished their lunch and Andrée and Alain put on their thick coats to protect them from the cold air. Hiding their faces with thick scarves to avoid being recognised, the Griotteray youngsters left their flat and hurriedly headed towards the Church of Notre Dame de l'Assomption off the Faubourg St Honoré where they had arranged to pick up Noël, Pascal and Jean. Friends joined them at different prearranged points and as they walked en masse towards the Arc de Triomphe, they were encouraged by the large numbers who had gathered on the surrounding streets. By mid afternoon the trains heading for the Pont de Neuilly were unusually full as more and more protestors got off at the Avenue Georges V *métro* station and made their way to l'Étoile. Others had cycled from the outskirts of Paris to the Place de la Concorde, where they left their bikes and walked.

The Champs-Élysées, one of the most majestic avenues in the world, waited for events to unfold. The streets emanating from the Étoile had borne witness for the last four months to the gloom of the citizens of Paris since the Wehrmacht had marched down the Champs-Élysées on 13 June 1940. Several buildings now carried the Nazi flag but, worst of all, the swastika was flying from the Arc de Triomphe.

An atmosphere of rebellion, defiance and resistance reigned as people started singing the 'Marseillaise'. By late afternoon it was estimated that up to 3,000 students, some as young as fifteen, were there, demonstrating against the German invasion.[4]

The success of the demonstration took everyone by surprise. By early evening, as the Wehrmacht and the Parisian police caught up with events, they began to take control of the crowds and break up the demonstrators. The retaliation was predictably violent and as the police began to break up the crowd, Alain, Andrée and their friends split up and moved away in different directions. Alain moved quickly on to the rue Avenue Georges V. From there he walked down and crossed the Pont de l'Alma. Once over the bridge he successfully made his way to a friend's flat on the Left Bank where he could stay the night. Most of the French police and German soldiers had stayed around the Place de l'Étoile, chasing people down the main avenues and onto the small streets off the avenues.

Andrée and Margit moved away from the crowd arm-in-arm and headed towards the Avenue Klébert. Should the girls be stopped, they planned to explain that they had been out walking along the Champs-Élysées, unawares, when they had been caught up in the demonstration. Andrée stayed the night at Margit's parents' place, not returning home until the following morning.

German soldiers moved in everywhere, breaking up the crowds. The *métro* stations were shut so that no one could escape to the trains. Many of the protesters were trapped. The soldiers drove their troop cars and lorries into the crowds of demonstrators, shooting indiscriminately. Some students were wounded by gunfire while others were physically attacked by the soldiers.[5] The French police recorded the names of the individuals they had rounded up, while some of those detained by the Germans spent weeks in the Cherche-Midi prison.

News of the demonstration and the vicious response of the German armed forces had quickly made its way around Paris and Edmond and Yvonne were beside themselves with worry about Andrée and Alain. They sat up all night, unable to sleep. At six o'clock in the morning, half an hour after curfew had been lifted, Andrée walked in through the front door.

Her calmness over the previous afternoon's events soothed her parents' worries, but Andrée had to move quickly. After reassuring her parents that all was well, she had to get ready for work. No one knew whether Alain had been arrested or escaped, nor was there any news of her other friends, although all had previously planned escape routes and earmarked several safe houses they could go to should events turn nasty. Andrée had a quick bath, put on a black suit and ate breakfast. She wanted to get to work swiftly to find out from her police colleagues the turn of events and the number of arrests.

As the news of the day started to circulate beyond Paris, the young knew the demonstration had been a huge success. They had shown the world their defiance and their willingness to fight for freedom. There were consequences, however. The chancellor of the Sorbonne was made to resign, and the university itself was closed. Those students from outside Paris were sent home while those living in the capital had to find work to stay on. Thanks to the help of his brother-in-law, Alain managed to find a position working at the ministry responsible for managing food supplies across France.

The demonstration may have been broken up by the Nazis, but many of those involved would go on to become the founding members of the French Resistance. It gave people the confidence they needed to believe that the Nazis could and would be defeated, though the Germans' retaliation and brutality towards the student protestors had been frightening to behold. As Alain would later be told by his new mentor, Henri d'Astier de la Vigerie: 'Your demonstration on the Champs-Élysées was perfect… Now you must start thinking about even more important things. It is revenge we must aim for.'[6]

# 8

# *Fighting Back*

Georges Piron was restless. His train was due to arrive in Paris late morning, but as with most wartime trains it had been heavily delayed. It was late afternoon as the engine noisily steamed into La Gare du Nord.

In Brussels everyone had heard of the success of the student demonstration at the Étoile on 11 November 1940, Armistice Day, and Piron knew the time was ripe to recruit younger members into his fold.

During the First World War Piron, while a serving officer in the Belgian Army, had been a successful British intelligence agent. After the war ended, he became President of the Belgian War Veterans' Association and also of the Belgium Reservists' Association. Now with Belgium and Germany again at war, Piron was once more working for the British intelligence services. Piron and Yvonne Griotteray were old friends: through her brother-in-law Major Auguste Geno, a close friend and fellow officer, Piron had met Yvonne Stocquart as a young woman, and was impressed by her language skills and assured confidence. She went on to work for him as an intelligence messenger on British ships, taking information from Belgium via Holland to England.

Following the German occupation, Piron went home to his family in Parmiers, near the French/Belgian border, where, over the next twelve months, he recruited thirty members into a Resistance group he had created after the fall of France. Piron and his team had been stockpiling arms left by the retreating forces in the area surrounding Parmiers, in the Ariège region of France, and over the next few months had conducted acts of sabotage with these weapons whenever the opportunity arose.

Protecting himself from the cold, damp December weather, Georges stepped off the train onto the platform wearing a heavy raincoat and his favourite check-patterned hat. In his hand he carried a brown overnight bag, out of which was hanging a copy of Belgium's national newspaper. He walked down the platform and out onto the Place Napoleon. He sensed the change in atmosphere since his last visit to Paris, before the fall of the city. As he turned towards the Place Roubaix, he decided to walk down to the Place de la Madeleine. It would take him over an hour, but the exercise would do him good. Arriving at the rue la Fayette, he turned into the boulevard Haussman and thought back to Paris at the end of the 1914–1918 war; the empty shops, the look of sadness on the faces of so many Parisians who had lost their sons in the Great War. History was repeating itself.

It was close to six o'clock as Piron left the Place de la Madeleine and continued the few hundred yards to the rue Godot de Mauroy. Between the two wars the Pirons and the Griotterays had seen little of each other, but they had kept in touch and only a couple of years previously the Griotterays had stayed with the Pirons in Parmiers on their annual trip to Brussels to visit Yvonne's parents. During their visit Piron had been impressed by Alain and Andrée's youthful confidence and intelligence. Climbing slowly up the stairs to the second floor, he wondered how Yvonne would greet him – he had not warned her of his impending arrival. The fewer written details or telephone calls about such meetings, the safer they would all be.

Piron knocked at the front door and found himself face to face with Mémé, the Griotteray's housekeeper, who had accompanied Yvonne to France when she married Edmond back in 1919. Despite the intervening years, Mémé immediately recognised 'Monsieur Georges' and was all smiles as she shook his hand, took his small case and led him into the small salon. Hearing the commotion, Yvonne came out into the hall and as she walked into the room was both surprised and delighted to see her old friend.

They were totally engrossed in conversation when Yvonne heard Edmond walk through the front door, followed by Andrée and Alain. Both youngsters were in fits of laughter as Andrée explained how at work she had jammed a window in an unsuspecting German officer's office, causing a cold draught to flow through the room throughout the whole morning, much to his annoyance.

As they toasted his arrival with a bottle of champagne from the cellar, Piron began to explain the purpose of his visit. Repeating the words of General de Gaulle, he declared: 'We have lost a fight but we have not lost the war.' He went on to talk about the need to recruit Frenchmen and women who could provide information on German activities in France, to be passed on to British Intelligence.

As Piron spoke, both Edmond and Yvonne knew what was happening. Piron had come to see them with the aim of recruiting their son and daughter to work for the British intelligence services. Their parents felt proud, but also anxious. Edmond knew about his wife's activities during the First World War, but neither had imagined that their daughter might follow in her mother's footsteps.

When Piron finished speaking, Alain immediately stood up. 'I will do anything I can to help.' Andrée wasted no time in joining in. 'Anything, anything to get rid of the Germans.'

Alain had just turned eighteen. Andrée was twenty. Neither could have any idea how their activities over the next four years would contribute towards the liberation of France. Neither could envisage the dangers they would face or the risks they would take. Their mother had often spoken of the German occupation of Brussels during the First World War, of the shooting of her brother, their uncle, as a spy by the Germans in 1916, and the way in which her mother, their grandmother, had reprimanded German soldiers on the streets of Brussels. Yvonne did not tell her family much of her own involvement with British Intelligence during the First World War, but they knew very broadly that she had made a contribution. They had grown up understanding that to submit to the occupation of one's country by a foreign power was not an option.

Edmond was nineteen years older than his wife. He had been born in Paris in 1874, three years after Bismarck's troops had marched in and occupied the city. During the First World War he had lost his only brother, Emile, at Verdun, and as he reached his sixty-sixth year the Germans had again invaded France. He was finding it difficult to cope with what was happening to his country and his family, and as the war progressed and his son and daughter became more involved in the Resistance, tensions would build in the Griotteray household.

The door flew open as Yvette and Claude rushed into the room. They were returning from an afternoon trip to the theatre and were eager to tell their parents about the play. The girls hugged their parents and, as they did so, Piron stood up and prepared to leave. He spoke quietly to Alain, asking him to meet his colleague Henri d'Astier de la Vigerie. Warning him to be discreet at all times, he turned to Yvonne and said, 'Remember, the rules have not changed.'

'I do not like it at all,' said Edmond after Piron had left.

'We have no choice,' Yvonne said simply. 'The Germans have to leave France.'

Yvonne knew her children well, and her daughter particularly – and her own past experience gave her an insight that Edmond could not understand. She and Andrée had always been close. When Andrée described the first day of the occupation of Paris in her journal, she compared her position to that of her mother's in 1914. 'It is ironic to think that when Maman was exactly my age the same thing happened to her. It was 1914, she was twenty-one and living in Brussels. It is 1940, I am nineteen and living in Paris.' The similarities between Yvonne and Andrée are astonishing: how young they both were when war broke out, how patriotic and determined to play a part, however small, in the liberation of their country. That Andrée should follow in her mother's footsteps and go on to risk her life to carry intelligence out of Paris is remarkable – and yet perhaps only logical, given the tight relationship they had.

In another diary entry, written the same year, she talked about her mother: 'My darling Maman is without any doubt the person I love and will always love more than anyone else in the world. She has always been so good to me; she is so uncomplicated and easy-going. She has such a very unpleasant life but she never complains about anything. She is an angel and, what is more, Renée simply adores her.'

Yvonne and Andrée's mutual deep love for England, its language and customs was another strong bond. Yvonne had taken Andrée to England aged sixteen to stay with friends Yvonne had made during the First World War. Just as Yvonne had immersed herself into English life years earlier, so did Andrée follow suit for the twelve months she stayed in England. She was young to be away from home for so long, but Andrée had already learnt much from her mother's confidence, independence and initiative.

During the war, her mother remained her primary role model, inspiring her daughter with her proud contempt for the occupying forces in her country.

Henri d'Astier de la Vigerie was demobbed at the end of the First World War with the rank of lieutenant in the French army. In 1918, aged twenty, he was given the Légion d'honneur and, between the wars, he had developed several business interests and worked as a journalist in New York. Henri was one of three d'Astier de la Vigerie brothers, who were all to play an important role in the Second World War. François, the eldest, worked in London from May 1942 onwards, at the right-hand side of General de Gaulle, while Emmanuel, the youngest brother, ultimately became head of one of the major Resistance groups, Libération-sud, helping thousands of men to travel from the Occupied to the Free Zone, among other achievements.

Henri helped to organise the first US landings in North Africa, in Algeria, in November 1942, and in August 1944 he commanded a group of French commandos he had trained, dressed in British battle-dress, who became the first Frenchmen to land in the port of St Tropez since 1940.

One of his first acts of intelligence gathering had been so daring that it was recorded for prosperity. In 1935 his brother, then General François d'Astier de la Vigerie, had met the future Nazi head of the Luftwaffe, Hermann Goering, at a shooting party in Bavaria. Over the weekend the two men had become friends and, on his return to Germany, Goering had sent d'Astier a small gift, a silver cigarette case onto which he had inscribed the words 'To my friend d'Astier' signed 'Hermann Goering'.

Thinking the case might come in useful, Henri had decided to adopt it as his own and, spending an afternoon in Amiens in June 1940, met and began talking to a German air force officer. As the two men got deeper into conversation, discussing the political situation of their mutual countries, Henri offered his new found 'friend' a cigarette, drawing special attention to his silver cigarette case with its inscription. The German officer was deeply impressed to discover that his new acquaintance was a friend of Goering's and invited him to visit the German air base just outside Amiens for lunch in the officers' mess.

While being entertained, Henri made a mental note of the number and type of aircraft on the base, along with how many aircraft would be flying out of Amiens that day. In the mess he had an excellent lunch of wild boar with sauerkraut and, after drinking several schnapps and beers, found himself chatting to several German pilots, who told him about their reconnaissance flights over England and what they thought about the strength of the RAF.

Henri was already thinking about establishing an intelligence-gathering network. In the summer of 1940, in Lille, he had met a demobbed army officer named Justin Fatigue, who shared his anti-Vichy sentiments. In July Fatigue established a Resistance group named Alibi, whose aim was to hide as much military equipment as possible to avoid it falling into the hands of the enemy. Fatigue asked d'Astier to visit northern France, including the area around the Somme and the Pas de Calais, and report back on any information gained about the German plans to invade southern England. D'Astier, meanwhile, was concerned about how to transfer his newly gathered intelligence to the right people in London. Following his visit to the Somme, Fatigue introduced d'Astier to Piron, who had links with the Resistance group Saint-Jacques, which, in turn, had contacts within British Intelligence in London. D'Astier and Piron soon discovered they had many Belgian friends in common and grew close. It was not long before they began working together, gathering information for British Intelligence.

In December 1940, Piron told d'Astier about his new recruits. It was time for them to meet.

Alain arrived at d'Astier's flat, aware of the concierge watching through the glass window of her ground-floor apartment. Andrée had not been invited, but told her brother to make sure he recalled every single detail of the meeting to report back to her.

D'Astier welcomed Alain into the apartment. He poured out water and then two glasses of Bordeaux. Passing Alain a glass, he invited him to look out of the window onto the street below to check his surroundings.

'We are alone and able to talk freely here. I understand from Monsieur Piron that both you and your sister would like to join the war effort as members of the Franco–Belgian Resistance movement. There are several of us here, in northern France and in Belgium, feeding British Intelligence with anything we can gather on the activities of the German forces which could be of interest to them.

'This is what we would expect of you. You would need to recruit young men and women who share our ideals, who want to resist the German occupation and fight for the freedom of France.'

D'Astier outlined a list of the intelligence they were looking for in particular:

1. The military fortifications around France.
2. Air movements around France.
3. German troop movements around the country.
4. The whereabouts of enemy agents around the country.
5. The way in which the Gestapo was organised and operated.
6. Information on the location and production of secret German arms.

In addition, they wanted to know more about the inner workings of the Vichy government (both military and political) and to find out whatever they could about German military plans in Algeria, Morocco and Tunisia. D'Astier and Alain discussed how agents needed to find ways to convey material gathered from Paris to Marseilles and on to Madrid, where it could reach the British Embassy. D'Astier was also keen to help encourage Frenchmen wanting to leave France and join up with the French army in North Africa and the Allied Forces in Britain.

Alain was well aware of the importance of the group he had been invited to join, and he was already in awe of the man who would become his mentor. After several hours, as he left, d'Astier warned Alain that the time had come to put aside what he described as silly acts of rebellion against the Germans, such as the time when Alain managed to steal a handgun from a German soldier's holster while they were on the *métro*. D'Astier had approved of the student demonstration at the Étoile, but was more dismissive of *La France*, describing it as a game for small children: '*C'est de l'enfantillage à nos yeux.*'[7] It was time for Alain and his friends to grow up.

*

At the end of 1940, on an intelligence-gathering trip to Boulogne in northern France, d'Astier was arrested by the Gestapo. He managed to escape, and returned to Paris, where he was able to warn Piron that the group had been betrayed, by whom they were never to find out.

Shortly after his escape, d'Astier decided that it was now too dangerous for him to remain in France. The Gestapo knew of his existence and of his involvement with the Resistance. In January 1941, he left for Algeria, North Africa. Before leaving, he met with Alain and spoke of his vision for prompting French North Africa to enter the war: 'You are now to go to Marseilles and set up a group which will work alongside the one you have built up in Paris … You must organise an escape route along the demarcation line and find a way of transmitting your gathered intelligence from Marseilles to Algiers and in reverse my mail in the other direction.'[8] D'Astier also warned Alain against meeting further with Piron. 'He could be arrested any moment and since your mother is Belgian, they may link the two up. Keep well away from him.'

After d'Astier's departure, the chronology of events is not entirely clear, but it certainly seems as though Alain did not sever all ties with Piron immediately. Piron continued to run his Franco–Belgian Resistance group for several months with Alain by his side, but in October 1941 Piron was caught, arrested and taken to Fresnes prison where he was badly tortured by the Gestapo. Although he admitted his involvement with the Resistance, he never betrayed any of his colleagues, nor did he disclose any information which could be of use to the Nazis.

Piron was eventually moved to Cologne by the Gestapo, where, on 15 October 1943, he was beheaded. In his memoirs, written over fifty years later, Alain Griotteray wrote that he learnt of Piron's murder on the day of his twenty-first birthday. For Yvonne, the brutal murder of her old friend Georges would stay with her for the rest of her life.

After Piron's death, Alain Griotteray remained in France alone. He was determined to build up his own group to supply Algiers with intelligence. At just eighteen, he was one of the youngest leaders of the French Resistance movement.

## 9

# *Working Amidst the Enemy*

In the autumn of 1940, Andrée watched helplessly, along with her fellow citizens, as the Parisian police force began to implement the Vichy government's anti-Semitic laws against every Jew living in France. After 3 October 1940, Jews were no longer able to join the army or the civil service, teach in schools, work in the media or go to university. Foreign Jews living in France could be interned. After 18 October, any property or business belonging to a Jew was to be confiscated by the state.

Working at Police Headquarters alongside members of the Wehrmacht was becoming increasingly unpleasant for Andrée. But it was hard for anyone in Paris, particularly this conscientious, naïve twenty year-old, to predict how the Parisian police force would move forward over the next four years.

For Andrée, there was no choice but to remain in her job; when the Wehrmacht had marched into Paris and taken over Police Headquarters six months ago, all employees who were categorised as civil servants were required to stay in place. Some of Andrée's colleagues had chosen to disappear rather than be near the occupying forces, but Andrée needed to earn a living. Somehow she and Alain instinctively knew, even in the early days of the occupation, that her position at Police Headquarters might bring certain invaluable advantages.

As the new laws came into force, many Parisians, shocked at the increasingly overt anti-Semitism on display, tentatively began trying to find ways of helping Jewish friends and colleagues leave the city. Some offered to take care of homes or help with businesses. But it was dangerous to stick one's neck out for others, and many Jews found themselves in dire straits. For those living in the poorer districts of Paris with fewer gentile friends, leaving their homes and jobs was not an option. They had nowhere to go.

Edmond and Yvonne were trying to lead as normal a life as possible while living at the heart of a city crawling with Germans, but they could not ignore what was happening. Their friends the Bernsteins had left Paris, but they had not yet had word about their safety. Meanwhile, another friend, Joseph Rubinstein, was preparing to leave his business (an antique shop near the Place de l'Opéra) with the almost certain knowledge that the contents would be pilfered. Edmond, now retired and in his late sixties, was desperate to work out how to help his friend. After much thought and with Yvonne's support, he decided he would offer to run the shop as his own until Joseph and his family could return to Paris.

Initially, all appeared to go smoothly, but within a month a mole alerted the Wehrmacht to the company's Jewish owner. One morning, as Edmond sat in Joseph's office reviewing the accounts, two SS officers and a Wehrmacht captain entered the shop. The officers demanded proof that Edmond owned the business; meanwhile they began searching the shop, looking for evidence that the company still belonged to a Jew. Edmond struggled to control his anger as files and documents were thrown carelessly onto the floor. As they went about their business, the captain accompanying the group moved quietly towards Edmond. Silently he passed him a Rubinstein wedding menu card, which the captain had picked up from the floor. Edmond knew that not all Wehrmacht officers were anti-Semitic, but was nonetheless shocked that the captain had been willing to turn a blind eye to such incriminating evidence. Fortunately he managed to maintain his composure and hid the card on his person.

The search lasted well over three hours, but eventually the officers left without finding any evidence to incriminate Edmond. It had been uncomfortably close though, as he told his family that evening, and there was no guarantee it would not happen again.

As the cold weather approached, Wehrmacht control over the citizens of Paris intensified and food shortages became ever more common. The winter of 1940–1941 was one of the coldest on record, with Parisians freezing without fuel to heat their homes, while also desperately trying to find food. François Clerc, a fit and healthy twenty-year-old member of the Orion Group, lost ten kilos in the four years after the winter of 1940.

In December 1940, Andrée was abruptly moved into a new section of Police Headquarters, referred to as Room 205, 'confection et renouvellement des cartes d'identités étrangéres', where she became part of a team responsible for renewing identity cards for the many foreigners living in Paris. Among them were a large number of Jews, many of whom had previously escaped persecution in other parts of Europe only to find themselves once again discriminated against in France.

Andrée met her new department head, Monsieur Pouillet, a rather dull but immaculately dressed middle-aged man, who in turn introduced her to Madame Caillé, his seemingly charmless yet (as Andrée was later to find out) warm-hearted assistant. It was she who took Andrée through the detailed running of the department. Preparing the cards appeared straightforward, but Andrée was curious to know why every single detail on every Jew living in Paris was to be recorded: they had special filing cards indicating their name, job, date of birth, occupation, address and their identity cards were to be stamped with a red mark to indicate that they were Jewish. Even more odd, every card was duplicated four times so that they could be cross-checked in different ways. Her new colleagues explained that the updating of these special cards had been ordered by the German commandant of Paris, who wanted immediate access to the whereabouts of all the Jews in the city.

After her first day in Room 205, Andrée returned home and, over dinner, explained to her family the manner in which the Jews were being carefully controlled and watched over by the Paris police force. Alain saw immediately that Andrée's new job might afford the chance to steal some identity cards for future use. Andrée, defiant of authority and keen for any opportunity to outwit the Germans controlling Police Headquarters, thought it was an excellent idea and agreed to see what she could do, much to Edmond and Yvonne's anger and concern for her safety.

Andrée soon began to relax into her new role, partly because she enjoyed meeting the large number of foreigners whose ID cards she had to renew, but also because she enjoyed being with a like-minded group of easy-going, gossipy, giggly, fun-loving girls. But that didn't prevent her from starting to think about whether it might be possible to acquire a few blank ID cards from the cupboard where they were stored. As the weeks moved on, she observed her colleagues carefully and noted that, although once completed, an ID card was carefully checked and signed off by the department head, the actual number of cards used did not seem to be monitored as carefully. Many were torn up if an error was made or the name or details of the holder were smudged. It was clear that here was the opportunity she had been waiting for.

By the end of December Andrée had started to help herself to a few blank ID cards, discreetly tucking them into her handbag and taking them home to be stored in the cellar before being passed on to her Resistance colleagues. She must have been aware that if she was ever caught there would be trouble, but she was undeterred. After alerting François Clerc that she had successfully taken an ID card, she would be instructed to deposit it a few days later into a particular postbox, from where it would be picked up, filled out and given to someone who wanted to leave the city and needed a false ID card to do so.

Alain, meanwhile, was now actively planning his move into the Free Zone while still trying to recruit new Resistance members into his group. He began to pressure Andrée to recruit colleagues to help with the theft of ID cards and to carry out some of the courier work which would soon be needed. Despite his pleas, Andrée was not ready to take this next step. Openly discussing one's political opinions and attitude to the invading forces within Police Headquarters was not safe and she needed to be far more confident of her colleagues' political views, let alone whether they would participate in Resistance activities.

On 4 December 1940, Andrée wrote in her diary:

*I am now working on the first floor of the building. My manager is M. Pouillet. We are responsible for renewing the ID cards for all the foreigners who are living in Paris. We have to keep careful records on these people and everything has to be double-checked. Once I have renewed their permit to remain in France, I do not see these foreigners again.*

*I work closely with Madame Caillé, the mother of the Deputy Manager, and three other women from the Western Room. [In 2010 Police Headquarters was still divided into north, south, east and* west sections.] *My colleagues include Marie Thérèse Jeanville, who is somewhat crazy, I like her but she is a flirt, she is tall, dark and rather overweight; Françoise de Boin, a blond girl who is very nice but a bit too fat; and Jacqueline Fresson, who is tall and fair and who I rather like. Today I bought myself a new record, the songs include 'It's a long way to Tipperary' and 'God Save the King'. I also bought a Judy Garland record.*

On 5 December 1940, she picked up her pen again.

*I am at work and here I am writing my diary again. In the last month I have changed departments four times. I will have a very clear understanding of how all these departments work. I am now in office No. 205, where I am issuing ID cards again. I wonder how long I will be here? Well, it is probably of no importance.*

On the evening of 6 December, Andrée was to join Renée for dinner. Her older sister was anxious to learn about how she was coping at Police Headquarters. She arrived at Renée's flat to be greeted by a long-haired dark Siamese cat rustling up against her feet. As she bent to stroke it, she looked up and saw Renée, who explained that its owners were Jewish and had left Paris, so she had taken the cat in to give it a home.

Andrée loved going to Renée's flat. She always enjoyed her elder sister's company, despite her forthright comments about Andrée's appearance and how she should organise her social life. In line with her sister's eccentric personality, the place had a very theatrical appearance and atmosphere. Her husband, Steve Passeur, had collected over the years an interesting collection of memorabilia, including photographs of the leading actors and actresses of the day. Many of these were framed and hung closely together on the walls, alongside copies of the programmes for the plays he had produced.

Andrée was looking forward to dinner, as Renée always managed to find food, and usually good food at that. As they sat down and Renée placed a salad on the table, she asked her sister how she was coping with her job. Andrée explained that she abhorred the whole set-up on principle, but that some of what she did she found interesting and she had made a few friends. She mentioned that she had been moved from one department to another without much time to implement the skills she had learnt in each place, which seemed a little odd.

Renée listened carefully before reassuring her sister that she knew Langeron well and that if Andrée was being moved around departments, it would be for a good reason. She felt it was likely that Langeron wanted Andrée to know as much as possible about what went on within the different departments so that she could get to know her colleagues and make herself useful.

On 8 December, Andrée enjoyed a little light relief at a concert, thanks to her sister. She loved music and was grateful for any opportunity for escape.

> *Renée managed to obtain some tickets for Beethoven's* La Messe solennelle [the *Missa Solemnis*]. *It was simply wonderful. Monsieur Leclercq was in the audience.*

By January 1941, the Wehrmacht had been in Paris for over six months and no Parisian was in any doubt about the meaning of occupation. Andrée had been working at Police Headquarters for over a year and knew her way around pretty thoroughly. She was trusted with full access to the ID card supply and was allowed to request further supplies from an orderly who would deliver them directly to her office.

Some of her colleagues were aware that she had been brought into Police Headquarters by Roger Langeron, but she never referred to it and since the unsuccessful attempt in getting the police archives out of Paris, many of the staff at Police Headquarters had been careful not to be seen to be too closely associated with anyone who knew him well.

Neither she nor Alain ever told me how long they went on producing copies of *La France*, though it is unlikely that it would have continued after Alain left Paris. Possibly Andrée was still typing and printing copies of

*La France* in early 1941, or perhaps it came to an earlier end. She looked back on the risks she took in working on the news-sheet with pride though: in later years she often spoke about the irony of working with members of the German military at the heart of Police Headquarters with no one ever noticing what she was actually doing.

On 1 February 1941, Andrée was moved to the Passport Department, as she described in her diary entry for that day:

> *I am now working in the Passport Department, where I have taken over from a woman who was responsible for those VIPs sent to us by the Head of Police who needed their passports renewed. She must have had a serious disagreement with the Germans. Monsieur Redon attempted to build up my confidence by saying that they needed a sophisticated and intelligent person to do this demanding job. Monsieur Leclercq is the manager. He is very intimidating, but I will not allow myself to be intimidated. It is going to be difficult getting around the building to see my friends and I am having trouble getting to the Copying Department, but I will now know how to prepare passports and I will have access to them.*

In stark contrast to her former gusto, however, by 3 February 1941 she was beginning to feel very low:

> *The first day in my new job here was a nightmare, the second was like being in hell. I have never been so depressed in my life. I am alone in my new office. Monsieur Redon has moved Madmoiselle Laederich to another department, which means I am totally alone preparing passports. Luckily there are two or three really charming women I can call on if I need some help.*

Not even her then-boyfriend Raymond could cheer her up:

> *Raymond wants to go to Tilleuls for the weekend, an auberge in*

*Bourgurail. I am not sure how I could explain this to Maman, so I had better forget about going away with him.*

Still, the weather had its upsides:

*Monsieur Leclercq is not coming in to work today. There is too much snow and he cannot get beyond St Cloud. I am delighted as I will be able to leave my office and move around the building.*

Andrée herself had not had much trouble getting to work that morning, despite the heavy snowfall during the night. In central Paris the roads and pavements had been cleared and the *métro* was running. Knowing that Monsieur Leclercq would not be at work, Andrée took the chance to return to the different departments she had worked in and talk to her former colleagues. On a sudden whim, she went into the 'Foreigners Department' and started to look through the files she had made on some of the Jews who had had to register their presence at Police Headquarters. She took out the files of three Jewish families, made a note of their names and addresses and then replaced the files in the drawers. Without quite knowing why, she had a feeling she might be able to help them one day.

One of her former colleagues, Clotilde, was sitting working at her desk but appeared to take no notice of what she was doing. Had Andrée been asked any questions, she might have backtracked quickly, but fortunately no one did. Andrée was well aware there was a difference between people who were actively prepared to work for the Resistance and those who were part of the passive resistance, who chose to ignore what was going on around them. Andrée decided to stop and chat to Clotilde and started talking about a Charles Trenet concert she had been to a couple of days previously at l'Olympia. Trenet had just released a new record and one of its songs, 'La Mer', based on a Debussy piece, was proving highly popular. Clotilde was also a fan and they had a friendly conversation about Trenet while Andrée wondered whether she could trust her.

Before leaving the office, Andrée took a calculated risk. She moved towards the ID card cupboard and took out a couple of blank cards. Calmly she said to Clotilde, '*Au revoir, à bientôt.*' Then she walked out of the room and back to her office.

## 4 February 1941

*I am so bored. I have some work to do but there is not very much. This morning I prepared a passport and a visa which was checked by Monsieur Leclercq who made sure I had not made any mistakes. He congratulated me and said I had done everything without a single mistake. But for how long are things going to be all right? He is always so very bad tempered.*

## 6 February 1941

*It is 11.00 and Monsieur Leclercq is not here. He has a meeting with the Germans. I have some time to myself. He won't be back until lunchtime.*

As Monsieur Leclercq was not around once again and Andrée had time on her hands, she thought she would return to the Foreigners' Department to see if she could get some more cards.

Clotilde was at her desk again and, as Andrée walked in, she stood up and formally shook her by the hand. Clotilde then began to talk about a play she had seen the previous evening at the Théâtre de Montparnasse – a new production of *Marie Stuart*. While showing her interest in the play, Andrée moved towards the cupboard again. This time Clotilde didn't ignore it. Instead, she warned Andrée to be careful, telling her that if the odd card disappeared no one would notice, but if she continued helping herself to them on such a regular basis someone might become suspicious and that she, Clotilde, might be in trouble. It was the first time any of her colleagues had openly acknowledged what was going on.

## 8 February 1941

*I never have a minute to myself. Today I finished four passports and four visas. I have my own office, which is lucky, as no one quite knows what I*

*get up to. Yesterday Jacqueline and I went to the officers' mess for lunch.*
*It was full of police officers but it was good value.*

## 10 February 1941

*There are times when I find working here so unbearable. I know what is*
*going on around me and yet I just do not know what more I can do to fight*
*it all. There are so many things worrying me and Alain keeps asking me*
*to do more and more and I know I must do as much as I possibly can but*
*I really need to unwind. I do prefer my new job and I do find the people I*
*deal with are more sophisticated. Yesterday an unbelievably good-looking*
*German officer came into my office. He did not take his eyes off me. He was*
*with a French chap I did not know.*

## 11 February 1941

*Tomorrow I am in sole charge of the Passport Office. 'Je fais la perma-*
*nence.' I wonder if it will all go smoothly. I am a little frightened.*

Andrée was feeling rather daunted by this point – both her work and personal responsibilities seemed to be piling up and at times she doubted her
ability to manage. But she did her best to soldier on.

The behaviour of the Wehrmacht in central Paris in the early days of
the war was considered acceptable by many. Yes, they were the occupying
forces but their behaviour towards the civilian population attracted little
criticism and at Police Headquarters, where they were ultimately responsible for the policing of Paris, they moved among the staff with respect. As
the Germans had become more confident in their handling of the occupation, the atmosphere had begun to feel a little more relaxed and some of
the officers were in the habit of asking the French girls working there out
on dates. Andrée had already received several invitations to dinner, but had
always refused them. Her diaries show that she had a casual boyfriend at
this point, Raymond (but she certainly didn't talk to him about what she
was doing with the Orion group), and in any case, for her, dating a German

would have been out of the question. Yet she realised that if she got into trouble, a German friend could prove extremely useful.

### 14 February 1941

*I have just had two dreadful days at work. My feelings towards the Germans are exactly as they were when I first started writing these diaries. Oh, I hope we can win the war and get rid of this despicable lot. I had better be careful what I say, I could be shot for writing what I think of them.*

### 15 February 1941

*Monsieur Mignonnet has a meeting planned with the Germans today. I will have some time to myself.*

On 21 February 1941, Andrée wrote rather cryptically: '*I got into trouble yesterday morning and again this morning. I am sick to death of it all.*' She doesn't refer anywhere to what happened, though possibly the ongoing smuggling of ID cards was taking its toll on her performance at work. Not long after that, on 7 March 1941, she made a similar comment: '*I feel ill every time I walk through the gates. This morning, as I arrived at work at 9.00 a.m., I got into trouble again.*'

There were still occasions to be enjoyed, however, amidst her work troubles, as her diary entry from 6 March showed:

*Alain and I went to the theatre last night with Steve's brother and his wife. It was great fun; they are both so charming. They invited us to join them for dinner at Graff's.*

This was also the first entry in which Andrée mentioned a name that was to crop up in future diary references:

*There is a Monsieur Tevel who is always hanging around at Police Headquarters for some reason or another. He told me that he works at the Belgian Embassy and so we started to talk about Belgium. About a week ago he invited me out to lunch to a restaurant called Le Cabaret. It is not often I go to a restaurant for lunch. We had a really good meal and in the evening I told Raymond all about it. He looked rather surprised and could not quite work out why I had gone out with him. The next day Tevel invited me to the Carnival and I was able to order a Camembert.*

Over the following months Andrée described the various meals she had with the mysterious Thévelle (as she later spelt his name). She never talked about him in more detail, though in February of the following year she referred to having sent Yvonne to the Belgium embassy to pick up some lard. The Griotterays may well have been hungry at that time, but there must have been more to a trip to the embassy than collecting lard. Given the family's Belgian intelligence connection, it seems likely that there was something more to this relationship than purely food.

### 17 March 1941

*I am so very busy at the moment and I am a little frightened. I wish the war would come to an end and that the Germans would leave France. If only life could be what it was in 1939.*

On 16 March, Andrée noted that she was now working with a new, senior colleague, a Madame Bacquias. On the 17th, she wrote:

*Madame Bacquias went off for lunch at 11.15 and did not return until 2.15 at which time she was quite happy for us to take the rest of the afternoon off.*

### 21 March 1941

*Monsieur Langeron, who was arrested a month ago, has just been released from prison and has resigned. Monsieur Marchenaud is to take over as*

*Head of Police. Renée is beside herself worrying about it all. She talks about nothing else.*

On 22 March, Andrée managed to articulate in a little more detail her feelings of ill-ease:

*I am frightened. I really do not know why. At work, apart from a few small things, I do not think I am in any danger. I do, however, argue a lot with Monsieur Leclercq.*

*No, it is a very strange feeling. I am frightened, but I am not quite sure why. It must be because Monsieur Langeron is no longer here. If I do something really stupid there will be no way out.*

Several days later, on 25 March, she mentioned a meal that one of her clients had invited her to:

*Last Thursday Madame Bacquias and I were invited out to dinner. I do like her; she is absolutely charming. Our host was one of our clients, who I had looked after really well. His name is Franck, spelt with a 'c', which means he is an Israelite, a Jew. He certainly needed looking after. He is very nice and invited us both to a restaurant called Magdalen.*

Her rather cryptic reference to his needing to be looked after may suggest that she helped him out somehow or simply that she went out of her way to be kind to him. During the following months of April and May, Andrée noted (in her appointments book, not her journal) ten meetings with a Madame Franck in various bars and restaurants in central Paris. There is no other reference to this woman, nor is it mentioned whether she was a relative of Andrée's client. Given Andrée's clandestine smuggling of blank ID cards, the most likely explanation is that Madame Franck was a contact to whom she passed on the cards for distribution.

While Andrée was working, Alain had not been idle either. At the start of 1941 he prepared to leave Paris and move to Marseilles, in the Free Zone. Given his known association with the Étoile demonstration in November, it was agreed that he would be safer away from Paris and that he would be better placed in Marseilles to build up his intelligence network and recruit people to join his group. François Clerc, meanwhile, would run the group in Paris. Alain's priority before leaving was to find couriers to carry the gathered intelligence between Brussels, Nice, Paris and Marseilles, and he was quick to realise that Andrée might be able to obtain *ausweiss* to facilitate this (*ausweiss* were permits issued by the police, awarding the bearer permission to travel around occupied France during wartime).

Following the fall of France and the formation in October 1940, by Maréchal Philippe Pétain, of the collaborating Vichy government, it had been agreed to divide the country into two zones, the Free Zone and the Occupied Zone. The Free Zone was administered by the Vichy/Pétain Government and allowed the French to move around the zone with a degree of freedom until early 1943, when the Germans invaded the Free Zone and division between the two was abolished. The Occupied Zone was administered by the Wehrmacht, with strict controls over the movement and lives of the population. Travelling between the two zones was hugely difficult and to do so an *ausweiss* was required.

Before he left for Marseilles, Alain asked Andrée to make friends with the police running the Ausweiss Department. Andrée responded that she would carry on stealing and making up false ID cards, but she was not prepared to fraternise with the Germans. Alain tried to persuade her by explaining that without access to the *ausweiss*, they wouldn't be able to get their intelligence out of Paris. If Andrée was prepared to do it, she might be able to get a pass for herself. It was the start of a new career – as an intelligence courier.

## 10

# *Taking Risks*

There were many reasons d'Astier had encouraged Alain to run his new Resistance group in Marseilles in the Free Zone, one of which was because he felt sure that there would be opportunities to transfer the material his agents were collecting to Algeria via the regular ships sailing from Marseilles to North Africa. They were already building up a dossier of information on the movement of German airforce and army troops, the location of German arms production and the presence of the Gestapo around France. There would be more to come as Alain grew his network.

Alain left Paris on a very cold January morning in 1941. He was travelling without an *ausweiss* and so was even more concerned than usual about the ad hoc controls by the Wehrmacht on the roads, in the towns and villages and at bus and train stations. He had to find a way of crossing the demarcation line into the Free Zone without being stopped or questioned. He decided to cross the border in the Bigorre area of south-west France, in the Pyrenees, and where he knew he would find a local who would help him reach the Free Zone.

He got off the train one station early, thinking that as he was still some distance from the demarcation line, there would be fewer police controls. He slipped into the crowds, trying to mingle unobtrusively. He was heading to a safe house where the owners had connections to help him cross.

In early 1941, the borders between the Occupied and Free Zones were carefully controlled. Crossing a demarcation line from one zone to the other was very difficult and there could be serious consequences if one was caught without an *ausweiss*, though people did still risk it and occasionally managed to get through. As the war progressed and especially after the German occupation of the Free Zone and the creation of the *milice française* (Vichy's infamous paramilitary force), it became ever more dangerous.

Alain's ability to find friends wherever he went did not let him down. He reached the auberge he was looking for and the owner found someone who would smuggle him over the demarcation line. They refused payment for their help, insisting that he was 'too sweet' and would need the money later. A week after leaving Paris, Alain arrived safely in Marseilles, impatient to start building up his group. Thanks once again to assistance from his brother-in-law, he managed to get a job at the Ministry of Meat Distribution. He knew virtually no one in the area, but one of his first tasks was to find a way to relay his group's gathered intelligence from France to North Africa.

Life in the Free Zone was more relaxed than in the Occupied Zone; few checks were made on people's movements and the police force were primarily concerned with maintaining public order. Alain began to frequent the bars of Marseilles, seeking out like-minded young men. People were on the whole much more relaxed about talking to strangers than they would have been in Paris. Along the way he managed to acquire a press card for a southern regional newspaper called *Le Phare*, which gave him entry to a large number of civic events taking place in the city.

Drinking late one night among a group of friends in La Cintra, a popular Marseilles bar, Alain fell into conversation with a portly, dark-haired, suntanned Corsican named Jean-Baptiste Biaggi. Born into an old Corsican family and graduating from officer training in Saumur in 1938, Biaggi (as he was affectionately known among his friends) had had to give up law school to enlist in 1939. One of Alain's most daring and intelligent recruits, they would remain close friends until the end of Alain's life.

Biaggi thought through everything he worked on in great detail. Despite his huge energy, he was quiet, had a calming personality and spoke in a very clear voice. During the four years of occupation he never stopped telling his Resistance colleagues about how careful and cautious they needed to be about everything and anything going on around them. He had been shot both in the stomach and in the back in 1939 and was given up for dead on the battlefield when an army doctor friend recognised him lying among a group of wounded soldiers. 'This one we have to sort out,' his friend was quoted as saying. Somewhat prematurely, Biaggi was awarded the Légion d'honneur 'posthumously', having been understood to have died in combat. As Yves de Kermoal wrote to me in 2012: 'Because he was expected to die from his wounds, he was given the Légion d'honneur, but once he recovered, the authorities asked him to return it to them!'

After receiving medical care from the French army medical services, Biaggi was transferred to a German military hospital. The Wehrmacht medical corps nursed him back to health before releasing him, as his German doctors believed the wounds inflicted on him were so great that he would be unable to do anything further to help the French war effort. He left hospital with two walking sticks and moved to Clermont-Ferrand in central France where, for a whole year, doctors worked to rebuild his shattered body.

As their friendship developed, Biaggi invited Alain to Vichy, promising to introduce him to some of his friends working at the heart of the Vichy government. Alain's government job meant he could now get the *ausweiss* required to move freely around the country and he jumped at the chance, playing up his relaxed 'Grand Bourgeois' manner to endear himself to Vichy society. The approach bore fruit – both young men managed to recruit a number of people on the inside who were willing to keep them informed on the inner workings and personalities of the Vichy government; material that Alain could then feed back to d'Astier.

One of their most important recruits was Martial de la Fournière. Born in 1918 into an old aristocratic family, he had graduated from Saint-Cyr as a colonel in the French army and before the war had been earmarked for the diplomatic service. In 1941 Martial was working in Vichy in the Colonial Ministry, headed by Admiral Platon, a close friend of Admiral Darlan, who was in charge of the French fleet. It was with Martial's help that Alain and Biaggi built up a detailed picture of the Vichy government. They also came into contact with some young men working for Jean Barthélemy, Minister of Justice, who gave them details of what was going on in the judicial courts of Vichy.

Alain and Biaggi had been trying without great success to find ways of sending the gathered information to the British intelligence services via d'Astier de la Vigerie in Algiers when Biaggi's brother-in-law, Toussaint Guidicelli, offered to help out. He owned the Société Hôtelière de Ravitaillement Maritime, a company that supplied merchant ships going from Marseilles to Algeria with food supplies. The system became so successful that in 1942 General Giraud* started sending his mail through the group.

As they extended their network, the boys met Marc Jacquet of the Banque National de Commerce et d'Industrie (today's Banque Nationale de Paris), who at great risk allowed their intelligence to be dropped at an agency in Marseilles and then taken on to Algiers through the bank's own couriers.

One significant difference between the Orion Resistance Group and others in its early stages was that they never used radio transmitters as a method of transferring gathered intelligence; Alain considered them far too dangerous because the signals could be easily picked up by the occupying forces. It was only later, in 1942, when Alain had recruited François de Rochefort into the group, that this began to change. François brought with him several military contacts and as a result they were able to gain occasional access to radio transmitters belonging to the resistance arm of the French army (l'organisation de la résistance de l'armée, or ORA). After the war, Andrée repeatedly stressed the wisdom of Alain's original decision, however: 'I was a member of the Resistance for several more years than most members of SOE and therefore ran the risk of being caught over a longer period, but I was always safer than they were because I was never asked to carry a radio transmitter or transmit information using one.'

---

* Later to become Commander-in-Chief of the French forces in North Africa.

# 11

# *A Dangerous Affair*

Alain's group of resistance fighters were recording information on a number of different areas, including the industrial production of certain targeted companies in France, the movement of German troops in the north of the country, and the inner workings of the Vichy government. François Clerc, now the Orion Group's leader in Paris and Alain's deputy, needed someone to type up the intelligence they had gained and prepare it for forwarding to British Intelligence.

At the start of the invasion François had attempted to escape France on a British ship to England. When that failed, he decided to remain in France and ended up working for a company that manufactured and distributed steel pipes across the Occupied Zone. Deeply patriotic, he worked tirelessly during the war years to gather information about industrial production in eastern France that might be of use to the British intelligence services and later to the US. Aware of how she had helped out with *La France*, he asked Andrée if she would be willing to provide similar assistance in urgent cases, taking dictation over the telephone and then delivering the typed material to agreed drop-off points. Once again, Andrée agreed readily.

Participating in the French Resistance was dangerous and, as their little group began to grow, Alain and his colleagues knew instinctively that they should draw up guidelines as to the precautions they should all take. Alain was adamant that strict rules were vital and it was mainly to his credit that only six members of his group were arrested over the course of the war. Two members lost their lives, including the group's original leader Georges Piron, while the remaining four managed to escape imprisonment.

The less contact members of the group had with each other and the less they knew about the others' activities, the safer they would be if questioned or arrested. Moving their acquired intelligence around was dangerous and they had to be careful, but an early axiom for the Orion Group was that personal safety was more important than the relaying of the intelligence.

Because of her role in typing up others' material, Andrée was potentially at greater risk than the others, although she always claimed she typed out the reports without paying attention to the contents. The group avoided written communication to minimise the chance of incriminating themselves. They rarely called each other at home or at work, they never met at each others' houses and they were always on their guard. One of their cardinal rules was never to meet in bars or restaurants because of the impromptu ID card checks and searches made by the Nazis. A preferred method of communicating was through coded telephone conversations; François Clerc might phone Andrée at Police Headquarters and ask about the weather. If the answer was 'It is a lovely day', François knew he could speak and arrange a meeting. If the weather was bad, he knew he had to get off the line quickly. François had set up a number of safe houses around central Paris where information could be delivered or picked up. The best places were those to which regular travel was entirely expected. No one would question a visit to a doctor, a lawyer or a priest. The confessional box was always considered a safe place to pass on messages verbally because no German soldier would dare eavesdrop on the confessional box; especially in Paris in the early stages of the war, when the behaviour of members of the Wehrmacht towards the civilian population was still restrained. François would indicate he was going to confession that evening and Andrée knew that he therefore had something to say to her. He gave his priest the message he wanted passed on to Andrée, who in turn would attend confession to receive the message. François told me, with characteristic French humour: 'I have never been to confession so much in my life as I did during the war.'

François went to great trouble to emphasise to me, in a conversation in 2010, the environment in which they operated. 'At any time you could be picked up off the street for no reason. It was only by having a sixth sense that many survived... We lived from one day to the next not knowing what might happen... we were terrified of the bombs, the exodus from Paris... The denunciations were horrendous. Often there was no reason. It could be that someone did not share a neighbour's political views or they were anti-Jewish, or they just wanted to make a bit of money on the side.'

He was contemptuous of the French police, whom he described as 'more laid-back about who they arrested' but who, nevertheless, worked hand-in-hand with the Germans. 'You had to be so careful about everything you did … the way you spoke, walked, ran, even your mannerisms. The way you lit and smoked a cigarette, how much money you spent, where you bought a newspaper – anything that might lead to someone noticing you.'

In May 1941, aged twenty, Andrée undertook the first of many trips on behalf of the French Resistance movement. Her only qualifications for her job as a courier were common sense, confidence and 'sangfroid'. Unlike the couriers working for SOE (Special Operations Executive, a covert British service designed to support resistance in Europe), she had been given no formal training to help her. In typical fashion, she was unconcerned about her personal safety. She never thought of the dangers, or the implications of being caught. She simply got on with what had to be done, motivated both by patriotism and perhaps an even stronger human urge – the desire to please her adored brother. In later life she described her work in the Resistance as a game, and often said, 'When you are young you do not think about the dangers or the risks you are running.' Yet a courier's job was inherently dangerous. Travelling around France in 1941 was not a safe adventure; a French citizen could be searched for no reason at all. To be caught with anything (such as information on German troop movements or industrial production, to give but two examples of the kind of material Andrée would carry) would inevitably lead to arrest and questioning under torture.

In the run up to her first trip to Marseilles, Andrée made an early-morning visit to her doctor, where she collected the information left by François Clerc the previous evening. She typed up the document at work, as usual making no duplicates of the report and taking the used typewriter ribbon with her, along with the document, when she left for the day. Once home, she carefully unstitched the lining in her suitcase to conceal within the 'post' she was taking.

She went to bed early, explaining to her parents that she would be going to Marseilles in the morning for a few days' holiday to see Alain. Her father, quick off the mark, said he would take her to the station in the morning; her parents suspected something was afoot but decided not to express their concerns.

The train left at 6.30 a.m. Curfew finished at 5.30 a.m. and by 6.00 a.m. both Andrée and Edmond were waiting in line in the station to have her ticket, *ausweiss* and ID card checked. Edmond hugged his daughter and waved goodbye, trying not to let his fears show as she handed over her documents and walked towards the train.

Because the Wehrmacht had requisitioned so many trains, transport around France during the war had been substantially reduced, and the regular bombing by the RAF caused endless delays. The operating trains were always overcrowded with large numbers of officers and soldiers travelling with the civilian population. Andrée made her way onto the platform and walked along the carriages looking for a seat, hoping she wouldn't have to stand all the way to Marseilles. Luck was on her side this time; she saw a fold-away seat by the carriage door and swiftly took it. Not long after, after the train's departure, as she was reading her book, a German officer walking through the train noticed her with a smile, saluted and said, 'Bonjour, Mademoiselle.' Attempting to be helpful, he picked up her small brown case and told her there was some room left in a compartment in the middle of the carriage and that he would be happy to place it there. There was nothing to be done; Andrée could only acquiesce as her suitcase was carried away from her. The young German officer was quick to return and, offering Andrée a cigarette, tried to engage her in conversation. He was slim and fresh-faced and Andrée had to admit that she found him attractive, but she wanted to read her book and be left alone. She also knew that if she engaged with him, the people around her might well frown upon this and should she need to ask for their help later in the journey, any request might be ignored or denied.

The passengers were tightly packed into the carriages, each with a look of quiet resignation; everyone was used to difficult journeys. With so many of the railway lines being arbitrarily bombed by the Allies, trains regularly ground to an abrupt halt and passengers had to climb off the train and make their way to the next station by foot.

Andrée was lucky that this, her first proper journey, passed without any problem. The German officer who had helped her with her case left the train after a few hours, at which time Andrée decided it would be safer to collect her suitcase, rather than leave it unattended any longer. Many hours after leaving Paris, the train steamed into Marseilles. There was a sense of excitement among the passengers as they emerged from the train into a southern town free from Nazi occupation. It had been a warm spring day and the warmth in the air could still be felt.

It was dusk and Andrée knew she had to move quickly. She had never visited Marseilles before. It was a huge and potentially exciting town, but she had to be careful. François Clerc had given her the address of a reliable hotel overlooking the port. Hoping there might still be a room for her, she asked a taxi driver to take her to the hotel. The station area was congested with traffic; cars, horse-drawn carts, buses and people had all arrived to meet the train and the crowds of friends and families showed no sign of abating. After much swearing in a strong southern French accent from her driver, they managed finally to leave the station's square.

Upon arrival at the hotel, Andrée was pleased to see that it was small and comfortable, and even happier when the owner showed her to a room overlooking the port. It was still early evening and Andrée enjoyed looking out onto the activity below as several ships were being loaded in preparation for their departure the next morning. Dinner was a bouillabaisse followed by a chocolate meringue cake. There had been so little food in Paris over the last few months that eating this southern dish of freshly cooked fish, mussels, shrimps and lobster in a wine sauce was a memory that stayed with her into old age. Feeling warm and more relaxed, Andrée went to bed and quickly fell asleep.

In the morning she woke early to the sounds of a ship sounding its horn in preparation for its departure. She dressed, paid her bill and left the hotel. She had Alain's address and had been told to wait for him in the café below the apartment block where he lived and where he usually started his day with a café au lait. As she made her way to meet her brother, Andrée absorbed the relaxed atmosphere that reigned in the Free Zone. There was food and drink available in the cafés, bars and restaurants, and there were few controls to restrict one's movement. The police apparently kept careful control of the port, but otherwise people were free to move around the city and the Marseilles police turned for the most part a blind eye to Resistance activities, only becoming involved if they were provoked.

Alain was relieved that Andrée had not encountered any problems and as she discreetly passed him the 'post', they arranged to meet later that day for lunch with his friend, Jean-Baptiste Biaggi. The three of them enjoyed themselves over the next few days, but all too soon Andrée had to make her way back home to Paris.

Between June 1941 and Christmas 1941, she made several further trips down to Marseilles. For obvious reasons, no records were kept of these trips nor of their exact dates. Like SOE, the Orion Group kept few records,* but well after the war Andrée often spoke to her children about her adventures during the war years. She always claimed ignorance as to the contents of what she carried though, saying: 'I had no idea what information I was carrying. It was far safer for everyone involved.'

---

* Many of the records that were kept of SOE's activities in France during the Second World War were mysteriously burnt at the end of the war – possibly explained by the fact that so many members of SOE continued to work for the British intelligence services after the war had ended.

## 12

# *The Birth of Orion*

In 1941, a new member joined the group: Paul Labbé, a small-built, thin and highly intelligent twenty-year-old whose family lived in the Béarn area of France, in the Basque country. He and his family, and their home, Le Château d'Orion, would play a vital role in the group's work.

Paul was a staunch monarchist, descended from a long line of devout Protestants, and had been studying law at the Sorbonne. Another member of the group, Yves de Kermoal, described him in 2012 as 'a small chap who looked like a monk who had walked straight out of the middle ages into the twentieth century'.

On 9 February, 1941 Andrée wrote in her diary:

> *Alain brought his friend Paul Labbé to my party. He asked me to dance with him several times.*

Alain, meanwhile, was sounding out Paul's political views to see if he could be trusted. As their friendship grew, Paul invited Alain to stay at his home, only thirty kilometres away from the Spanish border and a couple of kilometres away from the demarcation line into the Free Zone.

The château was a seventeenth-century manor house covered in thick ivy, situated on the edge of the small hamlet of Orion and surrounded by an overgrown formal garden overlooking the Pyrenees. It had been in Paul's mother's family for several generations. Madame Labbé had suffered more than most at that point: her husband had recently died; she had lost a son, Jacques, killed in battle at the beginning of the war; and another son, Jean, was an officer serving in the French navy. Although Paul was technically still at university, his mother knew it would not be long before he too would be fully immersed in the war.

Nonetheless she gave her son's new friend a warm welcome upon his arrival. The boys spent many hours walking in the hills surrounding Orion, soaking up the clean air of the Pyrenees and planning their collaboration. Paul's family was well known throughout the area and he was confident his mother, his sister Ninon, the château retainers and other locals would help them with their plans.

Madame Labbé had met and married her husband before the First World War – a Parisian doctor whose successful hobby as a watercolour painter had earned him a strong following in the area. After her husband's death at the beginning of 1939 and the outbreak of war once again, she left Paris and returned to her family home in the Basque country. She allowed her house to be used for Resistance meetings and as a drop-off and collection point for the couriers relaying intelligence documents, and she invited many of the Orion agents, particularly Alain and Andrée, to stay at the château. The whole group was hugely fond of Madame Labbé, whom they called Tante Marie – an unusually informal term of address in France at that time.

One of Henri d'Astier's directives had been to find a way of helping men escape France so that they could join the army and, in 1941, Alain and Paul set up a system which would ultimately allow over 1,000 Frenchmen to use the Orion escape route to leave France. The people of Orion and the surrounding region knew the Pyrenees well, and the best routes across the border and over to Spain. Smuggling had been a way of life for some of the local families for centuries and during the war years they familiarised themselves with the German patrol times and the number of border points.

Given Orion's rural location so close to the occupied zone, the locals regularly crossed between the two zones carrying out their errands – anyone crossing was required to carry an *ausweiss* and there were regular inspections by the local police or Wehrmacht. But according to Gandy, residents weren't always subject to full checks; this was a tiny community close to the demarcation line, and procedures may have been more relaxed on occasion. Paul was presumably hopeful that getting across the line in the surrounding area might be easier than elsewhere, whether with false papers or by crossing illegally, away from the checkpoint. That is not to say that it was risk-free, particularly as the war progressed. Moving between the zones became increasingly dangerous as the demarcation line began to be policed more heavily and escapees without the right permits were picked up and arrested.

Once would-be escapees had managed to get across the demarcation line, they were matched with a local *passeur*. The *passeurs* were local Basque men who lived in the foothills of the Pyrenees and whose job it was to know the best ways of crossing the mountainous range. Between 1940 and 1944, it is estimated they helped over 33,000 men escape France to gain their freedom. In winter the paths could be dangerous, but during the rest of the year the weather was generally clement and posed no problem.

Back in Paris, Biaggi met two men who would prove central to Orion's plans. Xavier Escartin was a deeply patriotic Basque whose business activities led him to travel regularly between Paris and south-western France. Michel Alliot was an energetic and enterprising young man from a small village near the Jura: at sixteen, he graduated from one of France's leading schools, the Lycée Louis le Grand. Aged only sixteen, Alliot had established his own Resistance group, Vaudevir, focusing on producing false documents, but also helping men to escape France through the Jura to Switzerland. Based initially in the rue Honoré Chevalier, Alliot's extraordinary operation, Vaudevir, had collected over a million false documents by 1945, including christening certificates, food and tobacco coupons, and even school reports. The group started by making stamps out of sculptured potatoes to forge ID cards, but later became a repository for thousands of genuine ID cards stolen from Parisian town halls. Vaudevir went on to supply Orion with additional ID cards and certificates, as their 'clients' sometimes needed as many as seventeen sets of false papers to travel from Paris to the Pyrenees.*

---

\* In 2013, Economica published a book on the definitive list of Resistance groups active in France, titled *Les réseaux de résistance de la France combattante*. In it Vaudevir is listed as a sub-group of Orion, though that was not how any of Orion's members described it to me.

Biaggi introduced his new contacts to Alain and Paul, and the five of them discussed their escape route plans and how they would recruit men in the capital who wanted to leave France. As Orion's reputation developed, Frenchmen from all over Paris started to approach them for help. Detailed conversations would then take place to discuss on what basis Orion would provide assistance, and after their credentials had been carefully checked, their names would be passed on to Orion's agents in the Basque country, who would organise their departure.

It was during Alain's first stay at the château that Paul had proposed a name for their organisation: le réseau Orion (the Orion Resistance Group). He told Alain, 'No one will ever think of the château or the village. They will think you are referring to the constellation.'[9] After the war the group was officially recognised by the Ministry of Defence as the Réseau Orion, in operation from April 1941. Between April 1941 and October 1942, its couriers delivered thirty-one pieces of intelligence from different parts of France to Marseilles, from where they were passed on to Henri d'Astier in Algeria and ultimately to the British and American intelligence services.

## 13

# *Courage*

After Alain and Paul set up the Orion escape route through the Pyrenees, Andrée began to travel down to the Basque country, carrying some of the gathered intelligence which needed to be taken through the Pyrenees to the US consulate in Santander or to Algeria by boat via Marseilles. She was now travelling as a courier between Paris and Orthez, as well as down to Marseilles. The latter route was becoming increasingly important as new agents were drawn into the Orion network in northern France.

Sometimes Andrée received dictated notes (in code of course) via telephone and sometimes they were given to her in note form. Once in Marseilles, 'the post' was taken by the sailors of the Société Hôtelière de Ravitaillement Maritime (a private company that operated in a similar fashion to the Merchant Navy's food supply ships) or by couriers of the Banque Nationale de Commerce et d'Industrie to Algeria.

As day-to-day life in occupied France became increasingly depressing and difficult, Andrée was intrigued when she returned home one evening from a music recital at the German Institute to find a letter addressed to her from her Belgian uncle, advising her that one of his friends would be arriving in Paris and would be inviting her out to dinner. She had not eaten a good meal since Christmas and Andrée's love of good food was legendary, so she was very excited at the thought of dinner at Prunier's, but curious as to why a friend of her uncle would invite her to join him in one of the city's best restaurants.

Andrée's diary entry for 14 May 1941 refers both to the daily problem of finding food and the luxury of a good meal out – a rare pleasure for the majority of Parisians by this point:

*Maman is leaving for St James at the end of the month. She is fed up with not having any food. She intends to find some food there and send it home so that we have something to eat.*

*I had dinner with a friend of l'oncle Auguste who was in Paris for a couple of days. He invited me to join him at Prunier's where we had a bottle of 1918 Bollinger, some excellent oysters, a delicious steak tartare and some frites.* *

On the evening of her dinner date, Andrée left the flat in the early evening and made her way to the *métro*. As she walked into Prunier's and took in the atmosphere, she could see a large number of Wehrmacht officers dining. She approached her host's table and was careful to respond to his welcome appropriately, as he stood up and kissed her three times on the cheek in accordance with Belgian custom.

As they finished eating, her companion quietly explained that he was carrying a number of documents which he had brought from Brussels and which he was going to hand over in a bag also containing a box of Belgian chocolates from Wittamer and a couple of historical novels for her mother. Over the last year Andrée had collected intelligence from many Resistance colleagues, but never so openly in a public place, and in full view of so many officers. She casually took the bag and placed it by her side. Basic common sense told her that her host might have been followed from Brussels and, although her brother's security rules did not allow meeting in public places, it was safer to stay away from the family flat. A meeting like this one, taking a young lady out to dinner, would seem perfectly normal.

As curfew was about to fall, Andrée and her host left the restaurant and said *au revoir*. They wouldn't meet again until long after the war.†

---

* Indicative of the lifestyle some people in Paris were able to have during the war years, especially the German officers, collaborators and members of intelligence services.

† Andrée's host might have been Raoul Maillard. Born in Liège, Belgium, in 1896, he was included in the list of the Orion agents recorded in the archives of the French Ministry of Defence. He came to visit Andrée in London many years later, bringing gifts for her children.

When she arrived home, she was met by Alain, who asked his sister how she felt about going on a trip to the Pyrenees to deliver some intelligence. He and Paul had worked out a new route from Orion to the US consulate in Salamanca. There was always danger, of course, but he was confident that they had a reliable channel in place. Andrée was to travel down to the Basque country to stay at the Château d'Orion, where Madame Labbé and her friends would ensure the onward delivery of the material she brought with her. Alain was keen for her to go as soon as possible; he was sure the material she had been given was valuable and wanted to get it to Salamanca swiftly.

Yvonne had been listening to her son and daughter's conversation from the adjoining room. She couldn't keep quiet any longer. 'You had both better be very careful,' she warned them, anxiously.

At Police Headquarters early the next morning, Andrée requested the application forms for an *ausweiss*. She had examined the map and the train timetables and asked permission from her department head to travel to Orthez via Bordeaux.

Her request went through without a hitch and soon the day arrived. Andrée was looking forward to meeting the Labbé family; she had come across Paul several times at parties in Paris, but knew little about the rest of his family. Alain had told her that Madame Labbé was the kindest, most generous and welcoming person she could meet, and that Paul's sister was around her age.

She stepped off the bus into the quiet Basque village of Salies-de-Béarn and looked around to see whether anyone from the château had come to meet her. As she held her little suitcase with her 'post' hidden within, she could sense the nearby group of German soldiers observing her. She stood quietly where the bus had left her and tried to look relaxed and naive as she soaked up the warm sun. She had put through a call to the château from Orthez that morning to let them know she was coming, but still no one arrived. She took refuge in a nearby café and sat with a tisane for a while until at last an old man approached her and asked in a strong Basque accent, 'Are you expected at the château?' Not waiting for an answer, he continued, 'I am Monsieur Flandé.'

Relieved, she responded affirmatively and followed him to his horse and cart. She kept a tight grip on her suitcase as she climbed up and settled into the seat at the top of the cart.

The horse jolted before starting its journey through Salies-de-Béarn, which was slowly coming to life after the arrival of the bus from Orthez. They trotted through the narrow streets and over the small bridge, covered in red geraniums; Andrée admired the little houses with their sloping tiled roofs and large windows with closed shutters hiding them from the outside world. This was a Basque town at its prettiest and she looked forward to the journey ahead. They passed an elegant and imposing eighteenth-century house, which Monsieur Flandé told her had been bought by a local family to house Russian refugees after their revolution. As they ambled past the town's school, he told her tales about some of the local families. The sun began to set as they moved out into the open country, but she could see the rolling hills and track which led to Orion. The peacefulness of the country-side left its mark on Andrée, especially given the tense atmosphere she had left behind in Paris, and slowly she began to relax.

It was not long before they were trotting into the tiny deserted Béarnais hamlet. It was almost dark as they went past the cemetery where so many of the villagers were buried, the tiny town hall which doubled up as the local school, and finally the church adjoined to the château. The horse turned through the wrought-iron gates and stopped in front of the château's main entrance.

Monsieur Flandé's wife, the château's housekeeper, ran out to greet the new arrival. A short woman with meticulously tidy hair and a dark Basque complexion, she prided herself on looking after Paul's new friends, conscious that those living in the cities were always hungry.

Madame Flandé apologised that Madame Labbé was not there to greet her guest in person. Her grief, the war and the presence of the Germans in the occupied zone only two kilometres from her home had left its mark on the châtelaine. She was resting in her room and would meet Andrée the following morning.

Madame Flandé showed Andrée to her bedroom, climbing the wide panelled staircase to the first floor. There was little light and Andrée was barely able to see the steps to her room, but she was happy to have arrived and she knew she was now safe. She had been offered a bowl of soup and some bread, but after such a long journey she just wanted to rest. She lay down on the bed, looked out at the clear night and bright stars through the large windows and promptly fell asleep.

The church bells started ringing at 7.00 a.m. It was time to get up and Andrée was eager to meet Madame Labbé and her daughter, so she dressed quickly and went downstairs to see who was around.

Walking into the kitchen she was greeted by Monsieur Flandé with scrambled egg made with fresh milk from the château's cows and eggs from the yard's hens. She had been expecting this treat, knowing that most farmers and villagers throughout France were still able to feed themselves, despite the Germans pilfering much of it. Madame Flandé was preparing the pastry for a tarte aux pommes as Andrée sat down at the long wooden kitchen table and waited for her mouth-watering breakfast.

As she ate, she marvelled at the view in front of her; the rolling hills were covered by deep-green meadows which spread into the distance. It was a clear morning and she could see the shape of every peak of the imposing stretch of mountains separating France from Spain: occupation versus freedom. Despite the arrival of spring, the top of the peaks of the Pyrenees were still covered in snow and she watched the changing landscape as the sun rose. She could see the fields divided up by the different crops, barley separated from wheat, and she wondered whether the owners of the farm in front of her were 'friends' of the château.

Breakfast finished, Andrée decided to explore the château and its gardens. She walked out of the kitchen, picked a small bunch of wild flowers in the garden and walked around the house to the front door, where she entered a small rectangular hall with an imposing but beautiful portrait of Madame Labbé in eighteenth-century dress. Opposite hung a portrait of Maréchal Pétain in military uniform. On another wall to the right of the painting of the châtelaine, a huge French nineteenth-century mahogany linen cupboard dominated the hall.

She admired Monsieur Labbé's watercolours hanging in the drawing room alongside several portraits of the Reclus and Labbé ancestors. She then moved into the formal dining room where several large mirrors adorned the panelled walls. Some of the family silver was lying on the table. She thought about the hours that would have been spent sitting around this dining room table, eating, drinking and discussing politics.

As Andrée bent to look at some of the books lying on one of the tables, she heard someone coming into the room; it was Madame Labbé, dressed totally in black. She moved towards Andrée to shake her by the hand and welcomed her warmly. Together they walked out into the garden and despite the cool May air sat down on one of the garden benches to get to know each other. Andrée told Madame Labbé about the documents she had brought down from Paris; her host was pleased that everything had reached Orion safely and assured her that within the next couple of days the information would be taken through to Spain by one of their trusted *passeurs*. Madame Labbé invited Andrée to stay as long as she wished but, unfortunately, she had to return to Paris the next day. Her guest ventured a question: why was there a portrait of Pétain hanging in the hall? Madame Labbé laughed, and explained that by doing so the Germans would think they were collaborators and if there was any trouble the château was less likely to be searched. Life in Orion was difficult, as it was everywhere in rural France during the occupation, but because the château was so remote, there were no Germans on their doorstep. German patrols however regularly visited the hamlet, stealing their food and ensuring their presence was felt.

All too soon it was time to return to Paris. Her mission had been a success, but this was only the beginning. As their intelligence-gathering grew in scope, she would not be able to manage alone; they would need more couriers to help with the workload. But recruiting other couriers was likely to be extremely difficult. The right candidates would need to be discreet but confident, naive in demeanour yet quick-witted, fiercely patriotic but never forthright in expressing their political views. It would be useful to know whether they had families in different parts of France as that would make it easier for them to get *ausweiss*, but at the same time it was always better for everyone involved to know as little as possible about other couriers in case they were caught. Alain was keen to recruit women because experience suggested that they were less likely to be stopped or searched by the Wehrmacht.

Who could she approach, who could she trust? As the train steamed into Paris, Andrée mentally considered her closest friends and decided she would speak to two people, Marthe Dramez and Margit Ehrart. Marthe, who chain-smoked Gauloises, was small and quiet; she was slightly older than Andrée's other friends, and had proved to be one of the most loyal. Marthe had begun her career as a history teacher in one of the most successful lycées in Paris and she had helped Alain pass his baccalaureate. Later she became headmistress at another leading girls' school, and was awarded the Légion d'honneur in the 1960s in recognition of her work for the Resistance and her contribution to education. Half-Austrian Margit, meanwhile, spoke impeccable German and looked like an Aryan with her blond hair and blue eyes; she would be the perfect candidate to transport any material from Nice. Her grandparents had always lived there, so she had a valid reason to visit and Andrée knew she would enjoy soaking up the warm Mediterranean sun and relaxing in the Free Zone. Margit was always keen to undertake a challenge.

As she arrived back in Paris, Andrée felt very pleased with herself. She had thought of two reliable friends who she was almost certain would help. The intelligence would be divided up and she wouldn't have to risk drawing too much attention to herself at work by travelling too frequently. But at the back of her mind, she knew that the risks were growing; if she was caught, there would be the added risk of betraying the others.

# 14

# *Imperilled*

In late 1941, finding food was a challenge for most Parisians and as the winter wore on, they began to endure food shortages which were at times so extreme that Andrée described eating several dinners of rat meat and beetroot, a vegetable she refused to touch for the rest of her life. Food rationing had come into force back in May: each person was given an allowance of 350g of meat, 70g of cheese, 100g of fat, 50g of sugar, 250g of pasta and 200g of rice per month. For those living in the countryside, a little more food was often available but the German soldiers were masters of the art of pilfering.

Unsurprisingly, food became one of the most important subjects of conversation for Andrée and her mother for the rest of their lives. During the war years Yvonne managed to buy food on the black market in La Vendée by selling much of her jewellery, several pieces of which had been in her family for many generations. She was also able to bring back food from the country, either from Rochefort-en-Yvelines, where the family owned a small house with a little vegetable garden, or from friends in Normandy who would arrange for parcels to be sent to Paris. Much later Andrée took her own family to visit the Normandy farm that had been the source of much-needed food at a time of deprivation; her four-year-old son refused to drink the fresh milk he was given by the farmer's wife, so different was it from what he was used to in London.

Andrée's diary entries from this period reflect their day-to-day preoccupations – trying to find food, to stay positive, not to dwell in detail on the difficulties of life in an occupied city.

## 8 December 1941

*Life is becoming so unbelievably difficult. There are some fools who have begun to assassinate German soldiers on the streets of Paris. This will not help our cause and because of this curfew has been set at 6.00 p.m. Monsieur Leclercq, the Head of my Department, has said the office will close at 4.00. It is good to be able to leave work early, but not much fun having to be indoors by 6.00.*

Around this time, communist activists across France had begun a policy of indiscriminately murdering German soldiers on the streets of the major French cities. The reprisals for these assassinations were horrendous; for every murdered soldier, the Commandant of Paris ordered groups of innocent French civilians to be randomly rounded up from the streets and shot at dawn. Andrée lost one of her closest friends in this way after he decided to risk breaking the 6.00 p.m. curfew following a birthday party. He was arrested on the streets of Paris and taken to a local police station. The following morning, in retaliation for the killing of a Wehrmacht officer or soldier, ten Frenchmen were shot without trial, Andrée's friend among them.

General de Gaulle intervened from London to order that the killing of Wehrmacht soldiers should cease, though perhaps even more effective was the weight of local opinion in areas facing reprisals, where people were angry and scared by the violence on the streets.

On 16 December 1941, Andrée wrote in her journal:

*I am organising a New Year's Eve party. There will be twelve of us, although sadly Serge will not be there. Serge has left Paris and has gone into the Free Zone. It was about time he left because there are hundreds of Jews being arrested all over Paris. Monsieur Bigard, Serge's father, has been arrested and Papa is beside himself with anger. Toto Bernstein, a friend of Renée's, has also been arrested.*

On Christmas Eve Andrée returned from the family home in Rochefort-en-Yvelines with a three-kilo turkey that she had bought at huge cost from a local farmer. This Christmas, despite the freezing conditions in their flat because there was no coal, the family ate a meal the likes of which they had not enjoyed together for over a year.

On 31 December, as the new year dawned, she was contemplative, writing:

*New Year's Eve 1941. I was thinking through yesterday what we did on New Year's Eve 1940 and the way so much has changed over the year. What will 1942 have in store for us? A big question mark. And the war? What is going to happen to us all?*

### 2 January 1942

*We rented a small house in Chaville where we enjoyed a lovely weekend. At midnight on New Year's Eve we all hugged each other and wished each other a happy New Year. We raised our glasses to Serge who had left us three bottles of 1923 Nuits St Georges. We danced the tango. Serge has always been such a special friend and I am going to miss him so much.*

On 3 January 1942, she referred to her friend Mado visiting her the night before: 'She told me in confidence that she also keeps a journal but that she writes nothing important in it.' It was risky to commit anything to paper, of course, Andrée knew from her brother's strict rules, but that did not deter her. As she reflected in her diary: 'I was a rather shy girl six months ago. How things have changed.'

### 7 January 1942

*I was given a small bottle of perfume today by the Avions Caudron Company to thank me for preparing their passports so quickly. I will have to find someone I can sell it to and make some money. It is so very cold.*

On 9 January she referred to yet another invitation from one of her German would-be suitors:

*I had a phone call from Schurr, my German friend, who wants to take me out to dinner. I will, of course, refuse but he is rather a nice chap.*

Nor was he the only one. A week or so later, she noted: 'Rohrbach [another German Wehrmacht officer] did not call to wish me a happy new year.'

### 22 January 1942

*We are unable to find any food at the moment. Maman has no more butter. Well, I might lose some weight!*

### 27 January 1942

*I went to a jumble sale with Renée yesterday and found a pig-skin Hermès wallet. I am going to do my best to restore it and give it to Lucien for his birthday. I was also able to buy a tin of sardines and some old gloves.*

On 4 February she wrote:

*It is so cold in the flat. We have no coal. This morning I worked so hard so that I could finish all the passports I was preparing for my clients who were going to the Leipzig fair.*

Some days later, on 12 February:

*We did not receive any food from Mémé this week because there are food inspectors in St James checking on whether food is being sold on the black market.*

There was better news on the 18th:

*I had lunch with Thévelle yesterday. It was wonderful. It is impossible to find food in the shops.*

On the 25th she made a rather cryptic entry:

*Thévelle promised to give me some lard. I sent Maman along to the Belgian embassy to pick it up.*

Impossible to know for sure, but was this hiding something more important taking place? It was not so long ago that Andrée had met a friend of her uncle, after all; over from Brussels with documents to be forwarded to Algeria.

Most of the available food in France was being used to feed the Wehrmacht and what little was left over was not making its way into the capital. It had long-lasting effects: Yvonne hoarded tins of food in her cupboards in Paris until her death in 1977, while Andrée's sister, Yvette, bottled vast quantities of food and vegetables and hid them in an outhouse in Normandy. Andrée stockpiled food in her cupboard and freezer in London well into the late 1990s.

In 2012, Jacqueline Fresson (a friend and former colleague of Andrée's) described to me a typical meal in 1942. It consisted of a tomato as a starter, a tomato as a main course and a tomato for pudding. They would regularly walk ten kilometres in search of a rabbit they could kill to eat for lunch.*

Finding food that winter was clearly a major challenge, but Parisians also had other problems to contend with, as Andrée recorded on 4 March:

*There was the most incredible noise last night, quite extraordinary. At 9:15 p.m we heard what sounded like bombs being dropped over Paris. The noise went on and on and when we looked out of the window to see what was going on we realised it was the RAF bombing the Renault factories. Lolo* [the family's nickname for Claude] *slept right through it, the dog was terrified and Yvette was beside herself with joy until we learnt that there had been thousands of casualties.*

---

* My then eighty-seven-year-old neighbour in France described a similar meal of cauliflower that same year; she still remembered how one day she had earned some beans by working for eight hours picking the crops on a farm outside Paris.

*I am going to the Edouard VII theatre tonight with Luc to see*
Une belle histoire.

## 9 March 1942

*Alain is back from Marseilles for a few days and he managed to get some*
*bread without having to give any coupons. We are now getting a litre every*
*day. Maman must have seriously bribed the milkman.*

*I am annoyed with Thévelle. He promised me some carrots but then*
*never gave them to me.*

Andrée was in search of other items, beside food. On 10 March she wrote:

*I am meeting a chap for a drink tonight who may be able to help me find*
*some shoes.*

A week later, on the 18th, she had a strange encounter:

*I was invited to dinner last night by a German woman I met at the office.*
*It was a rather odd evening. It seemed as if she wanted to introduce me to*
*a German officer friend of hers. The Germans want to meet young French*
*women who would be happy to date them. No wonder these girls are*
*referred to as 'des poules'* [hens].

But for many in France, the problem of finding food was overshadowed
by even greater difficulties. The atmosphere in Paris was becoming daily
more oppressive. German soldiers and French policemen were increasingly
arresting Jews on the streets without cause, while young men were subject
to multiple ID checks daily in a bid to track down Resistance members.
Despite this, Alain's group continued their work unabated and Andrée was
becoming more involved due to her courier role.

Andrée had always been left to do her work at Police Headquarters
unsupervised. Whenever a new ID card or a passport was issued, one of her
superiors had to authorise it, and ad hoc controls were nominally made by

**Top:** Edmond Griotteray, Andrée's father.
**Right:** Yvonne Stoquart Griotteray, Andrée's Belgian mother.

**Above:** Alain and Andrée Griotteray, ca 1936/7.

**Above and Left:** (top) Andrée's French ID card, front and back, and (bottom left) her police headquarters ID card.

**Right:** The Griotteray children on the steps of their house on the Promenade des Anglais, Nice, 1930. From front to back: Claude, Andrée, Alain and Yvette.

**Left:** Henri d'Astier de la Vigerie, one of the heads of the resistance movement in North Africa.
**Below:** Le château d'Orion; (inset) Yves de Kermoal, a member of the Orion group.

**Above:** Andrée Griotteray aged approximately twenty-six.
**Below:** Margit Erhart, one of the Orion agents, holding Andrée's baby daughter Francelle, 1951.

**Above:** Dance at the British Officers Club, Place Vendôme, 1945 – the night Andrée met her future husband, Frank White.

**Above:** Andrée and Frank, Promenade des Anglais, Nice, 1947.

**Above:** The author with her aunt and god-mother Yvette Griotteray Leclair.

**Above:** Andrée after she had been given the Ordre national du Mérite, Le ruban bleue, 1972.
**Left:** The Croix de guerre 1939–45 citation Andrée received in 1945, describing the details of her arrest.
**Below:** Two of the medals that Andrée was awarded for her actions, the Croix de guerre (left) and the Légion d'honneur (right).

RÉPUBLIQUE FRANÇAISE

Guerre 1939-1945

# CITATION

Translation of the citation: 'While undertaking an important assignment as an agent in occupied France, Andrée Griotteray was arrested in Bordeaux on 17 July 1944 by police officers of the occupying forces and questioned for several hours. Displaying an enormous degree of sangfroid and exceptional skill, she managed to talk her way out of the charges being levelled against her and to extract from her accusers information which allowed her to work out the exact reasons behind her arrest and why her Resistance group had been targeted. Her mission accomplished, she immediately alerted the head of her group who put the appropriate security measures in place. Andrée Griotteray continued to carry out her underground activities uninterrupted until the liberation. This citation confirms the granting of a Croix de guerre with a Silver Star.'

**Above left:** The unveiling of a statue of General de Gaulle at Carlton House Terrace, London, by Queen Elizabeth, The Queen Mother, 23 June 1993. Left to right: former French Prime Minister Pierre Messmer, Alain Griotteray, Andrée Griotteray White and Jacques Chirac.
**Above right:** The memorial to the Orion resistance group, which lies at the entrance to the village of Orion.

**Above:** Alain and Andrée in front of the memorial to the casualties of both World Wars, in Charenton- le-Pont, Paris, after Andrée had been given the Légion d'honneur, 8 May 1995.

a German army officer, but the process was automatic and no one checked very closely for whom the ID card was being issued or the way in which it had been drawn up. Andrée assumed that most of her French colleagues were doing something to help the Resistance, but no one discussed anything openly, of course. In early 1942 she referred to problems at work, however – perhaps because someone had noticed that a number of ID cards had been going missing:

### 14 January, 1942

*Things are not going at all well at Police Headquarters. Yesterday I got into serious trouble with Monsieur Leclercq. I really do not know what got into him. He has reprimanded me by cancelling my 'semaine anglaise'. I consider this to be a serious form of bullying. I cried all morning.*

Andrée could not hide the fact that she hated working at Police Headquarters. She was a civil servant, 'a fonctionnaire', and she did not like it. After Roger Langeron's arrest by the Germans in December 1940, she felt very much alone working in this government building, surrounded by Germans and unable to trust any of her colleagues.

On 29 January, Andrée was offered a chance to escape from her job at Police Headquarters:

*I had so much work to get through today but my thoughts were elsewhere. I was thinking back to the day I was so badly reprimanded by Leclercq when he cancelled my week's holiday. That day I was crying at my desk when Monsieur Caroff, who sits on the Textile Committee, happened to walk into my office. He asked me what was wrong and I told him. He immediately said, 'Come and work for me – I need a secretary.' I was so pleased I accepted immediately. Today he returned to my office and offered me a starting salary of 2,000 francs a month. I really do not know what to do. I hate it here and I want to give in my notice and he is offering me such a good salary. The trouble is, I would be working for a collaborator, the company where he sits on the board as a director is collaborating with the Nazis, but it does sound like such an interesting job. I am hesitant.*

That evening the Griotterays were all in Paris, Alain having returned for a brief visit (Andrée later told me, with a little sarcasm, that despite the danger in returning, her brother had to see 'his darling Maman'). They sat down to dinner together. There was little to eat but Yvonne served some pasta and Edmond placed a good bottle of wine on the table. Andrée began to tell her family about her conversation with Monsieur Caroff.

'Well, well, what a choice,' said Edmond angrily, 'you can either work for those bastards at Police Headquarters who are arresting Jews on the streets for no reason whatsoever, or you can work for a collaborator.'

'Edmond, keep quiet. Poor Andrée has no choice. She has to work, we need the money and I will not tolerate you swearing at dinner, especially in front of Yvette and Claude,' exclaimed Yvonne.

'You are unusually quiet,' Edmond said, turning his anger onto his son Alain.

'Those bastards have to leave France,' Alain said coldly. 'Andrée should never have been put in this position, but she has been and the choice she is now faced with is irrelevant.'

Andrée sat in silence as her family talked. She knew her brother wanted her to remain at Police Headquarters. The atmosphere around the table was intense. As the conversation momentarily came to a complete halt, Yvonne decided to change the subject. Her timing could not have been worse.

'Renée and Steve have asked if we could have a young Jewish friend of theirs to stay, Mademoiselle Jacqueline Weller.* Plans are being made to get her out of Paris, but she may be with us for up to three months. As you know, there are many groups throughout Paris helping Jews escape the city, but it is not easy; transport and safe houses in the Free Zone need to be found and organised before they can leave. Andrée, I would like you to help me clear up Alain's old room for our guest.'

---

* The family never recorded the real name of their guest, so this is an invented one.

'And where will her food come from?' asked Edmond sarcastically.

'We will have less to eat,' responded Yvonne firmly.

'Well, she had better be attractive and we had all better be very careful. I really am beginning to wonder whether I have any authority at all over my family,' Edmond retorted.

Yvette, fifteen and still at school, had been listening intently to the conversation unfolding around her. She burst out: 'But is it not very dangerous, helping a Jew and hiding them? We were told at school that anyone hiding a Jew could be immediately arrested and shot.'

Yvonne calmed her daughter, but held firm. 'Yes, it is dangerous but what are we to do? We cannot ignore the dangers the Jews are facing and if we all do our bit to help, many will be saved. Mademoiselle Weller will be given strict instructions as to how she is to behave while staying with us, and as long as we are all careful no one will notice.'

Dinner was coming to an end and Alain, wanting to talk to Andrée privately about her work, suggested they join their friends for a drink. As soon as they were alone, Alain said firmly: 'I am sorry, but you really have no choice – you have to stay at Police Headquarters. The supply of ID cards and the ease with which you can obtain *ausweiss* are priceless to us all.'

'And if I am caught?' Andrée responded. 'It is getting more and more dangerous. My colleagues do not seem to suspect anything but Monsieur Leclercq, I just do not know. He knows I am using up more ID cards than I need to, but I can't tell whether he thinks I am completely stupid and careless, or whether he suspects the truth.'

'But you must have some idea of where his political ideas lie,' said Alain.

'No, none at all. He never makes any comment about the political situation to any of us. Of course, it could be that as the Head of Department he thinks it better not to mix with us; the staff hierarchy at work is beyond belief. I just have no idea.'

Fearful of pushing his sister too far, Alain tried to reassure her. 'Andrée, I do not want to put any pressure on you. The decision is yours and yours alone. I trust you to make the right choice.'

The following morning, Yvonne began to plan in earnest for her guest's arrival. She had decided to go down and have a friendly chat with the concierge and his wife. While doing so, she would let them know that Edmond's niece would be staying with the family for a few weeks. Being open about her guest's presence would, she thought, attract less curiosity.

Later that afternoon Mademoiselle Weller emerged from the *métro* onto the Place de la Madeleine. She was tall and smartly dressed, with thick black hair and light-green eyes; her confident manner and noticeable good looks did nothing to help her blend into the background unobtrusively. She strode past a group of German officers who had just walked out of one of the square's restaurants and as she reached the Griotterays' apartment block she ignored the concierge's door and went straight into the building and up the narrow staircase to the first floor.

Yvonne invited her into the salon where, over a tisane and a biscuit, a delicacy rarely eaten by the Griotterays during the war, she explained the day-to-day way in which her family lived and how her guest would fit into their daily routine.

'There are six of us in the family. My husband, who spends much of his time in the country; my daughter Andrée, who works at Police Headquarters; my son Alain, who is living in Marseilles at the moment; my two younger daughters, Yvette and Claude, who are still at school; and myself. We travel a lot between Paris and our house in the country, but while you are staying with us I will not leave Paris. We have a spare bedroom for you as Alain no longer needs it. We only have one bathroom, so I suggest you use it late morning after everyone has left. I am delighted to be able to help you but please remember to be very careful and very discreet with your dress and where you go. Remember the Wehrmacht headquarters are only a ten-minute walk from here.'

As she spoke, Yvonne scrutinised the new arrival, painfully aware of Mademoiselle Weller's striking appearance. More worryingly, her guest could be described as looking Jewish, which was a good enough reason for her to be stopped on the streets and questioned by the Nazis.

'I know most of my neighbours,' Yvonne continued, 'and they are unlikely to ask any questions. I will keep you updated on the plans being made to get you out of Paris but I cannot emphasise enough how very careful and very discreet you must be in everything you do.'

In the days that followed, their new guest rarely ventured out and spent her time helping around the flat and looking through Edmond's vast collection of historical design books. But as time went on, she grew tired of being cooped up. She ventured out onto the streets, walking as far as the Tuileries Gardens and soaking up the beauty of central Paris. Her hosts were a little concerned, but felt reasonably confident that in this sophisticated part of the city her immaculate toilette would not attract too much attention.

For several weeks all seemed well, but at dinner one evening, Yvette mentioned that she had spoken to two soldiers who had been looking around the courtyard and talking to the concierge.

'What did they want, Yvette?' Edmond said sharply.

'When I came home this afternoon and was putting my bike away, the soldiers followed me into the courtyard and asked if I lived here. Claude was terrified and did not utter a word. I just said yes. They asked who else lived in our flat.'

'And what did you say?' asked Yvonne, in concern.

'I said there were just five of us: Papa, Maman, me and my sisters.'

'You did not mention Mademoiselle Weller?' asked Edmond.

'No, of course not,' said Yvette.

'This is worrying,' said Edmond. 'They must suspect something – what reason could there be for them to come here asking questions about us?'

'Leave it to me,' said Yvonne. 'If they return I will deal with them.'

For the next few days Yvonne carefully watched the street below to see whether any Wehrmacht soldiers approached her apartment block. Late one afternoon, several days later, she saw two young Nazi soldiers talking to the concierge. She swept downstairs and, in her most authoritarian manner, spoke directly to the soldiers. 'I understand you have been apprehending my daughters; how dare you go anywhere near them, let alone talk to them. If you ever come anywhere near them again, I will immediately report you to your commanding officer.'*

Utterly cowed by Madame Griotteray's anger and icy poise, the two

---

* Andrée told me that Yvonne's behaviour mirrored that of her mother's towards Wehrmacht soldiers stationed in Brussels during the First World War.

soldiers – neither of whom could have been much over eighteen years of age – stammered out a few words to say that they hadn't done anything wrong. Yvonne interrupted them fiercely: 'I repeat, if I ever see either of you anywhere near this building again, your commanding officer will be informed immediately. I suggest you leave at once.'

The soldiers, unused to such authority from a French civilian, hurried out of the courtyard on to the road and headed swiftly down the street towards la Madeleine. Yvonne could only hope they had not been ordered by their superior to check on her apartment block and were instead acting on their own initiative. She had no idea who or what had led them to her family, but she was only too aware that if caught the whole family could be arrested. It was puzzling; they had all been very careful since Mademoiselle Weller had arrived, so there should have been no cause for suspicion.

As spring 1942 arrived, the Wehrmacht's rounding up of Jews from the streets of Paris intensified, but the Griotterays continued to maintain their cautiousness and Jacqueline Weller's presence in the rue Godot de Mauroy went unchallenged. They assumed their guest understood fully the risk they were taking in helping her and that she also was taking all necessary precautions to avoid drawing any attention to herself or them. What happened next provoked such anger in Andrée that it would remain with her for the rest of her life.

Mémé, the Griotterays' housekeeper, had returned from Rochefort the previous day with some food, from which she and Yvonne had been able to make up a coq au vin. Everyone had been told dinner would be served at eight o'clock and so rarely were they able to find fresh food that the family was eagerly looking forward to the meal. As they gathered for dinner, they realised their guest was missing. Edmond questioned his wife as to her whereabouts, but Yvonne didn't know where she was.

'It is well past eight o'clock,' said Edmond impatiently. 'Where is she? Why is she not here? What is she doing out on the streets so late?'

'Be patient, Edmond. She will be back shortly.'

Yvonne opened the windows and leant over the balcony to see the street below. As she watched, she saw a *velo taxi* make its way towards their flat and stop right outside the door. A dark-haired, heavily made-up, beautifully dressed young woman stepped out. 'I simply do not believe it,' Yvonne muttered in astonishment, 'what does she think she is doing?'

Andrée joined her mother at the window to see what was going on. They both watched, speechless, as Mademoiselle Weller paid the carriage driver and made her way past the concierge's window into the building's staircase.

'That's it, she is not staying!' exclaimed Andrée. 'We are not running any more risks for that stupid woman. How could she possibly draw attention to herself in such a way when she knows that Jews are being arrested on the streets of Paris for no reason whatsoever? No wonder those soldiers were downstairs – someone must have noticed her and tipped them off. She has to leave.'

Andrée had stolen an unused ID card that afternoon; it was in her handbag, to be put into Jean Barbier's postbox the following evening. If the flat was searched because someone in the street had noticed Mademoiselle Weller and reported her to the authorities, Andrée might very well find herself before a firing squad, and so might her parents.

As their guest walked confidently through the front door, tensions were high. Edmond greeted Mademoiselle Weller calmly, 'Bonsoir, Mademoiselle, and where have you been today?'

Oblivious to the emotion she had aroused, Mademoiselle Weller replied that it had been such a lovely afternoon that she had decided to go out for a walk down the rue Royale towards the Louvre. She was tired of not being able to dress attractively and enjoy living in the centre of Paris.

Andrée was struggling to control herself. She said, sarcastically, 'Did you think of walking into the Hôtel Meurice?'

'Andrée!' her father interjected sharply.

Mademoiselle Weller was startled, but replied, 'Why, yes, I did; I walked right past it.'

'But the Hôtel Meurice is where the Wehrmacht Commandant of Paris is based,' Claude piped up.

'My eleven-year-old sister understands the dangers, but a grown woman appears not to,' Andrée muttered to herself.

Edmond spoke calmly. 'Do you appreciate the dangers we all face? You do realise what is happening to the Jewish people in Paris?' They were all struggling to understand how this intelligent, educated woman who had been given a safe house could be so carelessly indiscreet.

As it dawned on Mademoiselle Weller how upset her hosts were, she apologised quickly and promised not to do it again.

'You are right, Mademoiselle, it will not happen again. I am not prepared to risk my family's safety to help you when you behave in such an irresponsible way. It is too dangerous for all of us.'

The following day Yvonne made discreet enquiries among her friends and found her guest a new place to stay.

From 29 May 1942, every Jew living in France over the age of six was required to sew onto their clothes a yellow Star of David to indicate their ethnicity. The staff at Police Headquarters were instructed to distribute these across the city as well as to mark ID cards for Jewish citizens with a red stamp (JUDEN) to identify them. Of some 330,000 Jews living in France before the war, almost 25 per cent lost their lives between 1940 and 1945, according to the Jewish Museum of Paris. It might, however, have been even worse, were it not for France's vast rural countryside and escape routes via the Pyrenees and Alps.

Andrée was working at Police Headquarters during the spring of 1942 when plans were in train to round up thousands of Jews living in Paris and take them to the Vélodrome d'Hiver (always known as the Vel' d'Hiv, a bicycle stadium in the 15th arrondissement) on 16/17 July 1942, from where they were ultimately taken to Auschwitz and murdered. It is unlikely that anyone there would not have known of the plans, but Andrée was working in the ID and Passport Department, entirely separate from the department policing Paris; the German and the French police were also intent on keeping the round-up secret until the eleventh hour so that its implementation would be easier.

Theodor Dannecker, the SS captain who commanded the German police in France, had together with Adolf Eichmann decided to use the French police's records to round up the 'foreign Jews' living in Paris and its suburbs.

To enable the operation to succeed, they needed the cooperation of the Parisian police force, as they (not the German police) would be responsible for carrying out the raids; at a meeting with René Bousquet, then Secretary-General to the Vichy police force, and several of his colleagues, they agreed to put their plan into action early on 16 July.

It is recorded that Bousquet raised no objections to having to organise the arrests, but found it embarrassing that the French police would have to carry them out. After much argument it was agreed that the French police force would only round up foreign Jews and not French Jews. One of the reasons Bousquet gave for his complicity was that the Vichy government was intent on upholding its freedom as the government of France in the Free Zone and Bousquet had received his instructions directly from Pierre Laval, the Vichy government's Prime Minister. By helping the Germans, Vichy would be allowed to remain a sovereign state.

As the 16th approached, rumours began to spread around Paris. Many policemen did their best to warn Jewish residents, many of whom lived in the ghettos of the capital, of the impending arrests. Word spread fast, but the plans had been kept so quiet that there was little time for people to leave their homes before the police arrived at their doors.

The charge of overzealousness in the carrying out of their duties has been levelled at the Parisian police force. Many Jews did manage to escape, warned by members of the Resistance, while others were hidden by neighbours. But while some police officers disobeyed their orders and helped their fellow Jewish citizens, the conditions in which the detainees were held at the Vel' d'Hiv were inhuman, with very little food and few toilets available and in unbearable heat.

In 2008, sixty-six years after the event, an eighty-five-year-old friend of mine who had lived in Paris during the round-up broke down in tears as she described the events of July 1942. It took fifty-five years before the French government of Jacques Chirac finally apologised for the then police force's actions and the Vichy government's complicity. Previously it had always been argued that Pétain's regime was not the legitimate government of France, and that therefore the French government was not responsible for the actions of the French police force at that time.

On 16 July 1995, President Chirac made a speech to the nation, acknowledging the role that the state had played in the persecution of Jews and other victims of the German occupation:

These black hours will forever stain our history and are detrimental to our past and the traditions we cherish. Fifty-three years ago on the 16th of July 1942, 4,500 French policemen, under the command of their leaders, obeyed Nazi orders when over 13,000 Jewish men, women and children were rounded up in Paris and throughout its suburbs and arrested in their homes in the early hours of the morning. This happened in France, a country who bears in its constitution the declaration of the rights of man, a country which has always welcomed foreigners and asylum seekers, and yet on that night France broke man's civil rights and delivered those it should have protected to its executioners.

## 15

# The Allied Landings in North Africa

H enri d'Astier de la Vigerie was convinced that France could and would
defeat Germany, but he also knew that it would not be done alone.
France's North African territories were essential, as was the help of the
United States and Britain.

In 1941 the principal French North African territories were Algeria
(which at the time was part of France), Morocco and Tunisia; the latter two
were both French protectorates. Under the terms of the armistice drawn up
between France and Germany, these territories fell into the Free Zone and
were therefore unoccupied by German troops. The indigenous populations
and the French forces based there remained loyal to Maréchal Pétain and
the Vichy government.

In January 1941, aware that the Gestapo knew of his Resistance activities in northern France in the Pas de Calais, d'Astier decided it was time
to head to North Africa. He reached Algiers on 25 January. Not long after
arriving, he started work in the city of Oran, where he began to link up
with his fellow Resistance fighters. As he settled into that stiflingly hot,
dry city, d'Astier was well aware that there was little appetite in France's
North African territories for war and that most Arabs and French Algerians
supported the Vichy government. The prospect of fighting alongside the
British forces was not appealing to many, following the bombing of part of
the French fleet at Mers-el-Kébir, in which 1,290 French officers and men
had been killed. The attack had taken place because Admiral Darlan, head
of the French navy, had refused to allow several French ships to join the
Royal Navy – a plan concocted by Churchill to avoid French ships falling
into the hands of the German navy.

The political atmosphere in Algeria was stifling: anyone with any degree of authority had been appointed by the state; there were no free elections and anyone opposing Pétain was considered a traitor. Most foreigners were treated with contempt, with the exception of the Americans; in 1941 the US government formally recognised the Vichy government and were thus permitted to continue running several consulates in France's North African territories.

There had been sporadic attempts at setting up several informal Resistance groups in North Africa, but d'Astier's intention was to establish a more structured Resistance movement into which he could bring together all the anti-Vichy inhabitants of North Africa, some of whom had already started to supply the French and British intelligence services with material.

As d'Astier settled into his new life, he began to gather around him a group of friends, acquaintances and contacts from across the region who he knew and trusted. He wanted to show the American consuls in North Africa (who would report back to Washington and London) that his Resistance network comprised well-placed, useful, reliable people who would help the US if and when they entered the war. His contacts included a group of Algerians referred to as les Pieds Noirs (Black Feet), whose families had always lived in Algeria; Frenchmen based in Algeria for business reasons; and members of the French armed forces. He befriended members of the civil service, Jewish Algerians and members of the French intelligence services.

As in France, to be part of the Resistance was dangerous. Vichy sympathisers were quick to denounce anyone suspected of being involved in the Resistance movement, and there was at least one police inspector posted to Algeria with specific instructions to infiltrate the Resistance and report back. Arrests were common, but d'Astier's group persisted.

By May 1941, d'Astier was receiving regular intelligence reports from the Orion Group, including a briefing on the political views of several ministers at the heart of the Vichy government. They had identified a number of men who might be anti-Pétain and could potentially be persuaded to support the Free French. Alain's group relayed details of the movement of German troops around France, the numbers of troopers stationed in different parts of the country, records of the industrial productions of specially targeted companies, the amount of electricity and gas used by the German army, and the state of the railways and road networks. D'Astier could also relay messages back to his supporters in France via the postal service Orion had set up through Marseilles and the Pyrenees.

Between the wars d'Astier had worked in New York and he felt confident that he understood the American way of thinking and could use that to France's advantage. He set about using his skill and legendary charm to gather around him a network of political allies, including the head of the Algerian security forces and the Head of the North African youth camps movement. In early 1942, the latter invited him to become joint head of the movement, a position which involved travel throughout Algeria, Morocco and Tunisia, thereby helping him to build up his Resistance network.

D'Astier appointed Lieutenant Louis Cordier as his deputy, a vicar from Laon in northern France who had been wounded in 1940 and had returned to his parish following the disbanding of his regiment after the defeat of France. In Laon l'abbé Cordier had set up a Resistance group to help prisoners of war escape France; once the Gestapo became aware of his Resistance activities he escaped to Algiers, where he was recruited into the French intelligence services in Oran.

On 11 December 1941, a few days after the Japanese attack on Pearl Harbor, the United States declared war on Japan and Germany. Thanks to d'Astier's close links with Ridgway Knight, the US consul in Oran, the US armed forces were aware of his structured Resistance group when they started planning for what was to become Operation Torch, the Allied landings in North Africa.

D'Astier had also developed a relationship with Jacques Lemaigre-Dubreuil, head of olive oil company Huiles Lesieur, who had close ties to the US government and acted as a formal intermediary between d'Astier, his Resistance group and Robert Murphy, head of US consuls in French North Africa. The Americans were looking for a French general with sufficient rank and authority to ensure that French North African troops would accept a foreign landing without challenge. Initially Murphy approached Admiral Darlan, Pétain's 'dauphin'. Pétain was now in his mid eighties and a line of succession had been established; should anything happen to him,

Darlan would become head of the French Vichy government. Darlan had dreams of being admiral of a joint French–German naval fleet and refused to support plans for a US landing in North Africa.

Murphy then approached General Weygand, former head of the French armed forces in North Africa but who by the end of 1941 had been relieved of his command; the Vichy government thought he was too anti-German. There was also General de Gaulle, head of the Free French forces in London, but he was considered too divisive and difficult to work with. Besides which, he was intensely disliked by Roosevelt.

Finally an approach was made to General Giraud, a leading French general who, after the fall of France, had been held as a prisoner of war. From there he had escaped to Switzerland.

Lemaigre-Dubreuil offered to contact Giraud on Murphy's behalf. With Murphy's agreement, they met in Lyon and started to discuss the conditions under which Giraud might take on the leadership of the French North African army, working alongside the US and British forces. Giraud wanted the troops to land simultaneously in North Africa and on the French Mediterranean coast, but Eisenhower did not have sufficient troops to engage in such an operation. Giraud was forced to accept that the Allies would only land in Algeria, Morocco and Tunisia. On 17 July 1942, Eisenhower formally invited General Giraud to become head of the French army in North Africa; just over a week later President Roosevelt informed Winston Churchill of his plans to land in French North Africa. He summoned his military advisers to the White House on 30 July to tell them of his decision to defer plans for a cross-channel invasion in favour of Operation Torch, the Allied landings in French North Africa. On 13 August 1942, General Dwight D. Eisenhower was named Supreme Commander of the Allied forces in North Africa.

In early October 1942, Robert Murphy asked d'Astier to arrange a meeting between a group of French representatives and eight members of the US armed forces. The US contingent was headed by General Mark Clark, representing Eisenhower. The meeting took place in secret on 22 October in a villa on an isolated beach, eighty kilometres west of Algeria near a town called Cherchell. The Americans were brought to the Algerian coastline by a British submarine and taken ashore in a small boat. The French side included General Charles Mast, Giraud's personal representative; Colonel Jousse, head of the Algerian Resistance; a journalist named Jean Rigault, who wrote the minutes of the meeting; senior officers of the French navy and air force; and, lastly, d'Astier himself and a couple of trusted colleagues.

They discussed the help that the French army and Resistance groups could give their US allies as they landed in Algeria and Morocco, as well as the military plans drawn up by Eisenhower and the difficulties American and British troops might encounter from some of the French armed forces loyal to Pétain.

The lengthy discussions were interrupted by a security alert at 4.00 a.m. when two local police officers out on patrol were seen checking the surrounding area. To avoid an international incident, the eight American officers had to scramble back into the waiting British submarine.

Over the next two weeks the plans agreed at Cherchell were put into action as d'Astier prepared, following General Clark's request, to take control of Algiers for six hours on the day of the landings, which was thought to be sufficient time for the Allied troops to land on the beaches at the port of Sidi Ferruch.

On the night of 7 November, d'Astier's Resistance groups, headed by José Aboulker, successfully took control of the radio-transmitting stations at Mogador, cutting off most military communication networks. D'Astier's groups took over the marine and air forces headquarters of Algeria and arrested several high-ranking French army officers. They were determined to prevent the French forces loyal to Vichy from opening fire on the Allies as the landings took place.

Before General Giraud had even landed in Algeria, he was mysteriously heard to make a radio broadcast rallying the French army and civilians to support him. Meanwhile, d'Astier was faced with an unexpected problem: out of the blue Admiral Darlan had arrived in Algiers in a private capacity because his son was in hospital, seriously ill with polio. D'Astier and Colonel

Chrétien (the latter was responsible for the French intelligence services in North Africa) went to see General Juin, head of the French North African troops, and informed him that Eisenhower had agreed that General Giraud was to take control of the French armed forces, that US and British troops were about to land in North Africa. He asked Juin to try to convince Darlan not to stand in their way and instead to join them. Darlan refused to accept the situation without Pétain's full support, leaving Murphy and d'Astier fearful that the French armed forces would rally under Darlan.

D'Astier decided to take pre-emptive action; he placed Darlan under arrest. That night a British Royal Navy warship attempted to put ashore one hundred men but was shot at with canon fire by French soldiers, forcing the British to give up their planned landing. The Resistance forces had tried without success to take the Algiers airport of Blida; it remained in the hands of the Vichy French. Everywhere else in Algiers, the landings were delayed but ultimately successful, though in Oran and Morocco the French troops resisted and approximately 2,000 casualties were reported.

Conscious that the French armed forces were still loyal to Admiral Darlan, d'Astier's position was no longer tenable: he was forced to release Darlan. Murphy decided there was no other option but to recognise Darlan as the legal head of the French armed forces representing Pétain and to negotiate with him.

But the military advances were not over yet. Early on 8 November, a group of British and American commandos managed to capture the gun emplacements guarding the Eastern side of the Algerian bay; using these as their base, 25,000 US soldiers landed on the beaches of Sidi Ferruch, twenty miles west of Algiers, along with 7,000 British troops further west of Castiglione. Once Darlan learnt of the successful landings, he had no option but to negotiate a ceasefire as the US forces took control of Algiers. It had been a significant undertaking, with major consequences for the outcome of the war. Operation Torch 'was the first indication that the Allies could turn the tables on Hitler. Over 100,000 American and British troops and 100 ships took part in the invasion, which involved a massive parachute drop and five simultaneous amphibious landings along nearly 1,000 miles of the North African coastline.'[10]

Henri d'Astier de la Vigerie's dream had come true: the Allies had landed in North Africa and the French army would now fight alongside the Allies with Giraud as their head. Yet Darlan – and Vichy – were still in overall command of the French army and of French North Africa. What was to be done about Darlan?

# 16

## *Arrest*

In December 1942, the political situation in French North Africa could be described, with understatement, as difficult to understand. Instead of appointing Giraud, as per the Cherchell agreement, Robert Murphy and Eisenhower formally recognised Admiral Darlan as overall Commander-in-Chief for North Africa. Giraud in turn also agreed to accept Darlan's overall authority. It is possible that Murphy – still concerned by the hugely pro-Vichy North African population along with Darlan's arrival and three Vichy-appointed Governor Generals in Morocco, Tunisia and Algeria – thought it ultimately safer to deal with Darlan than with Giraud.

Henri d'Astier, meanwhile, believed that General Giraud had let the French and his Resistance fighters down because, having accepted command of the French forces in North Africa, he then made way for Darlan and accepted reduced responsibility for the Tunisian campaign. Darlan's politically shrewd tactics had paid off, and despite the Allied landings, he refused to make any further decisions without Pétain's consent.

D'Astier felt that overall power and control of Algeria should lie with the team who had supported and helped the Allies land in Algeria and Morocco. The French army, however, was deeply divided; many supported Darlan while others were unsure who to champion.

At that time many in North Africa did not want General de Gaulle taking control of Algeria and Morocco and refused to recognise him as a possible leader. In turn de Gaulle, leader of the Free French, was not prepared to accept the pre-eminence of Giraud, while Giraud himself, although acceding to Darlan as head of the armed forces, was angry at the US turnaround. Many within d'Astier's Resistance group saw Darlan as a traitor, especially those who had risked their lives to help the Allied landings.

The plan to assassinate Admiral Darlan is thought to have begun within a group of young Resistance fighters. Initially d'Astier and his deputy l'abbé Cordier rejected the prospect, knowing that the US would not look kindly upon the political assassination by a group of Gaullist supporters of a leader they had recognised. Instead they hoped to persuade Darlan to resign, leaving the territory without governance and thus enabling them to invoke emergency measures under the Loi Tréveneuc of 1872. Their intention was to appoint Henri d'Orléans, Count of Paris and pretender to the French throne, as head of a provisional French North African government. The Gaullist d'Orléans had the support of the republicans, the press, the Catholic clergy, the Masons, the Jews and even the head of the Algerian armed forces and the representatives of the general councils of the North Africa territories.

On 9 December 1942, the Count of Paris travelled from Morocco to Algiers; d'Astier's plan, once he arrived, was to have the Murphy/Darlan agreement declared void, clearing the way for the Count of Paris to be declared head of the Provisional Algerian government. D'Astier had some authority by this point; in the provisional government that had been set up in the wake of the Allied landings, he had been appointed joint Minister of the Interior. For his plan to happen, however, Darlan had to resign. He had no intention of doing so.

On 19 December 1942, Air Force General François d'Astier, Henri's brother, arrived in Algiers from London to meet Giraud, Darlan and some Gaullist supporters. De Gaulle insisted that if Darlan did not resign to be replaced by a Gaullist, perhaps the Count of Paris, it would leave France in a potentially dangerous political situation. He believed that if a fascist leader such as Admiral Darlan was still in power when France was ultimately liberated, the French Resistance might side with the Russians.

The popularity of the French Communist party had been a longstanding concern for the establishment and it was widely thought that the French were more likely to support the Communists if a Vichy leader was still in power in North Africa. François d'Astier gave Darlan one last chance to resign; he refused. It has been claimed that François d'Astier had received clear instructions from General de Gaulle to assassinate Darlan if he refused.

Records show that François d'Astier arrived in Algiers with US$80,000 – it has been argued that the funds were intended to be used to arrange for Darlan's assassination.* Henri d'Astier, meanwhile, was still trying to convince Eisenhower to accept his plan to position the Count of Paris as head of the Provisional government. Roosevelt, who had never liked de Gaulle and preferred to deal with Giraud, refused to agree to the plan.

On 23 December 1942, a resistance activist named Fernand Bonnier de la Chapelle, described by writer Charles Williams as one of many 'hotheaded young Gaullist paramilitaries', announced to l'abbé Cordier that he intended to assassinate Darlan. De la Chapelle was a member of the Corps Franc, a monarchist and ardent anti-Vichyiste: after the night of the US landings, when French troops had opened fire on the Americans, he and his friends felt betrayed by Darlan and subsequently regarded him as a traitor.

The following day, driven by Jean Bernard d'Astier (Henri's son), de la Chapelle arrived at Darlan's headquarters at the Summer Palace, where he shot and fatally wounded Darlan. De la Chapelle's plan was to escape to Morocco immediately afterwards, but he was caught and arrested. The next day, at noon, he was tried and executed.†

Following Darlan's death, Robert Murphy confirmed that President Roosevelt had refused to accept the Count of Paris as head of the Provisional government. As Roosevelt did not support de Gaulle, Giraud was appointed military Commander-in-chief of North Africa.

Politically, Giraud was regarded – possibly unfairly – by the Gaullists as nothing more than Darlan's successor, as he was still surrounded by Pétain's North African governor generals. Public opinion was, moreover, starting to shift in favour of de Gaulle, with many feeling that Giraud was marginalising members of the Resistance. Giraud was determined to hold

---

* Gandy, *La jeunesse et la Résistance*, page 70. The official reason for François d'Astier travelling with such funds was to support the ongoing Gaullist campaign in the region.

† Gandy, *La jeunesse et la Résistance*, pages 72–3. On page 77, Gandy explains that de la Chapelle was subsequently exonerated in December 1945 by the Court of Appeals in Algiers. A room in the Court of Appeals was named La Chambre Bonnier de la Chapelle in his memory.

on to power, and the Americans remained firmly opposed to the prospect of de Gaulle taking control in Algeria.

Seventeen Gaullist activists were arrested on 30 December, some of whom had helped with Operation Torch. Giraud's explanation for these arrests was that, following Darlan's murder, he was concerned more attempted assassinations would follow.

On 10 January 1943, Henri d'Astier and l'abbé Cordier were formally arrested and charged with plotting against the State and of being accomplices in the murder of Darlan.

Ten days later, Marcel Peyrouton, who in 1940 as Minister of the Interior had signed a decree stripping the Algerian Jews of their French citizenship, was appointed Governor General of Algeria at Roosevelt's request.

In February 1943, the seventeen political Gaullist prisoners were released, but d'Astier and Cordier were held for a further nine months, possibly because Giraud feared they would build up support for de Gaulle, thereby undermining his authority. On 25 February 1943, Algiers became the capital of Free France and the provisional government of the French Republic began to establish itself.

*The Times* reported on 1 January 1943 that: 'To the British, and apparently to the American peoples, the whole affair appears on first hearing to be wildly confusing. How is it that pro-Allied Frenchmen can be arrested?'

The mystery surrounding Darlan's assassination may never be solved, especially while the French intelligence records remain closed. A large percentage of the British Intelligence records were destroyed. There is no doubt that Fernand Bonnier de la Chapelle shot him, but was he acting alone or under instruction? Many believe SOE were ultimately responsible for Darlan's murder.

# 17

## *Escape*

A few months before the Allied landings, d'Astier had recruited into his group a twenty-two-year-old named Jacques Sauvage, who had been working as a double agent for the French and the Algerian section of the German intelligence services, the Abwehr. Sauvage was later described as the most daring of the Orion Resistance agents. In the autumn of 1942, Sauvage was instructed by the Abwehr to travel to Paris and advise the Parisian collaborators of the impending military activities in the Mediterranean. Granted an *ausweiss* by the German authorities, he reached Paris in late October 1942. His other mission, per d'Astier's request, was to find Alain and warn him of the dangers lying ahead.

After the North Africa landings in November 1942 and the defeats in Russia, the terms of the armistice between France and Germany were declared void by the Wehrmacht, who subsequently occupied the Free Zone and therefore the whole of the country. As the progress of the war changed, the Wehrmacht became ever more aggressive, increasing their indiscriminate searches and ID checks on young men in particular.

After arriving in Paris, Jacques found Alain through the underground movement and he agreed to work with the group as an Orion agent. Despite the many trips he carried out between Algiers and Paris throughout 1942 and 1943, his Orion colleagues never understood how he was able to deceive the Abwehr so successfully while still remaining loyal to France. But it was clear he was a brilliant double agent; he watched and listened carefully to everything around him, no matter how trivial. He was only twenty-two years old in late 1943 when the French security services decided to move him out of danger to Morocco, where he joined the French army.

Conscious of the heightened danger in Paris, Alain and Biaggi set up stricter security rules for their agents: retracing one's steps was forbidden, and all members were under strict instruction not to allow themselves to be followed – or if they were, to avoid their own homes and to make all possible attempts to lose their assailant. They were warned about the possibility of concierges acting as informers, spying on their movements, and they were told to keep well away from their friends, an order which must have been very difficult for a group of young twenty-somethings. They had to be more careful about the new friends they made, questioning rigorously the integrity and honesty of any new member they wanted to recruit. They were told never to meet openly in bars or restaurants unless there was an emergency. With the exception of Alain and Andrée, no member of the group was ever aware of the existence of more than two other members – so that if one of them was picked up by the Gestapo they would be unable to betray the group.

Towards the end of 1942, Alain was worried. He had not heard from d'Astier for some time and had no instructions as to how the group was to move forward. With no radio transmitters, they were unable to contact him directly. After much thought, he and Noël Le Clercq decided to leave France in search of d'Astier in North Africa. As Alain put it: 'We must leave France and head for Algeria where we will get a better picture of what is going on.'[11]

Although she was taking great risks at work and for Orion, Andrée was still just a young girl at heart, and one who couldn't help feeling frustrated at times. On 24th October she wrote:

*Well guess what, dear diary? Yesterday morning I had the honour of a visit from Rohrbach.*

*I was seriously surprised. He told me he had been trying to find me yesterday but because I was not around he gave up. He said he was looking for someone's file and decided he wanted to catch up with me. He invited me to dinner and I replied, 'Yes, I would like to accept your invitation but do call me on Thursday to reconfirm.' By saying this I thought he could get out of it if he is only trying to be polite.*

*I am dying of boredom. Rohrbach certainly picked the right moment. If I had a boyfriend I would never go out with him.*

It was not a great success. She updated her entry the following day:

*By the way, dear diary, dinner with Rohrbach was seriously boring. After dinner we went to the pictures. Luckily he did not make a pass at me, which is just as well because I have decided I do not like him.*

By Christmas, however, her indomitable spirit had prevailed. Andrée's diary entry for 25 December 1942 suggests that, despite their troubles, the Griotteray family were coping well:

*It is Christmas Day 1942 and as usual I am at work. Last night it was Christmas Eve and the whole family got together and we had the most wonderful dinner. As an hors d'oeuvre we had a vegetable salad with mayonnaise, the main course was chicken and potatoes, we had some cheese and for pudding Maman made a cake and a chocolate mousse. We had some real coffee and a liqueur. It was all thanks to Maman, who had gone to Brittany for a week and managed to find some food, which she brought back to Paris. Last week I bought myself a black silk suit with the money I got from selling two bicycle tyres and with what was left over bought myself some wooden shoes. Last Monday I was invited to a theatre gala where I won a hat from Lemonier in the tombola.'\**

### 12 January

*Tonight I am going to the Théâtre de l'Étoile with Margit. I have been several times to the cinema and have just seen* Un Grand Amour *with Zarah Leander, I also went to see* The Count of Montecristo.

*Yesterday I went shopping with Maman and bought myself a navy-blue suit. I was not asked for any clothes coupons, but I had to hand in two old suits.*

---

\* Lemonier was one of the leading hat designer in Paris during the war years. Despite the heavy rationing of clothes during the war, the leading clothes designers in Paris carried on their businesses, selling primarily to the occupying forces. The gala Andrée attended was held to raise money for French prisoners of war.

There was another reason for Alain's escape. On 15 February 1943, 'le service du travail obligatoire' became law. Its introduction meant that every man aged forty-five or younger was forced to do industrial labour in Germany. This latest assault on the French male population led to the creation of many more escape groups, helping men and women who wanted to join up with the Free French forces in North Africa or in London. Alain and Noël waited restlessly for the day of their departure via the route they had so carefully plotted for many others. On 21 February they finally left Paris, travelled down to the Château d'Orion before setting off to make the difficult journey across the Pyrenees.

On 22 February Andrée wrote:

*The news is far from encouraging. The Germans are enduring a large number of defeats on the Eastern front and have lost several major battles in Tunisia. It is now all-out war. They are picking up thousands of men off the streets in Paris and literally sending them off to Germany. Alain said he was not going to allow this to happen to him and has disappeared. We have no idea where he is or where he has gone. Papa is so unpleasant mainly because he is so worried and upset about everything going on around him. Maman is beside herself worrying about Alain and she certainly has every reason to be. As for me, I am praying for Alain.*

*Three weeks ago I was invited to lunch at The Claridge by Monsieur Machenaud's Secretary. We had a foie gras, a huge steak with béarnaise sauce and fried potatoes and for pudding a wonderful chocolate cake, the sort one could find before the war. A chauffeur was sent to pick me up from the office and, oh yes, I forgot to mention I was given two pears for Mother who was ill.\**

*I need to get my bike mended because it would save the soles of my shoes not to mention how much money I would not have to spend on the métro.*

---

\* Such a lunch was not usual. It was most likely a way of thanking Andrée for some assistance given to Monsieur Machenaud – perhaps connected to her Resistance activities.

Crossing the Pyrenees during winter wasn't the only challenge escapees faced. Arrival in Spain did not come with a warm welcome; 'mountaineers' were more often than not greeted by the Guardia Civil, who arrested them and placed them in prisons or holding camps. Meanwhile, in her book *Love and War in the Pyrenees*, Rosemary Bailey has estimated that in 1940 there were around 236,000 Spanish Republican refugees trying to escape Franco's Spain – often to end up joining the Maquis wing of the French Resistance. To prevent this, the French authorities set up similar holding camps on the French side of the Pyrenees, with similar living conditions – crowded, with little food and the poorest of sanitary conditions.* Among the escapees, Bailey notes that some 40,000 were anarchists, communists and republicans, whose civil war experience was vital to the French Resistance.

On 26 February, Andrée heard from her brother:

> *We received a note from Alain this morning. He says he is safe and has sent us his food and tobacco ration card but we have no idea where he is.*

Alain and Noël must have reached Orion by the 26th, before leaving France for the dangerous journey to freedom. The journey across the mountains took two whole days and nights; Alain and Noël knew the dangers better than anyone, but they were excited to be doing it themselves.

They left the château, wrapped up against the freezing conditions and carrying only a small shoulder bag, and made their way towards the mountains. Cold, damp mist had already settled and made it hard to see much, but their spirits were high, despite what lay ahead. Higher and higher they climbed through thick mud, with icy winds whipping their faces. As the altitude changed, the wet ground turned to ice and they started to slip

---

* When I visited the Château d'Orion to research this book, its German owner encouraged me to visit the camps to understand that it was not only the Germans who had run such places during the Second World War. In 2010, the French authorities began rebuilding the camps to help visitors understand what had happened in the area during the war.

and fall. Another few kilometres on and it started to snow. They stopped briefly at refuge huts along the way for a few hours' rest, before heading on. Although they felt confident that they were heading ultimately towards freedom, they knew that once they had reached Spain they would almost certainly be picked up by the Guardia Civil.

After forty-eight hours, the boys reached the Spanish border village; as they expected, they were arrested on arrival at the bus station and taken to the Miranda prison near Santander. It was renowned for holding political prisoners on a starvation diet of dry bread with little drinking water; serious episodes of dysentery were common, resulting in severe dehydration and weakness.

Thousands of young Frenchmen were similarly interned in various prisons by the Spanish authorities during 1943. Most were held for anything up to five months before being released – usually to make way for the next wave of French escapees arriving over the border. It was common knowledge that most of these men were heading for Barcelona or Malaga to board ships bound for North Africa; their detention was intended to be temporary, to control the number of people crossing the Spanish border.

Spain released detainee lists to US and British consuls: because Alain was known to be working for the intelligence services, they secured his expedited release on 23 May 1943. Luck was on his side. As he headed via Portugal to catch a Casablanca-bound ship, he met up with Yves de Kermoal, who had also gained early release from Pampelonne prison for the same reason. Noël was still in prison but Alain was confident that he would be out soon, and reassured Yves, who was concerned about their friend. 'Don't worry about him. He will join us shortly, he is not the sort of person to stay locked up for very long.'[12]

Alain's certainty was not misplaced; not long after he and Yves reached Morocco, Noël, Paul Labbé and Pascal Arrighi were released. They joined their friends in North Africa and all five signed up to the French army.

Many of the young men who escaped France to avoid the new forced labour laws were anti-Vichy and supported de Gaulle and the Free French, but once in Morocco they found themselves having to join a predominantly pro-Vichy French army. They, in turn, were regarded as deserters, often unwelcome, by the French troops they joined.

After de Gaulle's arrival in Algeria, d'Astier worked with the OSS and British intelligence services to set up and train Les commandos de France, an elite group of approximately 600 pro-Gaullist Free French army recruits (officially recognised by ministerial decree on 4 May 1944). Alain, Yves, Pascal and Noël were early enlisters.* After their training, Alain was recruited as an OSS agent and was later parachuted back into France to regroup Orion. Yves, Pascal and Noël meanwhile joined le Détachement Spécial – an even more elite group of forty specially selected commandos who were trained at Le Club des Pins, a secret Algerian training camp run by British Intelligence officers.

In early August 1944, members of le Détachement Special, under d'Astier's command and dressed in British battle-dress with berets that bore the Croix de Lorraine, left Algeria on board the *Marietta Madre*, captained by a Royal Naval officer. The ship was loaded with heavy arms and explosives. Their destination was the port of St Tropez, where they would become the first Frenchmen to land since 1940.[†]

Following their landing, the group moved north-east towards Colmar in Alsace, now dressed as civilians while working as intelligence officers for the Allied forces. In September 1944, as part of the French armed forces, they took control of Colmar. Alain later quoted Jacques Soustelle's tribute to the group, made at an event to commemorate Orion's achievements in September 1985: 'Thanks to Henri d'Astier de la Vigerie and his group of faithful followers ... the Franco–African Orion alliance was further crowned by the victorious fighting of the Commandos de France. They were there, right at the front, to deliver Hitler his final blow.'

From the winter of 1940, this Resistance network had followed France's long journey towards liberation.

*

---

* Paul Labbé was killed in a car crash in October 1943.

† At a celebration to commemorate sixty years since the landing of the *Marietta Madre* in St Tropez, my husband and I entertained many surviving members of the *Marietta Madre*, the Orion Resistance Group and the military representatives of the US and UK embassies to France.

Meanwhile, back in Paris, Alain's family still didn't know where he was but assumed he had headed to England, to join de Gaulle's Free French. On 6 June 1943, some four months after his departure, Andrée wrote:

> *Ils mobilisent la classe de 42 entièrement. Thank goodness Alain is not here. We have however received a reassuring message and hope to get more up-to-date news next month from a chap who has gone to Sweden and has promised to send a cable to the UK on our behalf.*

# 18

# *Illness*

In July 1943, Andrée was diagnosed with scarlet fever. The stressful conditions under which she and her fellow citizens had lived over the last few years, the food shortages, the cold winters and lack of fuel for heating, the risks involved in her Resistance work – they all took their toll on her health.

Scarlet fever was once a major cause of death; in Paris in 1943, treatment in the form of antibiotics was not available, making it a serious illness. The main symptoms are an extremely sore throat, high fever (at or above 101°F/38.3°C) and a rash, which usually starts on the neck and face and then spreads to the whole body.

During the summer Andrée had been struggling to earn some extra money by selling cigarettes and bottles of perfume, which she had been given by people she had helped to obtain passports and ID cards. Her journals during this period go into long, typically youthful descriptions about her difficulties in finding a boyfriend because so many young men had either escaped France, were planning to do so, or were prisoners of war. She also refers frequently to being very bored; her Resistance work in 1943 was less intense than it had been in previous years as while Alain was out of the country, the group's main focus was on recruiting young men who wanted to use their escape route. Several members of the group had left for North Africa and the army. Andrée felt frustrated by her inability to do more to help her country overthrow the Germans. She had lost several friends already and was fearful of what the future might hold.

It was on 29 June that she first reported feeling unwell:

*I am in bed, I am alone and I am feeling very depressed. Why do I feel like this? Is it because I am such a weak person? I have now been in bed for a whole week with a raging temperature and I have been reading Alain's diaries written back in 1940, just after the invasion. He is so very patriotic, so determined, so single-minded in everything he wants to achieve.*

*Oh, I hate the Germans so much. I hate what they have done to us all and how worthless we have been made to feel.*

*Alain has now been gone for over four and a half months. Where can he be? What can he be doing? We have no idea. Maman is very distant and I will never get on with Yvette,\* and as for Lolo, she is just a baby.*

*Earlier today an air-raid alarm went off. It was just dreadful.*

*It is 9.00 p.m. and I am so tired. Earlier today I thought about taking an aspirin overdose.*

*Last Monday night the Biaggis took me out to dinner. We had some liver pâté, tuna with mayonnaise, a chateaubriand with sautéed potatoes, asparagus, cheese, a coffee and rum ice cream, a peach and a Grand Marnier, but tonight I am at home alone in bed and the only thing I could find to eat was some cheese and a jam sandwich. M. Leclercq has been very kind because when I took six days' sick leave he did not deduct any of my salary.*

*I have very few cigarettes or perfumes to sell, which means I have no extra money.*

*Yvette has broken the TSF [the radio]. I cannot stop scratching. Could there be a flea attacking me?*

Her friend Mado came to visit while she was ill in bed. Andrée noted their conversation:

*We talked for a long time, especially about the political situation. It is impossible for me to describe how much I hate the Germans. I will never be able to say it enough.*

Andrée's doctor couldn't find anything wrong with her and she returned to work. On 1 July 1943, she wrote:

---

\* In fact, in later life, Andrée and her sister Yvette did become close, particularly after Andrée's husband Frank died in 1966.

*I am sick to death of working at Police Headquarters. I am always completely exhausted and I do not know why.*

*In a month's time I will hopefully be on the shores of Lake Geneva on holiday, that is if the political situation allows me to travel.*

*I have to find some money for my trip. I now have a few bottles of perfume which were given to me by some grateful clients and which I can sell, along with some cigarettes, which should give me enough money to pay for my train ticket.*

But things changed quickly, as she recorded a week later:

*It is just unbelievable, absolutely incredible. I have been in bed since Saturday with scarlet fever and that half-wit, Doctor Charles, who I went to see last week because I felt so awful was incapable of working out what was wrong with me. I was at work for four whole days with scarlet fever. How could this have happened?*

*One day after work last week I went to Marthe for dinner and I had the most awful headache. I noticed that one of the glands in my neck had swollen and Marthe said she was going to take me to her doctor. He kindly agreed to see us even though it was very late and, after giving me a full examination, announced that I had scarlet fever and that I was to stay in bed for the next two weeks. I am at home, all alone. I am really angry. What a time to be ill when I need to earn some money. Luckily I started saving a while ago and so I have a bit in my moneybox. I also gave Raffini four bottles of perfume and three cartons of Gauloise to sell, so I will make some money out of that. I will not be paid while I am off work. My salary will be stopped and I will only receive a little sick pay from the Social Services.*

*I am in bed reading all day and it is getting a little boring.*

*Margit took my sick note to Police Headquarters and Monsieur Richard sent me his good wishes, hoping I would be back soon.*

*I have been told to stay off work for a whole month, just in case. I do not feel ill, I just feel lethargic and have no energy.*

*I received a telegram from Longeain who said she could not pay me a*

*visit. She made all sorts of excuses. Everyone at work is terrified of catch-
ing scarlet fever and no one wants to come anywhere near me. So how about
me? I must have caught it from someone. If only being ill could help me lose
some weight but sadly I do not think it will. I am allowed to eat whatever
I want and I would love some chicken, but there is no food around and so
it will remain a dream.*

*Papanous* [a friend of Alain, whom Andrée described as 'very
kind'] *has just been arrested and put in prison, which is a nuisance because
he was going to arrange to sell some of our tapestries. We will now be
unable to sell them and we will therefore have even less money.* *

*Will I have enough money for my holiday to Lake Geneva? I still have
to pay for the two appointments I had with Dr Charles. What a fool! He
might as well have let me drop dead for all the help he gave me. The com-
plications arising from scarlet fever can be seriously worrying.*

*I am so miserable and breaking off with Lucien at the beginning of the
year is not helping. I have the phono on the bed next to me and it cheers me
up and I am reading lots of detective novels. I must write to poor Papanous
and I must write to Maman.*

*I wonder what sort of life lies ahead for me? At the moment it is imposs-
ible to predict anything. We could all be dead within days with the political
events unfolding around us. The RAF are dropping the most enormous
number of bombs over Germany and Cologne is in ruins. Margit's boss had
the nerve to say that bombing civilians is not what waging war is about,
but I am strangely happy about it all. Was war about bombing Rotterdam,
a city at the heart of a neutral country in 1940, killing over twenty thousand civilians and refugees, and what about the Blitz in London in 1941?
As for the Italians, I will never forget what they did on 10 June 1940*
[when Italy declared war on Britain and France].

---

* This may read callously to modern-day eyes, but shows the reality of the
times they were living in; Andrée was always forthright and pragmatic, and
surviving the war only hardened these qualities in her. And of course, this was
a private diary, in which she recorded thoughts not necessarily intended for
public consumption.

*Earlier today Marthe brought me some peaches and some celery. I am going to make a 'Tipperary' soup, which will remind me of my English girlfriends who gave me the recipe.*

*Before going to sleep last night I opened the windows and loudly played my record of the Royal Air Force march. It is highly unlikely that anyone could have heard it out on the streets and it was very uplifting.*

It took Andrée several months to make a full recovery in the end, but her strength and determination helped her to get back on her feet and return to work some four weeks after she first fell ill. She spent a week recuperating at Evian, at an auberge overlooking Lake Geneva. She later told me: 'Every evening I used to sit on a bench in Evian looking out onto the shores of Lake Geneva. Evian was in total darkness but Geneva was full of lights. It was so beautiful and I used to think if only I could get into Switzerland for a few days.'

Little could Andrée have guessed on that July night during her illness, as she turned off the light and listened to the RAF march music, that within two years she would meet an RAF officer who would change her life completely.

# 19

# *Betrayal*

Being caught was not the main concern of the Orion Resistance fighters; had it been they would perhaps never have achieved what they did. Nevertheless, the dangers they faced were very real and the possibility of betrayal, by an outsider or someone they trusted, was a serious concern.

Every Orion member was careful to follow Alain's strict rules, but they were young and inexperienced, and they could not always contain their impetuous behaviour. The 'game' was about taking risks and drawing more friends into their circle to join them, but the chance of recruiting a mole or a traitor into the fold was always high no matter how careful they were. In December 1943, something went terribly wrong.

Biaggi had taken on the role of identifying men they wanted to help escape to North Africa, recruiting them mainly from Parisian student circles (though the group was willing to help anyone who came forward and asked for assistance). There were huge dangers involved in working with these young men, arming them with false ID cards and arranging meeting points in Paris and the Basque country – not least the possibility of enemy infiltration. It was to Alain's great credit that, of a group of some seventy agents, it is believed that only one of his team – Jean Xavier Escartin, father of six and, at thirty-six, older than the others in the group – lost his life at the hands of the Gestapo.

Xavier, the owner of a haberdasher's shop in the rue St Martin in central Paris, was a lively and warm-hearted, generous man. He and Biaggi worked closely together to make sure their recruits were looked after; Biaggi handled the prospective escapees' travel arrangements from Paris to the Basque country, including all the necessary false ID cards and travel permits, while

Xavier was responsible for everything once they arrived in the Pyrenees and until they reached Spain.

They had detailed security rules. Besides Biaggi and Xavier, no one ever knew the name of the escapee, the *passeur*, or the safe house, until the very last minute. Meeting places and times were kept vague and always at night. No one working on the project ever had a problem recognising the men as they arrived from northern France because of their fair complexions and the way they dressed, but even so they were always asked for a password, which had been given to them just before they left Paris.

In the capital, depending on the personal circumstances of the escapee, a fee was charged. It covered the costs of their lodging, food, transport, ID cards, travel permits and some money for the guide who would help them cross the Pyrenees. The group was not out to make a profit; instead, as Biaggi once explained to one of his recruits, those who came from a wealthy background would be asked to pay for other recruits. Gandy notes that after arriving at their prearranged meeting places in the Basque country, 'clients' were taken to the village of Itxassou, from where their trip through the mountains to Spain would begin.

To celebrate her husband's birthday that December, Madame Escartin organised a dinner party at their home in Paris. Among the guests was le comte de Montreuil, otherwise known as Guy de Marcheret d'Eu, a recent acquaintance and newcomer to Paris who had made his way into Escartin's group of friends as a close friend of Madame B,* the wife of a famous sportsman from the Basque country. The ties between Basque people were famously strong, and such a connection was therefore treated as a seal of approval.

At the dinner, to which Michel Alliot had also been invited, the count told Escartin and his friends that he wanted to use their escape route. He explained that he had been born in Russia in 1917 and that, when the revolution began, his family moved to China, where he had been educated by the

---

* Her name remains unknown.

Jesuits. He said that he had returned to France before the war to claim the family seat, following his elder brother's death. Over dinner they discussed politics and de Marcheret described himself as a Gaullist.

There was no obvious reason to doubt his credentials, but when Biaggi met the count he sensed that something did not quite add up and stalled in organising his departure. He decided to make further enquiries into the man's background and phoned Madame B, who knew Escartin well. They arranged to meet at the Café Weber opposite the Tuileries Gardens on the rue Royale, so that he could question her in person about whether de Marcheret really was who he said he was. Unwisely, however, on this one occasion Biaggi did not abide by the usual rules that he and Alain had been so keen on enforcing. As he later explained, 'I was doing too much and wanted to find as many candidates as I could.' That same afternoon, he had also arranged a meeting at the same time and place with two recent recruits, Roulleaux du Gage and Guy de Frollé, to give them their papers and further details of their forthcoming trip. At this point it was not uncommon for Biaggi to have up to fifteen meetings a day in his never-ending search to find as many candidates as possible.

While Biaggi was meeting Madame B in the Rue Royal, Alliot had a rendezvous of his own – at La Source, a popular café in the Quartier Latin. He was meeting a man called Gosselin who, he had been told, was a member of the Mouvements unifiés de Résistance zone sud, a Resistance group based in the South of France. As Alliot walked into La Source, he was surprised to see de Marcheret there, talking to another man. Upon greeting him, he discovered that this other man was Gosselin. Alliot sat down at their table and as he did, de Marcheret gave him some leaflets to distribute to his friends. Alliot glanced at the papers, containing articles in support of de Gaulle and calling for Parisians to join the resistance. To be found with such material would mean instant arrest and likely death; exactly why most Resistance groups avoided such pamphlets. Alliot sensed danger. He left the café immediately, dropping the leaflets under the table, but outside on the street he was apprehended at gunpoint by three men who searched him roughly and, even though he had nothing on him, pushed him into a waiting car that took him to Gestapo headquarters for questioning.

While Alliot was being arrested, a Citroën drew up outside Escartin's shop in the rue St Martin and three men wearing Gestapo raincoats jumped out and forced their way aggressively to the front of a line of customers waiting in Escartin's shop. They grabbed him by the arms and pushed him out of his shop and into their car. Madame Escartin and her mother heard the commotion from their flat on the first floor. They rushed up to the maid's room at the top of the house* and were able from there to get into the corridor that linked the building to another block on a different street. They made their way down the stairs safely, and Madame Escartin caught the *métro* to Concorde and walked to the rue Royale to warn Biaggi. She was too late.

Minutes after Alliot's arrest, de Marcheret was taken by car to the Rue Royale where he joined Madame B; Biaggi saw them together in the café window as he approached, but did not have time to figure out what was going on. As he entered the café, he was grabbed by two members of the Milice. With no time to warn the two new recruits he was also meant to be meeting there, he was manhandled out to the street and into a waiting car. He recognised the Corsican accent of one of the Milice and tried to engage him in conversation using the local dialect as part of an attempt to persuade the man to let him go, but to no avail.

The coordination of the Gestapo operation to arrest Biaggi, Escartin and Alliot was brilliant; they had successfully picked up three leading members of the escape ring without any of the men being able to warn the others. Roulleaux du Gage and Guy de Frollé, along with everyone else in the café, had their papers checked and were searched by members of the Gestapo who were now crawling all over the building. Du Gage already had a false ID card Biaggi had given him a few days earlier. Both men were taken in for questioning; de Frollé was released due to lack of evidence, but du Gage was tortured to find out how he had obtained his ID card and was later deported to Buchenwald, from where he would not return.

The Orion Group was desperate to find out whether any of the men had

---

* It was customary in Paris for the maid's room to be located at the top of the apartment block and referred to as 'la chambre de bonne'.

talked – and indeed, how and why the group had been betrayed. They were worried, particularly, that Biaggi's war wounds might make him vulnerable to torture.

Several days later, they learnt that the three prisoners were to be moved from Gestapo headquarters to the prison at Fresnes (the main Paris prison where political prisoners were detained). Since no one else from Orion had been arrested and no one had paid the offices of Vaudevir a visit, they assumed the Gestapo had not been able to get anything out of the men. The person (or people) who had betrayed them was presumably still at large, however, and the group needed to find out who the mole was.

Andrée was hugely worried about Biaggi, of whom she was extremely fond. She decided that she would go to the prison to see if she might be allowed in to see him. It was risky, but the prospect of being able to find out any news about their betrayer outweighed the danger. She discussed the plan with her friend and Orion colleague Marthe, and also told her mother, hoping Yvonne would give her some practical advice; she was nervous, and wanted to make sure she looked utterly inconspicuous. It would be disastrous if she herself were to be suspected of working with Biaggi and subsequently arrested. To her surprise, Yvonne took the news calmly and without protest, possibly aware that there were many group members who could still be rounded up if they did not find out who had betrayed them.

Several days later, on a cold, damp morning, Andrée queued outside the prison wall with a group of women, most of whom must have feared that this might be the last time they saw their relatives. She wore no make-up and was dressed in an old grey coat with a scarf over her hair, hoping to avoid attention. She spent all day waiting but to no avail; the guards would not let her see Biaggi.* He spent ninety-five days in solitary confinement, after being questioned over several days by the SS, who used his old stomach

---

* Though not from Biaggi, Orion may have found out somehow who the mole was, as no one else from the group was subsequently arrested. There is no record of any form of retaliation by Orion against the count, though presumably they made sure that all agents were warned about him. Guy de Marcheret d'Eu was executed after the war. Madame B, meanwhile, was forced to make financial reparations to Escartin's wife and children.

wounds as a means to torture him. During one period he was put on a starvation diet as a punishment for having made contact, using Morse code, with his cell neighbour, the duc de Rohan-Chabot – President of the Red Cross.

Having tried and failed to get Biaggi to speak, the Germans eventually transferred him on 19 March 1944 to a holding camp near Compiègne. On 3 June, he was on a deportation train bound for Germany when he, with some of his fellow prisoners, jumped off the train to freedom. (By all accounts he had to threaten some of his companions not to raise the alarm.)* His story was not yet over. Alliot had been similarly transferred to the Camp de Royallieu, and had managed to escape a few weeks before Biaggi. Sadly Escartin was not so fortunate: he was sent to Germany on another deportation train, and never returned.

---

* Gandy provides an interesting account of the escape. There were roughly 100 prisoners in the carriage with Biaggi. They knew they were being taken to camps in Germany but many believed they would eventually be saved by the Allies. Biaggi and a few other prisoners, including a priest named Le Meur, argued that there was a strong chance they would die in the camps and that they therefore had to try to escape from the train. They had been warned by the guards that any such attempt would be met by the shooting of other prisoners in retaliation. A fierce argument broke out between those who wanted to take the risk and those who didn't, with Biaggi threatening to kill anyone who called the guards. According to Gandy, the abbé Le Meur told Biaggi that if he did kill another prisoner, the priest would give him absolution afterwards. Le Meur had previously bribed a guard to smuggle a small saw onto the train, which the prisoners used to unlock their carriage.

# 20

# *Secret Agent*

I n January 1944, after Alain had completed his training in North Africa, Henri d'Astier and the head of the French Security Service, Jacques Soustelle, introduced him to Henry Hyde, head of the Algerian section of the OSS. Hyde was looking for agents in France to work for the American intelligence services.

Hyde was aware of Alain's intelligence-gathering network in Paris and Marseilles and asked him to start an OSS network in south-western France. He promised to supply Alain with the money he needed to fund Orion, now led in Paris by François Clerc and in Marseilles by Raoul Maillard. It would enable them to bribe members of the Wehrmacht, pay their informants and cover their agents' expenses. Alain couldn't refuse. He was officially enlisted on 15 January. For intelligence purposes, occupied Europe was divided between SOE, the Special Operations Executive branch of British Intelligence, and OSS, the Office of Strategic Services branch of the US intelligence services. France mainly came under SOE, but the Americans wanted their own agents in the field. Under Alain's deal with Hyde, Orion would supply information to OSS.

On 4 April 1944, as he prepared to leave US Air Force base Blida, on the outskirts of Algiers, Alain met William Casey, head of OSS operations in North Africa and later to become head of the CIA in President Reagan's administration. Casey was eager to see this young Frenchman whose network was of such interest to Henry Hyde and who had been trained for several months as one of their agents. Casey was aware that, after a five-hour flight over Spain, Alain Griotteray was to be dropped 'blind' by parachute into occupied France with no one in the country aware of his arrival. It had been agreed that he would be dropped into the Pyrenean village of Orion, his Resistance headquarters and an area he knew well.

Alain was given a suitcase full of dollars by his OSS colleagues, which he carefully counted before leaving the hanger. He was also given a number of twenty-franc Louis d'or coins,* which he placed carefully in a purse in his pocket. In a smartly tailored Parisian-labelled suit belonging to his close friend Yves de Kermoal, he climbed up the steps into the waiting aircraft.†

As Casey wished him luck, Alain felt confident that he could find his way to the château. It had been a year since he had left France, and he was excited to go back. As the engines of the 'flying fortress' started up, he fastened his safety belt; the plane made its way down the runway and within minutes they were airborne.

It was nearly midnight when they approached the drop-off point. The pilot wanted to get out of the area as quickly as possible, conscious that the aircraft noise had to be kept to a minimum to avoid detection. Alain checked his parachute, threw out the case (which was attached to another parachute) and jumped out into occupied France. A few minutes later he was on firm land. Instinctively he knelt and kissed the ground beneath him. He was home. He couldn't waste time though; he had to get moving. He cut down his parachute, which was glowing cream in the dark. He started searching for his case and found several notes lying on the ground; its lock must have snapped and opened on landing. Alain was in a daze. Despite his training and his usual confidence, he was frightened. It was almost 2 a.m. and very cold, and he wasn't sure where he was – it was hard to get his bearings in the dark. If he didn't recover all the missing dollars, he would risk leaving

---

* Louis d'or coins were minted around 1793, when Louis XVI of France was still alive. As such they went on to be collectors' items. The French often referred to twenty-franc gold coins as Louis d'or, although technically they were not the same coins. Millions of twenty-franc gold coins were put into circulation between 1871 and 1940 and it is believed it was some of these that the OSS gave Alain to enable him to pay for intelligence, to bribe collaborators and for his expenses, rather than original Louis d'or coins as described by Andrée. Years later, in the 1970s, Yvonne Griotteray still kept a substantial part of her wealth in gold coins in her flat in Paris.

† The suit was Yves de Kermoal's idea; his reasoning was that if Alain should be picked up by the Wehrmacht wearing an expensive Parisian suit, no one would think he had come from North Africa.

a trail of evidence behind.* Fortunately, after a brief search, he was able to track down the broken suitcase and its scattered contents.

Taking stock of his surroundings, he decided that he must be some distance from the main town, Salies-de-Béarn, as he couldn't see any glow of town lights in the distance. It was therefore unlikely that the Germans had heard the plane but he could not be sure. He could, however, make out a small glimmer of light not too far away, which he thought might be a small farm; with no other choice, he made for it, hoping the owners would help him out. When he reached the house,† he knocked at the door and saw a man looking out of the window. Alain explained he was lost, that he needed help and that he was a friend of Madame Labbé, the nearby château's owner. The farmer, whose name Alain later discovered was Monsieur Laulhé, had heard the aircraft and assumed Alain was a member of the French Resistance who had been parachuted into the area. Bravely he opened the door and welcomed him into his home.

'You are only a kilometre away from the château and there are unlikely to be any Germans about, it is far too late. They are all stationed in and around Salies-de-Béarn, but it is possible they will have heard the plane. If so, we can be sure they will be out at dawn with the dogs. I will take you now to a safe hiding-place. You must stay there and at dawn I will go to the château and tell them where you are hiding.'[13]

No names were exchanged at that time – it was too dangerous. Together the farmer and Alain walked to a small field covered in bushes, where they hid the parachute and Alain settled down for the night. Despite the cold, damp air, Alain quickly fell asleep and did not wake up until well past dawn when he heard something moving nearby. He picked up his gun, ready to act, when he realised it was Marie Flandé, the château's housekeeper. She in turn was overwhelmed to see him. 'Mon dieu, it is Monsieur Alain!‡ How on earth did you get here? Where have you been? What are you doing wearing

* In 2010, when I visited the Château d'Orion, the current Madame Labbé told me all about the suitcase lock snapping and Alain having to collect up the notes, which were scattered all over the ground.

† The name of the house was Tambouri d'Andrein.

‡ 'Moun Diou! Moussu Alain!' – in her native Basque.

such a smart suit? We had no idea it was you hiding here.' She promised to return at nightfall to take him to the château, and to send her husband to collect the parachute separately.

While Alain waited in the forest, he started thinking about how to get the OSS money back to Paris. He couldn't risk the possibility of capture and the dollars being confiscated – the money was essential to their operation. It would be safer for a woman to travel with the money; Andrée was the perfect candidate for the job.

Eventually Marie returned to collect him; as they walked the few kilometres back to the château, he saw the building's lights in the distance and his confidence returned. He would be safe here.

Marie went ahead, leaving Alain to walk alone up the small drive to the manor house. He stopped outside the chapel and prayed that God would protect him, the Labbés and the Basque people who had helped him over the last twenty-four hours. On his arrival, Monsieur Flandé left to pick up the parachute. Alain asked him to destroy it immediately in case the château was searched.*

Alain was anxious to see Madame Labbé. He had wrestled with the question of how to tell her that her son Paul, his close friend, had been killed in Morocco. But the look on her face as she greeted him said it all; she knew already and she held him tightly without speaking, before abruptly changing her manner. Things were likely to turn dangerous in the morning as the Germans would surely come to ask questions about the plane. Alain was to stay in the attic until arrangements had been made to get him back to Paris.

Marie took Alain up into one of the main bedrooms. Behind a cupboard, a door led to a smaller room, which had once been used for ladies' maids or mistresses. Alain was allowed a warm bath and a new set of clothes before he went into the smaller room. Inside, a panelled door in the wall pushed open to let him climb a cobweb-ridden staircase up to a dark attic room that

---

* Forty-five years later, at a memorial reunion held at the château, Alain was shocked but amused to be formally presented with the parachute as a gift. Marie Flandé told him she had not obeyed his instructions because she wanted to keep it as a souvenir.

no one had used for years. It was to be his home for the next week while plans were made to get him back to Paris.

Andrée was due to travel to Orthez shortly, bringing the latest batch of intelligence from Orion's agents. Emile Flandé, the local town hall secretary, would arrange its transfer to Hendaye by Jean Elisalt and then on to Bilbao by Henri Etchepare – both reliable and patriotic locals. If Andrée missed her train connection she would bring the 'post' directly to Orion, although it was, everyone knew, safer for it to be left in Orthez.

Meanwhile there was the question of how to get Alain to Paris. In Algiers, OSS had supplied him with a new identity and matching ID card, but when Émile showed it to a local police officer, who was a member of the Resistance, the officer laughed and told him that the card had been so badly forged that it would barely get Alain beyond Salies-de-Béarn. A new ID card was made up. Alain adopted the identity of Adolphe Lambezat, the son of a local peasant, on the understanding that once in Paris he would destroy the card immediately and adopt a new name: Alain de Courcy de Brayance. He didn't want to risk being connected to his family in case anything should happen to them if he were to be picked up. Gandy refers to Alain staying with friends on his return to Paris, as part of his plan to protect his family and ensure his own safety.

New card in hand, Alain prepared to leave Orion. He was taken in the château's horse and cart to Salies-de-Béarn, where he caught the bus to Pau, then boarded a train for Toulouse and ultimately on to Bordeaux. There were lots of German soldiers milling around that morning but he stayed calm. His new ID card was credible and, as he later told me, his OSS training and the money he had gave him confidence that he could defend himself if needed.

Alain and Madame Labbé had discussed how best to transport their new funds back to the capital and had decided the safest plan was for Alain to meet Andrée in Bordeaux, where he could pass on to her some of the money. They did not want to risk either Alain or Andrée carrying the full amount at any one time. If either of them were to be stopped, they could lose everything. It would mean further trips and subsequently more danger, but Alain was confident his sister would not flinch at the task she was to be asked to take on.

## 21

# *Gold*

As the clock chimed six, Andrée left her office. She had had a difficult and tiring day and was eager to leave work on time. Pedalling home along the banks of the Seine, she passed the Louvre and thought how much she wanted to go in and enjoy some of the greatest paintings in the world. Sadly she was only too aware that its treasures, including 'La Joconde' (the Mona Lisa), had been packed up at the beginning of the war and sent out of Paris.*

Andrée carried on cycling and arrived home a little while later, storing her bicycle in the courtyard near the concierge's office. She stopped to collect the post and recognised, to her surprise, a note addressed to her in handwriting she recognised. She hurried upstairs; it was safer to open it in the privacy of her home. In coded language, the letter asked her to come as soon as possible to the rue de Bourgogne.

Changing into a casual pair of trousers and a sweater, she told her mother that she had to go out immediately to meet friends who lived on the Left Bank. Yvonne had wanted a family dinner that evening and sensed that something was going on for Andrée to be rushing out so quickly. She was therefore not pleased but, before she could object, Andrée was out of the flat, making her way across the river and towards François de Rochefort's flat.

Running up the stairs two at a time she was surprised to find the door to the flat slightly ajar. As she walked in, she found François de Rochefort sitting comfortably in an armchair and enjoying a bottle of 1926 Bordeaux.

---

* The Louvre moved most of its paintings out of Paris during the war. Safe storage proved challenging: they were transferred to a number of châteaux and museums. The 'Mona Lisa' was apparently moved five times – first to the Château de Chambord in the Loir-et-Cher, then to the Ingres Museum in Montauban to avoid damp, before being moved again later in the war.

Andrée knew how angry her mother would be if she was not back in time for dinner and demanded to know what was so important that he had summoned her so openly. She was given a small envelope containing some money, indicating that she was to go a hotel in Bordeaux where she would receive instructions from someone who would know how to find her. After checking the money, Andrée left, telling him she would let him know the following day whether she could get permission to travel and, if so, when. A few days later, documents in hand, she was ready to go. She packed lightly, assuming she would be picking up reports to be brought back to the rue de Bourgogne.

With ad hoc Nazi searches on travelling civilians increasing daily, Edmond and Yvonne were not happy as they watched their daughter prepare for her trip to Bordeaux. Alain had been gone for almost a year without direct contact or confirmation of his safety, and they didn't know the full reasons for Andrée's trip. Edmond insisted on accompanying her to the station, early in the morning. As usual it was over an hour late in leaving and full of soldiers, but Andrée felt relatively safe, knowing she wasn't carrying anything incriminating at this point. She never knew much about her trips to ensure that if she was picked up, she would not be able to disclose much sensitive information.

Once the train arrived at Bordeaux, Andrée moved with the other passengers down the platform, doing her utmost to blend in and avoid drawing attention to herself. She had spent some time examining a map of the town before leaving Paris, so that she would know where she was going once she left the station. She took a bus to the hotel, where a room had been booked in her name. The concierge greeted her formally, and after speaking to the reception clerk she was promptly shown to her room. Safely settled, she changed into a simple dress before returning downstairs to the main salon, where she ordered a glass of wine. For over an hour she waited, wondering who was going to meet her. The clock on the mantelpiece chimed every fifteen minutes. She knew she needed to look at ease and relaxed and had brought a Maigret story with her so that she could read while she waited, hopefully allowing her contact to find her without drawing attention to herself. Suddenly – unbelievably – she thought she heard the sound of her brother's voice. She almost jumped up in shock, but managed to keep her composure. She sat for a few moments observing her surroundings, then got up and walked to the main desk of the hotel. There stood Alain, checking in at reception. She felt a rush of emotion; here was her brother whom she had not seen since February 1943. Neither she nor her parents had had any news about him in over a year, yet now he was here, safe and well and almost at touching distance.

She managed to stay in control of her emotions. Alain turned as she approached; formally and without a trace of emotion, he shook her by the hand and told her quietly that they should meet in his room as soon as she was ready. Using the name he was travelling under, Adolphe Lambezat, he was confident no one would identify them as brother and sister. Once they met in the safety of his room they hugged each other tightly and began to catch up on all that had happened over the last year.

Meeting up in public places was not without its risks but, as Alain explained, it was unavoidable this time. He told his sister about the money he had received from the OSS, and how he needed her help to get the funds to Paris safely. Most of the dollars were still at the château, but he had some of the coins with him now to pass on to her; she would need to make several later trips to Orion to collect the rest over time. Andrée was worried. She knew the risks involved and the responsibility for carrying Orion's money felt like a big weight on her young shoulders, even though she always wanted to help her brother. She told Alain she needed some time to think. In the end, it was well past three o'clock in the morning before they finally went to bed.

The following day, after breakfast, they went for a walk, hoping a short stroll in the fresh air would do them good. As they wandered past a lingerie shop, Andrée stopped and stared at the window display, with its array of mannequins wearing girdles. Alain was restless but Andrée smiled to herself and told him she had the answer. 'I will buy a girdle and sew the coins into it. No one will suspect that and unless someone had a very good reason, they would be very unlikely to strip-search me.'

Alain couldn't understand how she could possibly manage to fit the coins into the girdle but he trusted his sister's judgement and they went into the shop. Andrée tried one on for size and pronounced it a good fit, so they bought it. That afternoon she spent several hours in her hotel room, sewing the coins securely into her new piece of lingerie. It was laborious work but she enjoyed sewing and liked a challenge. She managed to fix twenty of the coins into the girdle but, try as she might, could not fit the last one in. Instead, she put it in her purse, figuring that if she was searched, it was not likely that suspicion would fall on her for possession of just one coin.

The following morning Andrée awoke to strong sunshine filtering through the shutters. There was no soap in the bathroom for her shower. Soap was a luxury item in France during the war – one of the things most missed by the majority of the population. Andrée had hoped that this symbol of luxury might be available in the hotel, but it was not to be. She picked up the girdle and began to wrap it around her body. The small hooks had been securely sewn on and as she attached them, one by one, she felt confident that it would remain in place. Even though the weight of the coins was minimal (each one weighed approximately 6.45 grams and so in total, it was 129 grams,* the girdle was heavy and uncomfortable and she was not look-ing forward to the constraints it would make on her movements. She wore a thick, woollen navy pin-striped suit, which would hopefully cover up any bumps the coins might make in the girdle material. Once she was ready she went down to the hotel's dining room, where Alain was already eating breakfast.

The pair acknowledged each other formally. Andrée nodded to her brother to reassure him that all was well. Quietly she murmured as they sat at the table that her plan had worked, but that there was one coin left over. Both knew that the day ahead would be a challenging one. Keeping the conversation light, Andrée began talking about what she would buy if she had money of her own. 'I would love to buy a new pair of shoes. I am so tired of walking around in wooden-soled shoes. If only I had some money I would buy the shoes I saw yesterday in the rue St Catherine.'

---

* In 1944 gold was worth approximately US$33.85 an ounce; in 2013 gold was worth approximately US$1,250 an ounce. A twenty-franc gold coin would today be worth approximately US$272 in today's rates.

'Well let's go and have a look at them if you can walk that far in your girdle,' answered Alain.

They found the shoe shop and Andrée gazed longingly into the window. 'Let's go in and buy them,' said Alain, to her astonishment.

'But I have no money.'

'We can use the coin you couldn't fit into the girdle.'

'But it belongs to OSS and we need it to keep the group going.'

'Andrée, I do not think the OSS will know or mind if we spend a small amount on shoes for you. Besides, I think you deserve them in view of the risks you are taking for us.'

Andrée was happy to be persuaded by her younger brother. The sales assistant approached the young pair with a smile and asked how she could help. Andrée pointed to the black suede shoes with a high, thick heel and straps, which she had seen the previous day. The sales assistant took them out of the window so that she could try them on. She walked across the shop floor and twirled back, smiling with pleasure. 'They are simply wonderful, so elegant and so comfortable.'*

Alain paid the shop assistant in cash, muttering under his breath to Andrée that she could pay him back when she had converted one of the coins into hard currency. The pair then walked back to their hotel to pay their bill and collect their cases. They were to travel separately to Paris, as Alain was much more likely to be stopped at some point; Andrée would take the first train.

The girdle was heavy and uncomfortable and she was hoping to find a corner seat where she could settle down for the whole trip. The hotel had prepared a little food for her journey, so she went straight to the platform and onto the train.

It was late as the train arrived in Paris. Andrée moved swiftly and purposefully through the station and onto the *métro*. Spot checks on the street were increasingly common in Paris and she didn't want to be accosted so close to the end of her journey.

---

* The shoes were still in Andrée's belongings in London in 1996. As part of an interview for a school project, Andrée told her eleven year-old granddaughter: 'I will never forget how comfortable those shoes were.'

She reached her apartment block just before curfew and climbed the stairs up to the flat. She phoned a colleague straight away to tell him she had bought some shoes in Bordeaux; she made no mention of who her mysterious visitor had been. He understood on hearing her words that she had returned safely from her trip.

Andrée was pleased to find she was alone in the flat that night. Her parents and sisters had gone to Mesnil-le-Roi for a few days and she was thankful she would not have to lie about where she had been. Alain had made her promise not to tell anyone about their meeting but she was allowed to tell their parents that he was safe, and she knew they would be desperately relieved to hear it.

She went into her bedroom and undressed. She unhooked the girdle carefully, knowing she would need it again. Her skin was very red where her body had been restricted. She unstitched the coins from their hiding place and put them one by one into a smart silver-laced purse. They would be safe in her room until the morning, when she could hide them in the apartment cellar until needed.

## 22

# *The Cyanide Option*

Back in Paris, Alain wanted to go home to his family but he remained concerned that to do so might jeopardise their safety; he decided it would be better if he stayed for the moment with one of his couriers, Marthe Dramez, from where he could get back into the swing of things with Orion. Alain's ability to meet and endear himself to a wide range of contacts was already impressive (and only improved with age). One of his friends worked for Jean Bichelonne, whom Alain later described in his memoir as Vichy Minister for Communications and Industrial Production. Alain visited him regularly, and his friend passed on anything he had picked up, including data on the condition of the French road network, the number and location of blown-up bridges, the timetable of barges travelling the canals, up-to-date information on the condition of the railway network and details on the movement of German troops around France.

He was especially pleased to be reunited with his close friend, Orion's Deputy Leader, François Clerc, who with Andrée's help had kept the group going throughout 1943 and early 1944. It had been a difficult period for François, who had received no news from Alain or d'Astier and had been hit hard by the arrests of Escartin, Biaggi and Alliot. But despite the setbacks, he had continued to recruit new agents: in 1943 he met Patrick Dolfus, whose father was deeply involved with the Resistance despite having been forced to supply cars to the Germans from his manufacturing company.[14] Dolfus supplied Clerc with economic intelligence on Germany's industrial requirements throughout the country. François also met Claude Arnould, head of the Resistance group Jade Amicol. Under his assumed name of Colonel Ollivier, Arnould was one of SOE's agents. François's links with Ollivier and the ORA meant that both organisations allowed Orion access to their transmitters in order to forward on to British Intelligence certain time-critical information.

Andrée had matured considerably since 1940 and with her increased confidence she understood that, with Alain back in Paris and the group operating at full tilt once again, their new role supplying OSS with intelligence meant heightened risks for everyone. As lead courier she was now undertaking a trip every two weeks – mostly to Orthez or Marseilles. This must have been extremely difficult – to gain permission for each trip, obtain an *ausweiss* and to get any necessary time away from work without arousing the suspicion of her colleagues. Yet Andrée managed it somehow. Civil servants were not allowed to leave the country, but her diaries show that she travelled to Brussels at least once.

By May 1944, Andrée was relying on a group of women, some of whom had become agents in a sister group in Bordeaux named Cauderon. In Paris, her close friends Marthe and Margit shared courier duties with her, as did Ninon Pagezy in Orion (Madame Labbé's daughter and sister of Paul). Twenty-one-year-old Guy Mangenot had created the Cauderon Resistance group with a team of eight agents under his command. Mangenot* gathered intelligence on the naval movements in the port of Bordeaux and details of how much fuel the German navy was stockpiling and where their sailors were stationed. He discovered the defences the Wehrmacht had installed on the coast surrounding Royan and the timetables of the planes landing and leaving the airport at Mérignac. He was supremely impatient, as was evident when, after the US landings on the Mediterranean coast in August 1944, he got so frustrated while awaiting Andrée's arrival that he impetuously decided to give some gathered intelligence to a passing US Army Officer rather than waste more time waiting.

With the increased dangers agents now faced, Alain instructed the entire group – by now over forty agents – that they were to carry a cyanide pill with them at all times. The suggestion (and it is assumed the supply) had

---

* Guy Mangenot was awarded two Croix de guerre – one for the dangers he ran while running the Cauderon group and the other while serving in the army under General Leclerc in 1945.

come from OSS, who were concerned that if one of them was interrogated by the Gestapo, they might incriminate the others.

These lethal pills had an important psychological value for Andrée and her colleagues. The main advantage of carrying them was that they could be concealed more easily than other methods. They were small (about the size of a pea) thin-walled glass ampoules, covered in brown rubber (to protect against accidental breakage) and filled with a concentrated solution of potassium cyanide. They were never swallowed whole. Instead, the user had to crush them between their teeth to release the fast-acting poison. Brain death occurred within minutes and the heartbeat stopped shortly after. Field Marshal Rommel committed suicide with such a pill following his implication in the July 20th plot against Hitler, and Pierre Laval, France's Vichy prime minister, attempted to use something similar when awaiting execution after the liberation.*

Biaggi, Alliot and Escartin had not been carrying pills at the time of their arrest but managed to withstand their interrogation without giving anything away. Most people in the group, however, were unlikely to be able to endure prolonged torture, as Andrée often explained: 'It would not have been easy if they started to pull out your finger- and toenails.'

Andrée and Alain were particularly vulnerable because of their knowledge of the other agents operating in the group – although Andrée always insisted that she was 'merely' a postman who knew nothing of what the others were up to. In her typically unassuming way, she said after the war that she merely typed the reports she was given without reading them, though she must have retained some of the information. There were other central figures within the group who also knew a certain amount about other Orion agents.

Sometime in late June 1944, Andrée went to Marseilles on a courier trip to pick up some documents from a man named Albert Paoli. She was surprised and delighted when she arrived to find that her contact was none other than her old friend Biaggi, who now held a new ID card since his

---

* He may have been using a different type of pill, however, as when his guards realised what was happening, the prison doctor was instructed to pump the substance out of his stomach so that he could face death by firing squad.

escape from the train to Germany. In Vergèze, a town on the Mediterranean coast, Biaggi had met up with Monsieur Joel, the manager of the French water company Perrier, whose son Rodolphe had been arrested by the Wehrmacht. On his release he had been made to work at a building company making cement used to build garrisons along the coast. Biaggi never missed an opportunity and brought Rodolphe Joel into his espionage network. At great personal risk he supplied Biaggi with details of the garrisons the Germans were installing along the coast, information which Biaggi passed in turn to Andrée.

François de Rochefort had not been idle in Alain's absence either. He was a good friend of General Verneau, head of the ORA, and the relationship between the two men enabled close cooperation between the two groups. Following the sudden arrest of Verneau,* de Rochefort subsequently became close to a new group of former army officers who, having left the army after the fall of France, were willing to supply him with military intelligence they thought might be of interest to OSS. François's flat continued to be Orion's informal Paris headquarters – a place for the collection of intelligence and occasional meetings. It was risky though: ten years older than most of the others, François moved in a sophisticated circle of wealthy Parisians and his discreet friendships within Paris's gay community brought him into 'unusual' circles, including contact with Wehrmacht officers willing to exchange information for bribes.

Martial de la Fournière joined the Orion group in 1941; in 1944 he was still working at the Ministry of Colonial Affairs where, because France had been cut off from her overseas dependencies, he found himself with little to do. Instead he used his time and the *ausweiss* he could obtain to infiltrate other ministries, where he networked with a group of like-minded people who supplied him with information from other Vichy ministries, intelligence

---

* Verneau was arrested after the Gestapo managed to infiltrate the ORA. He died while awaiting deportation to Buchenwald. Alain felt Verneau and his ORA colleagues took far greater risks, with less security, than the Orion Group. In his memoirs he described his horror at discovering after the war that de Rochefort had carelessly kept a note (a 'pneumatique') from Verneau, cancelling a meeting between the two men.

they thought might be useful to the Resistance. Once again Andrée and her colleagues were there to take it to Orthez.

Within six weeks of Alain's return to Paris, Orion was running more successfully than ever before. With the money from OSS they were able to use informants more widely and pass on to other agents the skills Alain had learnt during his training.

## 23

# *The Brothel*

In May 1944, on what proved to be yet another delayed journey, Andrée arrived in Biarritz late in the evening. She had some 'post' stitched into her suitcase as usual and nowhere to stay, as she hadn't intended to have an overnight stop. She tried three hotels near the station, none of which was able to give her a room, and (unusually for her) she started to worry. She knew no one in the town, curfew was about to fall and she was carrying incriminating material. Desperate times called for desperate measures, as she later recorded in her diary:

> *I finally arrived at a brothel, 'Chez Denise'. I was so relieved to have found somewhere to stay, I did not even begin to start thinking about the dreadful smell. I undressed, washed, got into bed and fell asleep but, at around two in the morning, I woke up scratching. I turned on the light and saw that I had been badly bitten by some sort of insect and there were several large red spots on my legs and then what did I see? A flea, sitting on the sheet; it was huge. I did not give it the benefit of the doubt and killed it instantly. It oozed blood. I then saw two more fleas and they were subject to the same fate. Had I been able to walk out of the house there and then I would have done so but I had to wait until after curfew had been lifted. So I had to sit for the next three hours upright in the most uncomfortable chair because there was no way I was going to go anywhere near the bed. Needless to say I did not sleep a wink.*

Andrée had ended up at the brothel thanks to an unlikely source of help: the local police station. Trying to batten down a rising feeling of panic, she decided to take refuge there – reasoning that her job at Police Headquarters in Paris might cause them to take pity on her. The duty sergeant – over-weight, middle-aged and friendly – expressed concern at her plight. Briefly she hoped he might invite her to stay with his family, but to have invited in a stranger (even a charmingly naive young woman) was perhaps too great a risk for anyone to take. Instead he made a surprising suggestion.

'I have an idea, Mademoiselle. You will not like what I am going to say, but there is no choice. There is a brothel near here and I think that is where you should go and stay the night. I will give you a letter of introduction to its owner, Madame Denise. Please do not worry: we know Madame Denise well and she will take good care of you. She allows travellers to stay in her rooms occasionally and there is never a problem.'

Andrée was initially shocked that he would suggest such a thing. But she was a pragmatic young woman; the hotels were full and she had to be off the streets within fifteen minutes. She considered asking the sergeant whether she could stay in one of the cells, but then thought better of it: the Germans often visited police stations in the early morning and she did not want to risk an encounter. She would go to the brothel and see what happened. Her mind made up, she walked briskly out of the police station and to the address the sergeant had given her. She knocked on the door, which was opened by a peroxide-blond woman wearing a low-cut dress who looked at her sharply and asked her what she wanted.

Trying to conceal her hesitation and unusual shyness, Andrée told her: 'The sergeant at the gendarmerie gave me your address and said you might be able to put me up for the night. I have here a letter of introduction.'

Madame Denise looked at Andrée suspiciously as she opened the envelope, but after reading it her attitude changed. She ushered her visitor in. 'Yes, I can give you a room on the top floor; you won't find it very comfortable but you will be safe. I want twenty-five francs for it and I need you out by 5.30 in the morning.'

Andrée took the key, picked up her case and made her way slowly and somewhat hesitantly up the stairs. As she reached the first floor, she was quite taken aback by the huge number of mirrors hanging from all available surfaces. She was quickly brought back to reality as she came face to face with a couple of Wehrmacht officers flirting outrageously with two of the girls of the house. It appeared, however, that Andrée was totally invisible to them; they were off-duty, having a great time and uninterested in a shy-looking young girl who wore no make-up and was dressed in simple clothes.

She reached the second floor and unlocked her room, closing the door behind her in relief. There was no point in panicking; she was in a whorehouse, by herself, in a town with no friends or contacts. The most important thing to do was to get some rest so that she could leave early in the morning and get to Orthez as quickly as possible.

Andrée opened her little case, undressed and put on her nightdress. She hadn't paid attention to the room's decor until now but, as she looked around, she saw herself from every angle on a series of mirrors – covering not just the walls but the ceiling. She recoiled with surprise, but then suddenly started to giggle as she thought back to her smart English friends and wondered what they would have thought about the situation she now found herself in. She felt sure that an English brothel would not have been quite as opulent as this one. She looked at the bed with its silk sheets and started to laugh all over again.

She turned off the light, closed her eyes and tried to go to sleep, but it was difficult; she hadn't eaten and was hungry, but worse than that she could hear the sound of a couple making love in the adjoining room. What really upset her was knowing that the prostitute was French and the man was German.

The final straw – as her diary entry above records – was when she fell asleep at last, only to be woken a few hours later by fleas biting her. Once she realised, she scrubbed herself all over in disgust, and waited in a chair until she heard the church bells chime 5.30 a.m. As she came downstairs, she walked into the middle of a heated argument between Madame Denise and a German officer complaining about his bill. He had obviously had a bad night and was in a filthy temper. Andrée considered returning to her room, but it was too late; she had been seen. The officer wheeled round and asked Madame Denise who she was and what she was doing in the brothel. Madame Denise calmly explained that her guest had stayed the night with her because all the Biarritz hotels had been booked up the previous night and the gendarmerie had sent her to them. In typically abrupt fashion, the officer turned to Andrée and demanded to see her identity card.

Andrée put down her case, opened her handbag and took out her ID card. The card gave her occupation at Police Headquarters in Paris and upon reading that the officer's body language changed instantly. Possibly concerned that if he pursued his line of questioning she might have friends in high places and report him to a senior officer in Paris, he clearly thought it best to let her on her way. He returned the card without a word as Andrée thanked her host and left the building.

Relieved to have escaped a difficult situation, she made her way to the station where she ordered some breakfast and waited for her train. It wasn't due for a couple of hours and so it was not until the late afternoon that she arrived at Orthez and made her way towards the address that François had given her. As she approached, she saw a man working on a car on the side of the road. She greeted him politely and he replied without hesitation: 'Bonjour, Mademoiselle, and how is life in Paris?' This was her contact.

Within minutes she was inside the house, opening her case and handing over the documents. She was now desperate to get back to the bus station for the last leg of her journey to Salies-de-Béarn. Stepping off the bus in the small Bearnais town, she headed straight to a café to place a call through to the château. The housekeeper was delighted to hear Andrée at the end of the line, and told her she would be picked up within the hour.

Andrée sat down in the late afternoon sun and thought about the warm welcome awaiting her, along with a bath, the possibility of some soap, hopefully a dinner of fresh food and a good night's sleep. There was only one question in her mind. Should she tell Madame Labbé about the brothel?

## 24

# *The Arrest*

The largest military operation in history began on the beaches of Normandy on 6 June 1944 – codenamed Operation Overlord. Approximately 150,000 men landed or parachuted into the area and thousands lost their lives. As the liberating troops advanced, the RAF and US air forces increased their bombing campaign, leaving much of the French railway network destroyed. Communication and travel throughout France became more difficult, compounded by many acts of sabotage, and for twenty-four hours after the D-Day landings the trains were at a complete standstill. In a recording made some twenty years ago, Andrée spoke of the difficulty in getting around during this time: often she had very little notice before a trip and she frequently didn't know how she would reach her destination. She recalled once having to go to Bordeaux by way of Marseilles, a huge detour.

Between 6 June and 17 July 1944, Andrée made four trips from Paris to Orion. Each time she stopped in Bordeaux to link up with a Cauderon Resistance agent who gave her the Bordeaux post, which she then took down to Orthez or Orion. At other times she left the post she had brought down from Paris in Bordeaux for a Cauderon agent to take on to Orthez, in case anyone might have followed Andrée from Paris. One diary entry referred to a train journey back from Bordeaux to Paris where she said she was 'joined in the carriage by members of the Berlin Philharmonic Orchestra. They had been playing in Spain. They were such fun but I will not admit this to anyone.'

The intensity of Andrée's travelling during this period proved exhausting – she was still working at Police Headquarters while obtaining permission to travel and coping with the unavoidable delays. The tracks were damaged so the trains were overcrowded, subject to air attacks and very hot due to the summer temperatures. Carriages were often requisitioned by the Germans. It was a punishing schedule and she was feeling the weight of her responsibilities. Her diary entries from this period were torn out of her journal and weren't always dated, making it difficult to assess exactly where she was at any one time. They are surprisingly – even shockingly – detailed (though without, of course, referring to the real purpose of her travel), full of information about her journeys, including first names of people she was due to meet. Given everything Andrée had absorbed from her brother about the need for discretion and secrecy, it seems incredible that she should have written so much down: her journals would have been potentially damaging evidence, had they been found, but possibly her whirlwind activity and subsequent exhaustion meant she was not fully on her guard. And, of course, she was not a professional agent: she was a twenty-three-year-old young woman, charged with huge responsibility. On one trip to Orthez, undated but most likely sometime during the first half of June, she described the difficulties she had in returning to Paris:

*I had been travelling all day and as we waited for a train heading for Paris, we were told that the only one coming through was now only going to Poitiers. I was about to give up when some of my fellow passengers suggested we go and look for a lorry or car heading for Paris, which might give us a lift. As we went in search of one there was an air-raid alert. As we walked, we met a group of people who had recently arrived from Paris. They told us the city was besieged and that the Germans were shooting indiscriminately on the streets. I did not believe it but we were so worried that we stopped for a drink – first one glass, then another, till we finished several bottles of wine.*

*Finally we found a driver taking a lorry to Paris. He was prepared to take us if we paid for the petrol. After four hours we got only as far as Orléans, and we were packed in the back like sardines, but at least we were 200 kilometres closer to Paris. Orléans was completely deserted due to the intense bombing. We stopped and found a hotel but I could not sleep; I could not get the bombs out of my mind. There was another air-raid warning after midnight; if I had been alone I would not have had the strength to get up, but my new friends and I went together to the shelter. The temperature in the shelter was below zero and the bombing lasted half an hour. We went back to bed but within half an hour we were back in the shelter. Finally, back in bed for the third time, I got to sleep, only to be woken at 7 in the morning.*

*Now, let me describe my travelling companions. There was Michèle, a strange girl who I suspect has no morals. She is obviously someone's mistress and runs an American bar – La Racasse – in Montmartre. She has invited us all to join her for dinner if we ever get back to Paris. She has short hair, dresses in a very masculine way, and although she says she is 25 years old, she looks much older. Next, D'Artagnan – a rather stylish insurance salesman, and a perfume salesman who is seriously charming!*

She was in trouble at work due to the delays on the trains, which led to an extraordinary diary entry dated 15 June – the only time she comes close to explicitly recording her Resistance activities:

*Little diary, you will not believe the trouble I got into when I finally made it to the Préfecture. Monsieur Leclercq was absolutely furious and made me do all the filing. He wanted to send me to the rue des Ursins [where the police archives were kept] but there was absolutely no way I was going there because it is essential that I can be contacted and important that I am near a phone.* [I assume this refers to Resistance colleagues who may have needed to reach her.] *What is more I am being watched very carefully and apart from the filing do not dare to do anything else. Michel wants me to leave and I would really like to leave this disgusting place. I had dinner with Michel on Tuesday night and he wanted me to say 'Merde' to Monsieur Leclercq ... he has made it clear that if I want to resign I can ...'*

The only consolation was that she had a new boyfriend, Roger, with whom she was due to go out later that week, and who she thought was 'just great'. Was the Michel she mentions above her Resistance colleague Michel Alliot or someone else? She doesn't say, but there is no mention of a Michel in any other context so I have assumed so.

On 16 July, Andrée left Paris early to travel to Bordeaux, where she was to meet Guy Mangenot to collect some reports for onward delivery to Marseilles. Unusually for her, she was carrying no documents from Paris. The train was held up just before Poitiers due to sabotage on some of the tracks around the city, and passengers had to spend several hours walking to the next point from where they could resume their journey. In the end, they arrived too late in Angoulême to continue, so Andrée found a hotel for the night and returned to the station the following morning, to continue her journey.

She knew there was a problem almost as soon as she stepped off the train at Bordeaux. A Wehrmacht officer and two soldiers were carefully scanning the passengers as they made their way into the station's terminal. Something felt wrong. As she walked towards them as coolly as possible, the officer approached her and addressed her by name, asking for her papers. Showing her surprise at having been singled out, she did her best to stay calm and handed over her ID card. The officer looked at it carefully, then informed Andrée that he had been awaiting her arrival and that she was to follow him to the stationmaster's office.

Andrée remained seemingly composed, well aware how important it was for her to appear guiltless. But inwardly she was in turmoil. She had no idea why she had been stopped or why the officer knew her name. Nothing had been done differently on this particular trip, yet they knew she was coming. Someone must have said something.

Once in the small office she looked around the room, conscious that she had little time in which to assess the situation and therefore deal with what might lie ahead. Distrustfulness was not a typical trait for her, but this was no time to be naive. She thought about Guy Mangenot, and whether he or any of his agents had been picked up. In accordance with Alain's strict rules, she knew nothing about Guy's own operation, but it was clearly important or else she wouldn't have been sent to Bordeaux so frequently to meet his agents. She considered the possibility that she could have been followed to Orion, and if so whether Madame Labbé and her family and friends could be at risk. It was impossible to know anything for certain at that point.

Andrée's suitcase sat open on the table in front of her as the officer searched through its contents carefully, examining each item meticulously. At least he would not find anything; that was a relief. As his search came to an unfruitful end, his irritation began to show. He looked up at last and asked her what she was doing in Bordeaux.

Andrée was used to dealing regularly with officers of the Wehrmacht and was therefore not discomposed by his questioning. She responded calmly to his questions, which unsettled him further. He told her sharply that she was to be moved to the police station for further questioning. With a display of sangfroid that belied her years, Andrée demanded to know on whose authority she was being detained. He ignored her, and instead she was escorted out of the station and into a waiting car.

By this point Andrée was feeling rattled but tried to hold on to her belief that the officer had no evidence to suspect her of anything. This was probably just a fishing expedition; if he knew something about her, wouldn't he have tackled her with it already?

She was led into Bordeaux police station by two soldiers, and followed by the captain. Standing before the duty sergeant, she was informed that she was being charged with the crime of working as an agent for the Allied intelligence services. It was a brutal shock, but she was determined not to reveal anything. She was taken into a formal interview room, and told to sit down in front of a table in the middle of the room. A young woman in the corner looked ready to take notes.

As the questioning began, Andrée tried to stay calm and respond as briefly as possible, to avoid giving anything away inadvertently. Clearly, the captain was annoyed that she was not carrying the compromising material he had expected to find on her. But where had his intelligence come from? She needed to find out who or what had led to her being identified as a suspect, and how much of what she was doing was known to them.

She answered the questions politely and slowly, working hard to appear both surprised and a little naive. She explained that she was travelling through Bordeaux to Orthez, to visit her aunt who was not well, and that she had been given permission to do so by her employers at Police Headquarters in Paris. She addressed the officer as 'Captain'* throughout, careful to emphasise his rank. He was not diverted, however, and asked her why in that case did she stop off in Bordeaux and take the bus into town? Andrée was horrified. Someone had observed her going into the centre of Bordeaux? How could she explain that?

She smiled at the officer, doing her best to work her charm on him. She told him that she had not told her employer the exact truth; that she travelled regularly to Orthez because she loved the Basque countryside and wanted to enjoy it. She had told a fib about an ill aunt, so that her manager would feel sorry for her and give her permission to travel. Sometimes she had to wait at Bordeaux for a connecting train and so, to kill time, she went into town.

The captain watched her broodingly. He did not appear to be won over. Abruptly, he changed tack. He warned her that if she did not comply with him and answer his questions truthfully, he would have no choice but to bring in the Gestapo. Andrée fought to hide her fear, protesting that she was not hiding anything. She had now been detained for almost three hours. The captain stood and told her she would be placed in a cell to reconsider her story.

Alone in her tiny cell, Andrée focused on remaining positive. She knew that she could not afford to give her interlocutor any room for doubt; she had to convince him that they had the wrong person. She would not allow herself to even think about the possibility that they might round up the rest of the team. If all else failed, she still had her cyanide pill, safely stitched into her bra. But she was not ready to accept defeat just yet.

The hours went by slowly. She had nothing to do; they had not given back her handbag or her book. She knew she was being watched at regular intervals through the hole in the cell door. She could hear crying coming from somewhere, and the smell of sewage was strong. She focused on what she was going to say next; her colleagues' lives might depend on it.

---

* 'Captain' was the rank Andrée used when telling me the story – I assume she identified his rank from his uniform.

Eventually, the cell door was unlocked, and she was led out. The captain was waiting for her. The Gestapo had arrived to question her, he said. Andrée's ability to block out the negative was a huge strength; she would not allow herself to imagine what terrors might await her. She was taken to a different room and left there to await the SS officer. Mentally and physically, she braced herself for the encounter.

She was expecting a tall, physically intimidating officer and was somewhat surprised to be faced with a tired-looking, overweight man well into his late thirties. It was, she felt, to her advantage. Again, her questioner did not expect her to maintain her composure in the light of forceful and direct interrogation. She remained composed, answering only when she had something to say and otherwise remaining silent. After a while he stopped and looked at her. She seized the moment.

Imitating her mother's authoritative manner, she stood up and looked at him directly. She informed him that if he had been professional in his questioning of her, he would have contacted one of the Wehrmacht officers at Police Headquarters in Paris to confirm her respect of the Wehrmacht, her total lack of interest in politics and her non-involvement in any Resistance activities. The officer was noticeably taken aback, and she felt confident she had the upper hand. She suggested he contact Captain Rohrbach to corroborate her claims.

There was a somewhat startled silence, then the captain stood up and indicated that the interview was over. She was taken back to her cell to wait, desperately hoping that they would follow her suggestion.

Years later, Andrée told me what she thought had happened next.

*It took several hours but they finally got a call placed through to Paris and Rohrbach told them there was absolutely no way he could possibly imagine I was involved in the French Resistance, little did he know. He told them I had worked solidly at Police Headquarters for four years and that I had always gone out of my way to help them out with any administrative or language difficulty they had. I was never unpleasant to any of them. They always treated all of us politely and with respect. There was never any animosity among us. Rohrbach was always chasing me. I flirted with him and he often bought me chocolates. Your grandmother would have been furious had she known where the Marquise de Sevigné chocolates I gave her came from. He helped me sell the presents I had been given by my clients. It was all very innocent. He was not a Nazi. I never knew what happened to him after the war, but he saved my life.*

Eventually, Andrée was returned to the interview room, where the Wehrmacht captain informed her she was free to resume her journey. He gave no explanation for their change of heart. Inwardly, she was jubilant, but conscious that she was still no wiser as to who had informed against her. Without a name, Orion would remain vulnerable. It was worth a try, at least.

As she walked with the captain to the duty sergeant's desk to retrieve her possessions, she asked him for the name of the person who had caused so much trouble, explaining that she intended to report him or her to her superior at Police Headquarters. To her surprise, the captain told her the name of the informant.* His name meant nothing to Andrée, but at least they would now have something to go on.

It always remained a mystery to Andrée's Orion colleagues that the SS officer did not pursue his questioning further, and did not torture his prisoner. For her part, Andrée suspected that this particular officer had other pressing matters to deal with and decided to leave the case to the Wehrmacht officer who had originally brought her in. By this point, in July 1944, France was in upheaval five weeks after the Normandy landings. There was fierce fighting throughout the country and the liberation of Paris was only a few weeks away. In that sense, she could not have chosen a better time to be arrested.

Andrée wrote nothing of her arrest in her journal but she did mention meeting François de Rochefort in Paris at 18.15 the following day, making

---

* Andrée didn't recognise the name the captain gave her, and she never wrote it down anywhere, but she told me years later that she passed it on to Alain and the others as soon as she got back to Paris. When I asked what happened to the informant, she told me that her Orion colleagues had arranged for someone to 'slit his throat'. I can't find any corroborating evidence for this, however.

it unlikely that she went on to Marseilles as planned. The details of what happened are recorded in her Croix de guerre citation, as well as extensive conversations with me and some of her English friends. Yet it is not mentioned in Alain Gandy's history of the Orion Group, *La jeunesse et la Résistance*. Why? She was always modest about her own achievements, but surely this would have been worth talking about when she was interviewed – certainly other colleagues went to great length to describe their exploits. Over lunch, in April 2010, I talked to François Clerc about the omission. He responded by urging me to understand the very different position of women in French society at that time: 'Andrée simply accepted and agreed unquestioningly to do anything and everything Alain or any of the team asked of her... She would not have wanted or expected any acknowledgement because she knew she was only a woman and therefore would not have thought she had achieved anything or deserved any recognition.' In his own memoir, her brother described how he thought Andrée was more frightened of what he might say to her if she failed in something he had asked her to do than of being caught or interrogated by the Wehrmacht.

## 25

# The Cat with Nine Lives

Neither Andrée nor the rest of the Orion Group had the time to stop and reflect on her narrow escape, still less to scale back their work. She had been very lucky; their friend and fellow member, Martial de la Fournière, had not been so fortunate. He was being held in Fresnes prison awaiting deportation to Germany. Alain and François de Rochefort, meanwhile, were determined to find a way to rescue him before it was too late.

Martial had been arrested at dawn on 2 June. Three members of the Gestapo had driven to his flat on the rue d'Amsterdam near the Gare St Lazare, parked their car on the street and rushing through the main gate of his apartment block made their way up the stairs and smashed down the front door to his flat. At gunpoint and without giving any reason for their actions, they forced him into the waiting car. He was taken to SS headquarters for questioning.

For Alain, the news of Martial's arrest was serious – not only because he feared for his friend but also because he and Martial worked closely together. As Alain later wrote: 'He knew everything about me. I put the whole group on alert, expecting some of us to be arrested.'[15] Martial was loyal, but to assume he could resist Gestapo torture would be naive. It was therefore quite likely that other members of the group could be tracked down and questioned.

Over the next few days they waited anxiously, but the feared action never came. It was to Martial's extraordinary credit that, despite being tortured, he did not give up any information about Orion. Meanwhile, the group was doing its best to find out on what basis he had been arrested. Eventually they learnt that back in 1941 Martial had helped a Jew remain in Paris by helping him alter his ID card to conceal his ethnic origin.

In June 1944, the Germans arrested the man he had helped and under questioning he had given up Martial's name. Assuming that this might indicate subsequent involvement in the Resistance, the Gestapo had gone looking for Martial.[16]

After being interrogated, Martial had been taken to Fresnes prison, where he was kept for a month. Then news got through that Martial was to be deported to Buchenwald,* on what would prove to be one of the last deportation trains to leave the capital.

Martial was one of Alain's closest friends. Alain and Biaggi had met him and become friends while in Vichy in 1941, and he often joined the Griotterays for lunch or dinner in Paris during the war years. Classically handsome, Yvonne and her daughters swooned over him, and the prospect of him dying in a concentration camp was unthinkable.

On a hot summer evening, François sat in the drawing room of his flat in the rue de Bourgogne, waiting for Alain. The windows were wide open, but there was little relief from the heat. Living in Paris was becoming ever more dangerous for young men in their early twenties. The Germans assumed that every youth on the streets of Paris was involved in some form of underground activity and would search and arrest them under the slightest pretext.

François heard someone coming up the stairs. He recognised Alain's light, determined step and the pre-arranged coded knock on the door. Safely inside the flat, the men embraced. It had been a long time since they last met and François was eager to hear Alain's news. But the main purpose of their conversation had only one aim; how they were going to save Martial. François had been busy with his own contacts, and he thought he might have access to a general who might prove amenable to helping them – for a decent price. Alain confirmed that they could use the OSS money. First,

---

* In late July 1944 it was becoming clear that the Nazis were losing the war; with the American forces almost in Paris, the Gestapo decided that all remaining political prisoners in Parisian gaols would be deported to concentration camps in Germany to prevent them falling into Allied hands. The prisoners at Buchenwald were not liberated until 11 April 1945 by the US Third Army division.

however, they needed to know exactly when Martial was due to be deported. Here, Alain suggested, Andrée might be able to help them.

Throughout July 1944, Parisians were living in anticipation of an Allied victory. The success of the Allied forces in making their way through occupied France had given the French a new-found confidence and as they awaited their arrival, eagerly yet nervously, new Resistance groups began to emerge all over the country. Paris, a city downtrodden by German occupation for four long years, was awakening from a nightmare.

Andrée was feeling optimistic as she walked to work. She had got up early to attend mass at Notre Dame before going into work. She wanted to thank God for helping her to talk her way to freedom and pray for the Allied victory and the Liberation of Paris. The cathedral was buzzing with nervous excitement and as she emerged into the July sun, she sensed that something interesting might be about to happen.

At work she made her way up the wide staircase to her office, opened the windows and looked down on to the river, at the barges negotiating the fast-flowing Seine. As she later wrote that night: *'It won't be long now before I will be able to stop working in this dreadful place.'*

It was mid morning when the phone rang. She picked up the receiver and was surprised to hear François de Rochefort at the end of the line. After exchanging pleasantries, François asked if he could have back the novel she had borrowed from him and suggested that they meet at lunchtime in the restaurant adjoining the Châtelet. Andrée agreed at once, knowing it was serious. Never would any of her Resistance colleagues normally arrange to meet her so openly in the middle of the day in a public place.

She found it difficult to concentrate after the call, wondering about what François might want and whether she would be off on another trip soon. Then the phone rang again, bringing her back to reality. This time it was Rohrbach with yet another dinner invitation; her courteous prior refusals had not dampened his enthusiasm. Andrée was reluctant, but felt that she ought to agree, given his helpful intervention in Bordeaux. Arranging to meet a couple of days later, she decided they would go to the Quartier Latin, where hopefully no one would notice she was having dinner with a German. His French was excellent, which certainly helped.

The rest of the morning went by slowly, but eventually it was close to noon. She left the building, emerging into the midday sun, and crossed the bridge leading towards the Châtelet, Paris's leading musical theatre.

François had chosen the restaurant carefully. Despite the war, he was still a wealthy man and a frequent visitor to the best restaurants in Paris, where more often than not he knew the head waiter and could be sure of getting a good table. As always, he was exquisitely dressed in an immaculate suit, though he had lost weight over the last four years. Andrée wondered where his soft black leather shoes came from.

Within minutes of her arrival, a thick piece of Charolais rump steak with some frites and mayonnaise appeared on the table. In her head she tried to work out how many food coupons and how much money would have gone into this meal, but it didn't stop her from enjoying her lunch.

As they ate, François said casually and quietly that he had invited her to lunch to discuss Martial. Andrée was, of course, aware of Martial's detention at Fresnes and of his imminent deportation to Buchenwald. She and Yvonne had talked of little else since hearing the news. But she had no idea why François would want to talk to her about the situation, still less in public. She tried not to let her concern for Martial show in her voice or countenance; clearly François did not want to draw attention to their conversation.

François continued to talk lightly, as though discussing the weather. 'We have a plan which may help to stop Martial from being deported. There is a German general who may be able to help us, but it is vital that no one else knows about this. I need to give him some of the gold coins you have in return for his help.'

'How on earth did you come up with that plan? Does anyone else know?' asked Andrée with surprise.

'No. As always, the fewer who know about our plans the better.'

'I can get you the money, of course. But surely you didn't need to invite me here just to say that?'

'No, I also need your help. Firstly, when I have the meeting to discuss the terms I will need an interpreter on hand in case the German prefers not to speak French. Alain tells me you speak German?'

'Yes, and no. I used to be quite good, but have not spoken German since I left for England in 1936.'

'But would you still understand enough to act as an interpreter?'

'I think so. I have heard German spoken around me solidly at Police Headquarters for the last four years and always understand what is going on.'

'Perfect, then would you agree to join us for lunch?'

'Of course, if you think I can help.'

'Thank you. You will be an asset; I am sure the general will enjoy dining with you.'

'What else can I do to help?'

'My second request is a little more complicated,' François explained. 'We know Martial is being held at Fresnes. If we can agree a price with the general, he will need to know when Martial will be moved from Fresnes to the Gare de Pantin. He is not prepared to make any enquiries himself. We therefore need to find someone else who can tell us in advance when Martial will be moved.'

'I understand – but what can I do? I work in the Passport Department.'

François was confident that there were some German officers who could be bribed. He was sure she could find someone at Police Headquarters who would help.

Andrée was taken aback by his request. She told François that, firstly, it was far too dangerous to even attempt such a thing and, secondly, even if she was prepared to do it, she had no idea who to approach.

François had ordered for both of them and a large pear was now placed in front of each diner. Andrée could hardly believe her eyes. She had not seen a pear for months. Finding fresh fruit was almost impossible.

They ate in silence. Andrée knew that without a plan, Martial would likely die at Buchenwald. But could she do what they asked? Before she left, François urged her to think carefully about it. They had money; they could afford to pay handsomely for the right person. Andrée smiled at her friend; she would do her best.

Later that week, Andrée was preparing to have dinner with Rohrbach. She had brought the outfit she planned to wear that evening with her to work. She had only recently finished making it and to do so had used some material she had bought in exchange for two old suits. She slipped on the black cotton dress and looked down at the large white collar she had had such difficulty sewing on. The dress had a wide belt which accentuated her waistline and several large white buttons down the front. She looked at herself critically in the mirror, smiled and walked out of the building on to the Cour de Notre Dame, where she had arranged to meet Rohrbach.

He was waiting for her, and they greeted each other with a formal handshake. Had their countries not been at war, a close friendship might have developed between them, but both understood it was not that straightforward.

Andrée liked her colleague, but she also knew he could be useful. Although a Wehrmacht officer, Andrée believed that he was not a Nazi. Despite many exchanges at work, this was the first time they had met outside the confines of Police Headquarters. They walked to the Quartier Latin to take advantage of the lovely summer evening, stopping at a café along the way to enjoy the sun and drink an aperitif.

Rohrbach could tell that something was worrying Andrée. She was not her usual smiling self, despite her best efforts to appear so. He asked her whether anything was wrong. He did not point out that, with the imminent arrival of the Americans, she ought to be feeling positive, but he may well have thought it. She began to cry and he tried to comfort her, asking if he could help her in any way. Drying her eyes, Andrée told him about her close friend, Martial de la Fournière, due to be deported from Fresnes to Buchenwald. She explained that Martial had been arrested on the grounds that back in 1940 he had helped a Jewish friend escape from Paris. This had never been proved, but his name had remained on the Gestapo files. As the Allies approached Paris, many people were being arrested, often with little grounds for suspicion. Beseechingly, she asked him whether there was any way that he could find out the planned day and time of her friend's departure for Germany.

Rohrbach was forever trying to create a closer friendship with Andrée.

He listened intently and, after hearing the whole story, said he would do his best to help her. In fact, he promised her, he would personally attend to it the next morning. Andrée could not believe that it could be so simple. She composed herself, smiled warmly and thanked him for his help. She tried very hard not to show her enormous relief at the help he was prepared to offer without pressing her more on the subject of why she wanted to know so badly – and without the question of money being mentioned.

They ate dinner at a restaurant on the rue Montalembert, followed by liqueurs and coffee. Andrée made sure to keep the conversation light and friendly, as they talked about their families and where they had been brought up. Rohrbach walked Andrée to the *métro*, told her how much he had enjoyed the evening and said *au revoir*.

True to his word, a couple of days later, when Andrée was sitting in Rohrbach's office waiting for one of his colleagues to sign her batch of passports, he gave her a piece of paper with the date and time that Martial and other prisoners held in Fresnes were to be moved to the Gare de Pantin (a small station on the outskirts of eastern Paris, not generally used by passengers – prisoners bound for deportation were assembled here).

The Claridge Hotel* was a few minutes' walk from the Champs-Élysées. François and Andrée were to meet the General in the main dining room of the hotel. Andrée had worked through the weekend and was looking forward to some time away from the endless preparation of passports. She was also looking forward to a good lunch. As Andrée lay in bed thinking about the day ahead, she wondered what to wear. She wanted to look attractive, elegant and professional. Looking good would make her feel confident

---

* Andrée told me about the lunch they had together with a general to discuss Martial's release. She didn't name the hotel but I have assumed here that it was The Claridge – a small, discreet hotel in the smart part of town. In February 1943, Andrée was invited to the hotel for a sumptuous meal with the hotel manager's secretary. She didn't know the hotel management personally, and there was no obvious reason for such an invitation (she doesn't say why in her diary), so she may well have had some Resistance-related connection to the establishment.

and it was confidence that she needed most. The lack of coupons or money with which to buy clothes over the last four years had made it difficult for a young twenty-three-year-old to dress well, but Andrée had been clever in making the best of what she had and she was lucky enough to have a generous older sister. Renée had given her a navy-blue Lanvin dress a few years ago; that would hopefully do the job.

The dress was made of fine, almost silk-like, navy-blue cotton. Large pearl-coloured buttons were sewn down the front, and the material was gathered at the waistline. She also had a hat from Lemonier, one of Paris's most famous hat designers, which she had won in a raffle in aid of prisoners of war at the races at Le Tremblay.* To complete her outfit, she had her shoes from Bordeaux and the brown crocodile handbag she had been given for her twenty-first birthday. All in all, considering what lay ahead, she looked remarkably poised and calm as she ate her breakfast.

Yvonne, who suffered from asthma and was not feeling well that day, sensed that something important was happening. Andrée had not told her parents anything about the plan, to avoid any risk to them, but her mother suspected that it was to do with Martial. She watched her daughter nervously as she dipped bread into her coffee. Edmond, who had returned unexpectedly the previous evening from Rochefort, was restless. He had wanted to listen to a BBC broadcast, but as soon as Yvonne realised that he was setting up the radio, she told him furiously to put it straight back in the cellar. If the flat was ever searched and a radio was found, there would be serious repercussions for the whole family.

Andrée looked at herself in the mirror, adjusted her belt and felt confident that the result was what she had hoped for. Edmond looked up from his paper and complimented his daughter. Yvonne sensed danger, but hugged her daughter goodbye and didn't ask questions.

---

* Although horse racing in France was widely interrupted during the war, some races still took place. Normally held at Longchamps, the prestigious Prix de l'Arc de Triomphe was moved to Le Tremblay – a small racecourse on the outskirts of Paris – in 1943 and 1944. Photographs from the period show attendees enjoying a rare day out in elegant attire. The course at Le Tremblay no longer exists today.

Andrée walked purposefully into The Claridge and made her way to the large salon. The General* had been asked to stand by the mantelpiece and wait for a young lady to approach him. The Claridge was unusually quiet. Andrée saw the tall, stiff military-looking man and felt sure he was her target. She walked towards him and greeted him confidently. Despite wearing civilian clothes, he looked so German. The cloth may have been British, but the suit had not been made in Savile Row.

Andrée suggested they move into the restaurant and as she led the way, the General asked where she had learnt her German. François was already at the table. He stood up to greet his guests and as they sat down they took stock of each other discreetly. The dining room was small, with only a few tables, spaced to give guests some privacy. The tables had been formally laid with thick white linen tablecloths. The head waiter did his best not to show any surprise at the young French pair having lunch with a German who appeared to be in his late forties.

François offered the General a drink and they settled on a bottle of Bordeaux. He was pleased to see that his guest appeared to know his wine. The hotel was noted across Paris for its foie gras, and so it was agreed they should start with that. François told the General that the béarnaise sauce was also outstanding and suggested Charolais to follow. As they discussed the menu, Andrée forgot to be nervous; she was too busy contemplating the amazing meal they were about to have.

After ordering, François came straight to the point. He spoke quietly but clearly in French, which Andrée translated. After assuring the General that they were in a trusted environment where no one could overhear them, François explained that a friend, Martial de la Fournière, was to be taken to the Gare de Pantin within the next few days and put on a deportation

---

* Much about the General remains unknown, including his name. As Alain said in his memoir, 'No one has ever been able to explain this extraordinary story. Martial is dead, Rochefort is dead, and my sister remembers nothing about anything.' He first described it in another book as 'a miraculous escape organised by François de Rochefort and Andrée'. [*Qui étaient les premiers résistants?*, page 247.]

train for Buchenwald. They were prepared to offer the General a substantial amount of money in return for his help in securing Martial's escape.

The General was prepared for the proposal. He named his figure, to which François agreed, and he said simply that he understood the request and knew how he would implement it. Andrée opened her handbag discreetly and passed to the General a piece of paper with the date and time that Martial and the other prisoners were to be moved. They agreed to meet at The Claridge Hotel on the day the train was due to leave, from where they would drive together to the Gare de Pantin.

François stated rather delicately that the General would only be paid once Martial had been freed. The General agreed. As the foie gras arrived and they began to eat, Andrée and François exchanged glances; both knew they had no option but to trust their dining companion.

The day arrived. Their pre-arranged plans began smoothly; the General picked up François from outside The Claridge. That morning Andrée went into her father's study and took the key to the cellar from his desk. In the cellar she carefully moved aside the wine bottles and took out some of the gold coins. Back upstairs she packed a bag with some of Alain's old clothes for Martial. Then she left for François's flat on the rue de Bourgogne; once they had Martial, they would take him there to rest for a few hours before moving him to a safer location.

With a soldier at the wheel, François and the General drove to the station. They arrived on the platform as the prisoners were herded onto the carriages. Soldiers were shouting at the prisoners to move faster and François was alarmed at the chaotic scene; how would they even find Martial in the midst of all this, let alone extract him? But the General seemed to know exactly where to stop the car. Telling François to remain seated and on no account to draw attention to himself, he stopped a German army captain and demanded that prisoner de la Fournière be brought to him immediately.

The captain was taken aback. He protested that he had not received any orders instructing him to hand over any of the prisoners. The General shouted at him to obey the order immediately or face the consequences:

'I want that prisoner handed over to me. We have not finished with that one yet.'[17]

The captain did not dare to argue further with a general of the Wehrmacht, and called for Martial de la Fournière to be found and brought forward.

Unshaven, hungry and weak, Martial did not understand what was happening when he was pulled out of line and marched away from the train. He assumed he was about to be killed as he ended up in front of the General, who promptly told him to get into the back of the car. He was so disoriented that when he saw François in the car he simply did not react at all.

The General instructed the driver to continue to the rue de Bourgogne. As they drove off, he muttered to François that he had taken a great risk and that the rest of their plan had better go smoothly. François assured him that they would meet Andrée with the money as promised.

Andrée was waiting anxiously inside the entrance to François's flat. She was worried the concierge might take an interest in what was going on, despite François's assurances that, although he might be curious, he was trustworthy and discreet. She listened for the car's arrival, hoping desperately that the general had not betrayed them. François was confident that money was the motivating factor at play and had told Andrée he expected no trouble, but she still feared a trap of some kind. As the car drew up, she took a deep breath and stepped out onto the street. The General and François got out of the car. Andrée handed over the gold coins, which she had placed in a small black bag. The General picked a few out and looked at them in silence for a while. He then gave the bag to François, saying he needed no payment. François, utterly taken aback, quickly opened the car door and ushered the bewildered Martial out.

The General reminded François and Andrée of their agreement. No one was ever to mention his identity to anyone. 'I kept my part of the bargain. I hope you will always keep yours.'[18] They assured him that this would be the case and the General departed. François left immediately; it was too risky for them all to be seen together.

Still in shock, Martial followed Andrée into the flat. She led him into the bedroom and explained they had little time to waste. She ran a bath, told him to shave, wash and then put on Alain's clothes. They were to leave shortly for her parents' flat, where Martial could stay for a little while.

Within the hour, they left the flat. Martial was able to walk to the *métro* and in total silence the two friends made their way to the Griotterays' residence. As they walked through the front door, Yvonne came out into the hall; she had been waiting for her daughter to return. As she saw Martial, she gasped, before hushing herself from asking any questions. Instead, she took him into the kitchen, sat him down and prepared an omelette, assuring him that he would be safe with them and could stay as long as he wanted.*

It was an unlikely happy ending, but one that – as with many episodes in François de Rochefort's complicated life – raised questions that remain unanswered. How did he know the General? Why did this German officer decide to help a Frenchman at great personal risk – and why did he negotiate payment, then refuse it? None of Martial's colleague's ever knew exactly what had happened, as François refused to discuss it. Alain simply described it as 'a miraculous escape organised by de Rochefort and Andrée with the help of a German officer.[19] In 2004, Biaggi asked me if I could shed any light on exactly how François had managed to pull off this extraordinary escape. Andrée knew her part of the story but could offer no further explanation in later years; at the time she simply accepted it at face value, feeling it could only be dangerous to think too much about it. Besides, there was no time to waste.

---

* Martial de la Fournière was like the proverbial cat with nine lives. After his escape from the deportation train to Buchenwald, he was the only person to emerge alive from a burning apartment block in Hanoi in 1956. In yet another extraordinary event, he survived a helicopter crash in Vietnam in 1957, where all the other passengers were killed. He became a member of the Orion Resistance Group at the age of twenty-three after he and Alain Griotteray met in Vichy in 1941, and throughout the war he supplied the group with intelligence from the heart of the Vichy government. At the end of the war he received no award or recognition for his wartime services from the French Government. He did not want any. Eventually, twenty years after the end of the Second World War, Pierre Messmer (Prime Minister from July 1972 to May 1974) arranged for him to be awarded the Légion d'honneur for services rendered to his country.

## 26

# *Liberation!*

On 10 August 1944, many of the railway workers in and around Paris went on strike, followed by many utility workers. When Yvonne returned home on 13 August from a trip to Rochefort in the countryside near Paris, it was to a city with virtually no electricity, fuel or gas, let alone food.

Andrée arrived at work on the morning of 15 August to find the building occupied by the Forces françaises de l'intérieur. To reach her office, she had to walk past a group of Resistance fighters shooting – and being shot at – from the streets. As she tried to take stock of what was happening so that she could report back to Orion she was relieved, although unimpressed, to learn that the Parisian police force – which had openly collaborated with the German occupying forces and the Vichy government for the last four years – had finally decided to change sides and support de Gaulle and the Resistance.*

From mid August, open fighting broke out on the streets of Paris. Alain and his male colleagues were keen to be a part of the action. Andrée, meanwhile, remained focused on her role as the group's Chef de Liaison, coordinating activities and attempting to continue normal life as far as possible. Despite the events unfolding around her, she recorded in her journal going to an Edith Piaf concert on 18 August with her boyfriend Roger at the Moulin Rouge.

On 20, 21 and 22 August 1944, Andrée noted that firecrackers ('péta-rade') were being set off in the streets. Despite the gunfire and the grenades

* When I visited the archives of the Préfecture de Police, I was shown documents testifying that some policemen were part of the Resistance, but they were few and far between.

exploding on the streets around where she lived and worked, she still felt safe enough to cycle to work on 22 August from her flat near the Place de la Madeleine to the Place de la Concorde and along the Seine to Police Headquarters, where Matthew Cobb noted, in his book *Eleven Days*, that fighting had erupted in certain parts of the building (although Andrée doesn't mention this in her journal).

Together the US and French armies, which had fought together through northern France, moved into the outskirts of the city, as thousands lined the route to cheer them on. The German forces had been fighting hard to maintain control over Paris, and it was a dangerous time for civilians and soldiers alike. The FFI were armed with guns and grenades and wore armbands to identify themselves as such. They helped the American and French armed forces enter Paris, fighting on street corners in an attempt to take over the capital's strategic landmarks.

It was feared that the German military governor of Paris, General von Choltitz, was planning, on Hitler's instruction, to lay waste to Paris before his final surrender. 'Paris is not to fall into the hands of the enemy except in a heap of rubble,' the Führer's order of 23 August instructed. There has been much debate as to the part played by the Swedish Consul, Raoul Nordling, in persuading von Choltitz not to follow Hitler's orders, but certainly Nordling's attempt to arrange a peaceful surrender was unsuccessful. As the American and French forces entered the city centre, there was heavy gunfire and shooting around central landmarks including the Invalides, the École Militaire, the Arc de Triomphe, the Jardin du Luxembourg, the rue de Rivoli, the Hôtel de Ville, and the Naval Ministry.

By this point Andrée was no longer writing her journal; instead she kept a simple diary, which noted simply meeting times, places and the odd word to represent what she was doing.

On the afternoon of 25 August 1944, General Billotte of the Deuxieme Division Blindée (the Free French 2nd Armoured Division) took over the Hôtel Meurice, headquarters of General von Choltitz. His troops arrested von Choltitz and took him to Police Headquarters, where he signed the act of surrender. The document described General Leclerc as the Commander of the French forces in Paris and Leclerc signed it in the name of de Gaulle's

French provisional government. As Cobb put it, 'This was a Free French triumph'. There was no mention of the role of Resistance fighters in the document, nor would de Gaulle acknowledge their existence in the historic speech he gave later that day. De Gaulle had been fighting with the Allies (and the Americans in particular) over who governed France, and he was determined to resume what he saw as his rightful position, regardless of national politics or the Allies' views.

The Free French were worried that Roosevelt wanted to install an army of occupation in France until an election had been called, but de Gaulle had other plans. He wanted the world to recognise him as the only leader of the French Republic, and to acknowledge that the Republic had continued to exist in London under his leadership in the name of the Free French. Legally, therefore, Vichy had never represented the French government. It was an argument that resonated with many French citizens, not least the Griotterays, who refused throughout the war to acknowledge Pétain as head of state.

Despite the Germans' formal surrender, the fighting continued. Andrée described the Wehrmacht's departure as more frightening and dangerous than its arrival.* Yet the end was in sight.

The streets of Paris throbbed with excitement on 26 August 1944, as hundreds of thousands of people made their way into the city, lining the streets of the capital to celebrate its liberation after four years of Nazi occupation. On that day, General de Gaulle was the first among the Allied

---

* As did a friend of mine who lived on the rue Royale at the time, Jeanine Nouveau. Jeanine was about four years younger than Andrée and lived only five minutes away from the Griotterays' flat, though they never knew each other. Like Andrée, she watched cautiously as the events leading up to Paris's official liberation unfolded. She saw members of the FFI out on the streets carrying white flags while German soldiers took shots at them, and her family feared that Paris was about to be bombed. She said of de Gaulle's arrival in Paris: 'I watched General de Gaulle drive along the rue de Rivoli from the balcony of our flat. He was driving past a group of German prisoners when suddenly snipers started shooting at him. He did not budge an inch.'

generals to march down the Champs-Élysées, with General Leclerc, General Koenig and Georges Bidault (President of the Comité National de la Resistance) at his side. This was a pivotal moment, as both Churchill and de Gaulle were well aware; by walking down that iconic street before the US Army, de Gaulle was sending a clear signal to the world: 'to demonstrate and cement his importance and to show that French unity and power had been restored.'[20]

The crowds clapped, laughed, shouted and cried as they watched the parade at street level, from their balconies, windows and from rooftops. At the Place de la Concorde, de Gaulle stopped and got into a waiting car; people climbed up the statues and the lampposts to get a better view of their leader. Andrée and her friends had made their way into the square: they watched in amazement as snipers fired at the vehicle from the rooftops of the Hôtel de Crillon, yet de Gaulle showed no fear.

It was a heady time – watching the Wehrmacht leave the city was exciting. As Andrée later said, 'It was just so wonderful to see them leave with their musical instruments, with their bikes and on horseback'. But as her diary of the time recorded, it was also an extremely dangerous period. Paris was still effectively a warzone in the days during and after the liberation. After acknowledging the crowds at the Hôtel de Ville, de Gaulle went to Notre Dame for a thanksgiving service; halfway through, gunmen fired within the cathedral, bringing the service to an abrupt end.

There was much anger and resentment aimed not only at the Germans, who were still in Paris, but towards those who collaborated with them. Parisians wanted to settle their grievances. Biaggi later told me: 'It was those people who during the four years of occupation never did anything to help the Resistance who were the most vindictive.' Many were anxious to retrospectively join the winning side. As Andrée put it, 'There were so many people after the war who claimed to have been part of the Resistance, but most of them only joined up after the landings and they therefore ran far fewer risks than those of us who joined up in 1940.'

On 28 August, the US Army marched victoriously down the Champs-Élysées to the applause and cheers of the crowds. That day Yvette, Andrée's eighteen-year-old sister, met a US army officer whose name was

Wally Petterson. She brought him home to meet her parents, and they went on to form a close relationship. Indeed they nearly married but, after a trip to New York, Yvette decided the American way of life was not what she wanted and she returned to Paris.*

Shortly after the liberation, Alain managed to get yet another press card and became part of a group of youngsters who took over the offices of the newspaper *Paris Soir*, which had been under German control. One day he and François de Rochefort were out driving when they hit an obstacle. Crowds of Parisians surrounded two trucks in which forty German soldiers were holding several Frenchwomen hostage at gunpoint. Alain and François pushed their way to the front, accosting the soldiers and insisting that they release the women immediately. The soldiers refused, saying they were about to be killed by the crowds and the hostages represented their only hope of freedom. Alain found himself negotiating a deal with members of a defeated army in order to save the hostages, and had to agree to give the Germans a safe passage to the north of the capital. The hostages were released safely, but Alain wrestled with the moral dilemma of allowing forty soldiers to go free in order to save several civilians.

On 29 August, Andrée celebrated her twenty-fourth birthday at the Hôtel Scribe. Two days later, on 31 August, disaster struck. Margit Ehrart, one of her closest friends and trusted couriers, was arrested by the French police. Andrée referred briefly to the arrest in her diary but gave no details. That day she went to the Commissariat de Police on the rue Cambaures to see Margit, after which she went to do some shopping on her behalf. The following day she returned to the Commissariat. Her diaries say nothing more about her friend for two weeks, then, on 16 September, she records Margit's release from Drancy, one of Paris's largest holding prisons.

Margit's arrest is difficult to understand, and there are no official records to clarify it. Under what is presumably her married name of Hutton, she

---

* In 1952, Wally rekindled his friendship with Andrée and her husband Frank when he returned to London as a leading cast member in the musical *Oklahoma!*

is registered in the Ministry of Defence files at Vincennes as having been a P2 agent, which means she was regarded as a full-time agent for Orion from 1941.

Her 'proper' job, meanwhile, was at the German administrative headquarters in Paris (the 'Kommandantur'). As such she may well have had good access to information of use to Orion. She was half-Austrian and spoke perfect German, and – according to Andrée – she dated German soldiers more often than she should have done.

After the liberation of Paris, the backlash against women who had (or were perceived to have had) relationships with Germans was vicious and cruel. It is possible that she could have been wrongly informed upon as a German collaborator or sympathiser, and thus arrested. Sadly she and Andrée lost touch some years after the war.

## 27

# *Life After Liberation*

'I simply cannot take it any more,' Andrée exclaimed as she walked into the family flat one day in summer 1945, slamming the door behind her. Her parents were in the drawing room discussing France's recently formed provisional government under Charles de Gaulle. Edmond, not surprised by his elder daughter's outburst, stood up and gave her a hug, asking whether she had just been out with Karl.

'Yes, and he has been crying on my shoulder for the last three hours. It is the same every time we meet. It is horrendous for him, and now he has been told he has to return next week as part of a US military team questioning those inhuman Nazis about what happened at Buchenwald. He tells me every tiny, horrific detail and I know it is very selfish of me but all I can think is that I could have been deported there and I can't bear it.'

Karl Weyner was Andrée's boyfriend at the time, and one of the first American GIs to enter Buchenwald. Her parents tried to calm her. 'Darling, we all need to do our part to support the Allies now. These men have fought so hard on our behalf and the Americans are so far from home.'

'I cannot sleep, I am having nightmares. I know it must be terribly hard for Karl, and his being Jewish must make it even worse. I want to help him but I don't know if I can cope much longer.'*

---

* Andrée and Karl's relationship was serious; he asked her to marry
him several times, and she considered doing so, but ultimately could not
countenance leaving Europe for America. Years later, in the 1970s, Andrée
visited New York and looked Karl up in the phone book. They went out for
dinner and she subsequently got to know his family, becoming close friends
with his sister in particular.

'There is a letter addressed to you in the hall,' Yvonne told her daughter, trying to diffuse the conversation.

Andrée picked up the engraved envelope, wondering why they would write to her. It was an invitation to a ball at the British Officers' Club. She showed her mother, smiling; her troubles temporarily eased. 'What a lovely invitation and such a perfect opportunity to meet some of the British officers now here in Paris.'

Life was slowly beginning to return to normal for the Griotteray family. Andrée had resigned from Police Headquarters in late 1944; the relief at no longer having to work for an organisation which had effectively collaborated for four long years with the Wehrmacht had been tremendous.* Instead she was now working for the Ford Motor Company, which, following the end of the war, had re-established its presence in France. The energetic, resourceful François Clerc had been appointed head of its operation.

In the days after Liberation, the streets of Paris had been full of Allied soldiers intent on enjoying themselves after their long, arduous journey over the Channel and the intense fighting on the Normandy beaches and through northern France. For Parisians, long-awaited celebrations had been enhanced by the availability of some good food – the Americans brought with them provisions which most of Paris had been denied for a long time. The Griotterays had welcomed Americans into their home warmly and sincerely as their liberators, but like anyone else they were not immune to the lure of the Americans' supplies.

Returning home early one evening, Andrée found another letter awaiting her, this time bearing the emblem of the French Republic. Edmond was waiting patiently in his study for his daughter to return home so that they could find out what was inside.

Andrée opened the letter slowly; her eyes immediately jumped to the end, where appeared the name General Charles de Gaulle. On the personal

---

* Every gendarme joining the Parisian police force is today given a one-day training session on the shameful involvement of the Parisian police force in the round-up of 13,000 Jews on 16 July 1942.

instruction of the leader of the provisional French government, she was to be awarded the Croix de guerre, a medal traditionally awarded for a single extraordinary act of bravery by the French government while the nation was at war.

She began to cry softly as the letter's contents sank in. Secretly she had dreamt of being given the Médaille de la Résistance, but this was an even more prestigious award, and one she never even considered. Ecstatic at the honour being bestowed on her, she called out to her parents to tell them the good news.

Giddy with excitement, Andrée hurried along the boulevard des Capucines to the British Officers' Club. It was a night that would eventually change her life. She was introduced to a tall, slim and smiling Englishman whose well-trimmed auburn moustache caught her eye. She and Flight Lieutenant White hit it off immediately. As their friendship developed, Andrée introduced Frank to all the fun Paris had to offer: French food, the nightlife and long walks around Europe's most stunning city.

One month after they met, Alain told his sister that she was to be awarded the Médaille de la Résistance for services rendered to France during the war. The official announcement was made on Saturday, 20 October 1945 in *Le Journal officiel de la République française*. Frank was intrigued by his new beau's war record and to help him understand more about what she had done, Andrée asked Madame Labbé to invite him to stay at Château d'Orion.

The following year, Frank was demobbed from the RAF and returned to London in June 1946. In December, Andrée was invited to spend Christmas at the Chantry, near Slapton Sands in Devon, to meet Frank's family.

Frank was waiting to meet her when she arrived at London's Victoria station, but her pleasure at seeing him gave way to shock and sadness as they left the station. Andrée stared at the rubble and the bombed-out buildings around her, the destruction of a city she loved so much. Trying desperately to find a landmark she recognised, she began to tell Frank tearfully what she remembered of Victoria and the surrounding area when she had last been in England, in the spring of 1939. In France they had heard of course about the air raids, the bombings and the long nights that Londoners had endured, but she never imagined it was so dreadful. By comparison, she felt, life under the occupation in Paris had been relatively safe. Many years later, she told her granddaughter Chantal: 'When I came to London after the war and I saw the destruction, I was shattered. There was no Southampton left. I had seen it when I left England by boat in 1939. London was destroyed in the most horrible way, and Coventry and so many English towns.'

Trying to reassure her, Frank took her case and they walked to the Goring Hotel, a small family-run establishment a few minutes from the station. The Goring had escaped any major destruction during the war and Frank had got to know the owners through his shipping company, Gander & White. As the first place Andrée stayed on her initial post-war trip to London, it was a hotel she remained fond of all her life.

Andrée returned to England several times before she married Frank in Paris on 29 July 1947. After their wedding the pair started their married life together in London, where they raised their family. Frank White died in 1966 and, with no prior experience, Andrée took over the running of his business, Gander & White Shipping Limited. Today Gander & White is one of the world's leading fine art shipping companies, with subsidiaries around the world. Ten years after Frank's death, she introduced her daughter and son to her German boyfriend – their relationship a symbol of how much times had changed (though Yvonne and Alain were never to know of his existence). Andrée, who has suffered from Alzheimer's for the last eighteen years, has now been living in England – a country she has always loved – for over sixty-five years

## 28

# *A Just Reward*

In October 1972, Minister of Defence Michel Debré (formerly Prime Minister of France, 1959–1962), awarded Andrée Griotteray White the Ruban Bleu, L'Ordre National du Mérite – the Order of Merit. The ceremony took place at the Ministry of Defence in Paris and all the living members of her family were there to witness it: her mother Yvonne, her two sisters Yvette and Claude, her brother Alain, her brother-in-law, her two nieces, her daughter and son and a group of British friends who had travelled especially from London to witness the event.

It was an occasion of pomp and ceremony, but equally of warmth. Andrée, aged fifty-two, stood between two soldiers in the formal drawing room of the Ministry of Defence as Debré pinned the medal to her navy-blue dress. Some years later, in recording the events of that day in his book *Qui étaient les premiers résistants?*, Alain said of his sister that, in his eyes, she had earned the Légion d'honneur many times over for her actions, completing numerous dangerous missions calmly and courageously. However, as François Clerc pointed out to Alain, Andrée had no need for medals to show off, she never expected any recognition for her actions.

> Her extreme kindness and her level-headed personality meant that wherever she went she was welcomed with open arms with no one ever suspecting her of anything. She was so natural and never worried about anything going on around her.[21]

# *Epilogue*

I first learnt of my mother's exploits in the French Resistance when I was six years old. I had watched my parents getting ready to go to the British Antique Dealers' Association ball and the following morning I was keen to know how the evening had gone.

'It was great fun, darling, but all my friends were examining Mummy's cleavage very closely,' he answered, with characteristic humour.

'What do you mean, Daddy?'

'Well, Mummy had a low-cut dress on and she was wearing her war medals and they were all having a good look at them.'

'Why was she wearing medals?'

'Because she won them bashing up the Germans during the war.'

From then on, throughout my childhood and teenage years and into adulthood, my mother talked to me about her adventures in the French Resistance during the Second World War. She described 'those dreadful people I had to work with at Police Headquarters' and how much she hated working there. She told me how she typed up and distributed the underground news sheet *La France*, how she smuggled the Orion group's intelligence reports out of Paris, about the double life she led working at police headquarters while also acting as Orion's Chef de Liaison, and she described the events of 11 November 1940 when she, Alain and their friends demonstrated against the occupation of France at the Étoile in the first major act of defiance by French citizens towards the Nazi occupation of their country.

She told me about her travels around France during the war years. She could have described herself as an agent, a spy or a courier, but the term she preferred was 'postman'. She spoke of having to stay the night in a brothel or on the geriatric ward of a hospital because she had missed a train connection and curfew was about to fall. She described day-to-day life in Paris, the food shortages, the difficulties of living under the occupation and her hatred of the German occupying forces. Whenever we went to Switzerland she recounted tales of her holiday in Evian in 1943 when she looked longingly across the lake to Geneva, ablaze with lights and freedom.

She told me about Alain's disappearance in 1943 when he escaped France for North Africa and about his imprisonment and starvation diet at the Miranda prison near Santander; about her numerous visits to the Château d'Orion and her fondness for Madame Labbé and the kindness of everyone at the château. Andrée told me about how her parents had hidden a Jewish girl in their Paris flat, a girl she described as 'very nice but very stupid' and how terrified her sister, Claude, was of the Germans soldiers on the streets of Paris. She always claimed that she herself was never scared, declaring instead: 'I always looked down on them with contempt.' When her grandson Alexander asked her if she had been frightened during her arrest, she was slightly more equivocal, telling him 'Yes and no – but if you showed you were frightened, that was the end.'

Most of her stories she told lightly, with humour, and she always focused on how she had outwitted the Germans. But beneath the humour there were glimpses of the darker side of her adventures. I never forgot the sadness with which she told me about a close friend who had been shot by the Germans after deciding to ignore curfew following a party. And she never wanted to speak about what happened to the Jews in France during the occupation; there was no lightness there. I once asked her about the Vel' D'Hiv round-up and she went into a kind of trance as she referred to the horror of family friends the Bigards, Bernsteins and Rubinsteins disappearing. She never spoke of her close friend Serge, who escaped into the Free Zone in 1942 and was never seen or heard of again; it was only when reading her journals that I learnt about him. She did, however, tell me about a Jewish girlfriend in the recorded interview she gave my then eleven-year-old daughter Chantal in 1996. She said her friend 'simply disappeared' one day and then she added strangely, 'but I did not know she was Jewish'. Perhaps this was because her disappearance was a part of the infamous pogrom, that part of history the French are so ashamed of and about which I knew so little until I started to research this book in 2009. Indeed I initially only discovered what my mother had done to help Jews in Paris during the war from one of her friends.

I knew that my mother had been given the Médaille de la Résistance and the Croix de guerre because the small ribbons testifying to these were always sewn onto her suit jackets, coats, dresses and blouses, as is the custom in Europe. The first time I was properly able to gloat with pride, however, was in 1972. Andrée was awarded the Ordre National du Mérite, le Ruban Bleu, by former Prime Minister Michel Debré; both my brother and I clearly remember the event and the party afterwards, which was held at the Ministry of Defence in Paris. We met several of her Resistance colleagues and, at a time before good food had made its way across the Channel, the elegance of the surroundings and the excellent dinner that followed still stands out.

In 1985, Alain organised a memorial service at the Château d'Orion, the group's headquarters during the war: a chance for old friends to reunite and to explain to the younger generation what the French Resistance had been all about. Over a thousand people came, including Orion Group members, Madame Labbé's family, several leading members of the French Resistance movement including Marie Madeleine Foucarde (head of the Resistance group Alliance), former Prime Minister Jacques Chaban-Delmas and Jacques Soustelle, who had been head of the French intelligence services in Algeria 1943/44. Several members of the French air force parachuted into the village during the day to commemorate Alain's 'blind' drop in April 1944 by the OSS. Andrée behaved with intense dignity as she fought to control her emotions.

It was the first of several events intended to help subsequent generations understand in more detail what Resistance groups like Orion had accomplished. Alain had been shocked to discover that my brother and I still did not feel we knew much about what he and Andrée had done during the war. Yet it was not always easy to understand. Each member had different memories and their stories did not always line up with each other – unsurprisingly, as they had all been working on the basis that it was safer not to know what the others were up to. In 1990, Alain talked to a friend of his, Alain Gandy, about the possibility of a book on the group's exploits. *La jeunesse et la Résistance: réseau Orion, 1940–1944* was published in France the following year.

Although at times I found Gandy's book difficult to follow – especially when he attempts to explain the politics of French North Africa (a contemporary report in *The Times* in November 1942 also acknowledged the difficulties they had reporting the events) – it was essential when it came to writing my own book. Gandy spent many hours interviewing the key Orion players, especially Andrée and Alain, and without his book, I could not have written mine.

On 22 September 1990, in Coole near Châlon-sur-Marne (today Châlons-en-Champagne), there was a thanksgiving service, which Alain organised with the abbé Le Meur. The event was intended to commemorate forty prisoners, including Biaggi, who had escaped from a train to Germany in 1944. It was at that dinner that I first met Yves de Kermoal, who has been such a help with my research.

Five years later, in May 1995 – more than fifty years after the end of the war – my mother Andrée was given the Légion d'honneur, described at the beginning of this book. By July 2000 she had begun her long descent into darkness and Alain invited me to take her place at a wreath-laying ceremony at the tomb of the unknown soldier under the Arc de Triomphe.

In 2001, we were invited – as Andrée's family – to a lunch given by Jacques Chirac at the Élysée Palace to celebrate Alain's appointment as a Grand Officier de la Légion d'honneur. Alain asked me whether I had told Andrée of the occasion and the honour shortly to be bestowed on him by the President of France. I hadn't; she might not have understood, but it would have been worse if she had. She should have been there to watch her brother: it was her right. My eighteen-year-old son Alexander was introduced to the President shortly before the meal, who asked him if he spoke French – to which Alexander rather impudently replied, 'Mais naturellement!' President Chirac promptly begged his pardon.

I smiled to myself. Andrée's English grandson's love of France had made its way into the Élysée Palace straight to the head of state in the same way as Andrée's love of England had reached out into British society when she was sixteen.

In 2004, as France celebrated her sixtieth anniversary after her liberation from Nazism, there was yet another commemoration service, this time in St Tropez, where a plaque was unveiled in the harbour to commemorate the landing of a group of Frenchmen in British battle-dress (Henri d'Astier de la Vigerie and Yves de Kermoal among them): the first Frenchmen to land at the port of St Tropez since the war began. My husband Martin and I later held a party at our home in Ramatuelle, which included members of the CIA and military representatives of the British and American embassies, as well as many of Andrée and Alain's friends and colleagues.

Alain died in 2008 and his funeral was held at la cathédrale Saint-Louis des Invalides, attended by numerous politicians as well as friends and family. We grieved as Alain's body was draped in the Tricolore and carried by thirteen soldiers. The Minister of the Interior, Michèle Alliot-Marie, took the salute and a military band played while more than fifty members of the armed forces saluted Alain's coffin.

Writing this book has been a long and emotional journey. It has taken me about four years – roughly the same period of time that Andrée, Alain and their friends endured in occupied France during the war. How to compare the last four years of my life in the twenty-first century to that of a group of youngsters living in an occupied country among Nazi soldiers, collaborators, double-crossers, traitors, informers and their own police force, in constant fear of being watched and betrayed, risking their lives on a daily basis?

During the course of my research and writing, I have learnt much about Vichy, Pétain and particularly the horrors suffered by the Jewish people in France. And although I have spoken to people who were heavily involved in the French Resistance, I have also been told several times not to judge history, not to criticise Pétain's decision to sign an armistice nor to form a government of collaboration because I was not there. It is neither my place, nor my intention, to judge political decisions taken over seventy years ago, but I note Max Hastings' observation in *All Hell Let Loose*: 'The plight of the Jewish people under the Nazi occupation loomed relatively small in the wartime perception of Churchill and Roosevelt. One seventh of all fatal victims of Nazism and almost one tenth of all wartime dead, ultimately proved to have been Jews. At the time their persecution was viewed by the Allies merely as a fragment of the collateral damage caused by Hitler.'

There have been other discoveries that have surprised me. I was always aware of Andrée's staunch, unrelenting admiration for General de Gaulle, whom she always considered to be one of France's greatest leaders. I remember the fierce arguments between my parents in 1963 when de Gaulle vetoed Britain's entry into the common market and the ensuing arguments during his presidency. I had not expected to find myself admiring him also – but through her eyes I have seen more of le Général, a man who gave hope to the French people during their darkest years and who fought fiercely against Allied proposals to impose foreign control over France following its liberation. A man who never accepted the legitimacy of the Vichy government and who eventually restored France's honour and status.

I was also surprised to learn from Andrée's diaries that she had gone out to dinner on two separate occasions with a German Wehrmacht officer from Police Headquarters. In conversations with me she had always been so insistent that she never fraternised with the enemy, but here was an indication that life is nuanced, not black and white. Perhaps under other circumstances she might have developed a relationship with one of them. And perhaps – had she not been friendly with him and other German colleagues at Police Headquarters – she might not have escaped her interrogators in Bordeaux all those years ago.

There are many questions that remain unanswered. As I wrote more though, I found myself returning to one particular question repeatedly. Why had it taken so long for Andrée to be given France's highest award, the Légion d'honneur?

There were not many people left to ask, sadly. During our conversation in 2010, François Clerc had stressed the gender differences back in the 1940s: how dominant men had been and how women were simply expected to fall in line with their male counterparts' instructions, and certainly not to demand recognition for their achievements.

In his book *Qui étaient les premiers résistants?*, Alain described his sister thus:

She is a pretty brunette and her views on life are simple. When it comes to discussing the political situation, she happily takes on my views. She always thought that it was completely normal to do whatever I asked of her because she knew that waging war was something the men had to deal with… She is French through and through and that means everything to her. You know exactly where you stand with her, she was always there, ready to help us, and what was an even greater asset to us was that she never initiated anything.

My initial reaction was anger in response to such an arrogant, chauvinistic and misguided attitude. But over time I have mellowed: I have known Alain and François all my life, and some of the other members of the Orion Group for many years. They are some of the bravest and most resourceful men of their generation – and their views on woman were of their time. Once the war ended, they had careers to build and they were determined to establish their achievements in the Resistance as an important foundation for future life. As Hastings has observed: 'The manner in which they had conducted themselves defined their standing in their societies for the rest of their lives.' Women like Andrée were not expected to behave similarly, and she herself was so modest about her own accomplishments that it never occurred to her to put herself forward in the same way.

Alain once wrote that Andrée had confessed to him that she was more scared of his disapproval than of the Nazis. It is typical of both her fearlessness in the face of great challenges and her enduring adoration of her brother. I decided to write this book as part of my efforts to raise money for research into Alzheimer's and to support those suffering from the disease. I have set up a fund in my mother's name: the Andrée Griotteray White Charitable Trust. I can only hope that, if Andrée knew about this book, she would approve of me using her remarkable life as a platform to raise awareness of a very cruel disease.

*Francelle Bradford White*
*London, May 2014*

The Andrée Griotteray White Charitable Trust (Registered Charity No. 1157258) has been established in Andrée's name to fund research into any form of Alzheimer's disease or dementia and to provide support to those suffering from it. All royalties and any net profit the author receives from sales of this book will go directly to the charity.

# Intelligence Gathering in France

Because Andrée Griotteray married an RAF officer in 1947, it has often been assumed in Britain that she was an SOE agent. This was not the case; le réseau Orion was a France-based resistance network which operated independently for much of the war. Afterwards, Orion was officially listed by the authorities as falling under the direction of the Bureau Central de Renseignement et d'Action (the intelligence section of the Free French Army), which was headed by Colonel Passy and General de Gaulle in London.

While there were, of course, similarities between the work of SOE and that of a network like Orion, there were also some significant differences – and it is for that reason that I have included this section comparing the two.

SOE agents received over six months' intensive training in the UK before being parachuted into or travelling by sea to France. Orion agents, by contrast, had no formal training; this was a non-professional network set up and managed by Frenchmen and women living in their own country, working in surroundings familiar to them. Despite the lack of professional training, Alain enforced strict rules about security – some essentially common sense, but others based on advice given to him in Marseilles in 1941 by the brother of his brother-in-law, Jean Morin, who had been a member of Sinn Féin. Despite its different methods, SOE felt similarly about security; Dr Hugh Dalton, Minister of Economic Warfare, was quoted as saying: 'We have got to organise movements in enemy occupied territory comparable to the Sinn Féin movements in Ireland'.[22]

SOE sent 470 agents into France during the Second World War: 118 did not return. Of the total 470, thirty-nine were female agents, thirteen of whom died in action.[23] Orion, meanwhile, lost only two of their eighteen full-time agents listed in the records at the Ministry of Defence. They were a young bunch; by the end of the war, all but four were still under twenty-four. The group also worked with about sixty other agents, all of whom it is believed survived.

Resistance groups supported and cultivated by the SOE needed to maintain wireless contact with their handlers, and this was often achieved with the help of specialist wireless operators. Without the wireless they had no means of coordinating their arms and ammunition drops, for onward delivery to the French Resistance for acts of sabotage. To relay intelligence back to London, they had to use radio transmitters. The wireless operator was always the agent's weakest point; the Germans kept a close watch on every wireless wavelength. It could take a team of armed direction finders as little as twenty minutes to get within a few yards of a radio operator.[24]

The Orion Group never used radio transmitters; Alain considered them too dangerous. They were bulky and heavy, so could not be disposed of quickly, which made them risky to use. Instead, he used couriers. Through their extensive native network, Orion agents passed their material from one to another and ultimately out of the country and into the hands of the British and US intelligence services. It was a slow process, admittedly. When, on occasion, speed was of the essence, they used transmitters belonging to the Resistance arm of the army – the Organisation de la résistance de l'armée. ORA members always handled the actual transmission, as Orion couriers weren't trained to use a radio transmitter. Orion's main instructions, given by d'Astier de la Vigerie, was to make contacts and obtain information which they thought might be useful to British intelligence and the Overseas Strategic Services, but this was a general guideline rather than a specific command, as may have been more common for SOE agents.

All Resistance agents in France during the period had to be on their guard for moles in the pay of the Gestapo or Vichy; there were roughly 2,500 German agents active in France, some 6,000 French agents, and an estimated 24,000 people informing on their friends, neighbours and colleagues.[25] Orion couriers didn't need to worry that the Germans would suspect they were not French, but otherwise they ran similar risks. The only protection they had was basic training in operating a pistol, but they rarely carried guns. Instead, Alain schooled them in the importance of simple rules – changing meeting places regularly, avoiding restaurants and bars, exercising due caution when meeting strangers, never giving away much about themselves. Most importantly, if an Orion courier ever felt he or she was in danger, they were to destroy immediately any intelligence they were carrying: the safety of each agent was more important than the intelligence they carried.

Andrée always said she knew nothing of SOE's existence until after the war; when she learnt of their work she felt she had been safer than them because she never went near a radio transmitter, a fear confirmed by Clare Mulley in her book about SOE agent Christine Granville, *The Spy Who Loved*: 'wireless operators had a life expectancy of only six weeks'. It is worth remembering, however, that Andrée served in the Resistance for the entire duration of the war, running a far greater risk of being picked up over the longer period. There was no set period for SOE agents – it depended on their mission, though Mulley says: 'France was one of the most dangerous theatres of war where few SOE agents were expected to last more than three months before being brought back to England if they had not already been caught'.

Andrée was always able to talk openly about her Resistance work, and her efforts were recognised by the French and US governments after the war. Yet her son's mother-in-law, Lady Meriel Howarth, née Brabazon, was not allowed to talk about the four years of work she did at Bletchley Park for many years after the war, as the thousands of people who had been employed at Bletchley were forbidden from discussing it. It has been hard for our family to accept that Andrée and Meriel's grandchildren will know much about what one grandmother achieved, but very little about the other's personal contribution.

# A Note on the French Resistance

In researching and writing this book, I have been struck by the complicated concept of 'the Resistance'. Despite being referred to as a single entity, it was never that straightforward. Andrée's story is one small part of a bigger web of many, many individuals, each determined to defend their country with countless acts of courage, large and small. With that in mind, I wanted to add a brief note (and by no means an exhaustive or definitive account) about the various spontaneous and individual forms of protest in occupied France, which later became collectively known as the Resistance.

A 2009 television documentary made by one of France's leading television channels showed how, a few days after the Germans invaded France, French men and women all over the country almost instantly began to carry out small acts of defiance against the occupying forces. There was no formal structure or organisation at this point – this was individuals using their own initiative, with no idea of what others elsewhere were up to. Without knowing it, these men and women became the founders of what would later become known as the Resistance movement.

Actions varied enormously, from small gestures such as ignoring a Wehrmacht soldier by crossing the road so as not to have to look at or acknowledge him (as Andrée records doing in her journal in Paris a few days after the city had been occupied) to small acts of sabotage such as putting sugar in the petrol of a Wehrmacht car or cutting down telephone wires. Some openly insulted German officers or soldiers while others gave cigarettes or food to prisoners of war. Members of the trade unions went on strike and people started creating false identity certificates. A form of passive resistance began to develop as men and women all over France observed neighbours or colleagues, but deliberately turned a blind eye to anything that might be related to resisting the Germans. As François Clerc, Orion's deputy leader, said: 'You might not go into work for three days but no one ever asked where you had been.'

In the early days of the occupation several groups of people started to produce anti-Nazi pamphlets and news-sheets, similar to Alain's *La France*, both to inform readers about non-censored information and to encourage them in turn to resist. After the protest on 11 November 1940, when 5,000 youngsters rallied at the Étoile to demonstrate against the occupation of their country, the Head of the Gestapo in Paris sent a note to Berlin on 12 December 1940 to inform them that: 'The French population is not under control.'

From his base in London, General Charles de Gaulle exhorted his country to resist and organised La France Libre – the Free French Resistance movement. Over time, larger groups emerged in France, such as Gilbert 'Rémy' Renault's Confrérie Notre-Dame, Marie Madeleine Fourcade's Alliance and Maurice Duclos's Saint-Jacques were born.

In December 1940, Georges Piron and Henri d'Astier de la Vigerie recruited Alain and Andrée into their Franco–Belgium resistance group. Piron had contacts with British intelligence from the First World War, and as early as June 1940 he was back in touch with the Resistance group St Jacques, run by Duclos. The following year, Alain Griotteray formed his own Resistance group, Orion, in April 1941.

Resistance groups spanned the political spectrum, from de Gaulle's conservatism to the involvement of the Communist and Socialist Parties, who became more prominent in the Resistance after Germany attacked Russia in June 1941. There were Jewish Resistance groups, German anti-Nazi groups, Italian anti-fascist groups and SOE (see the Epilogue). Once America joined the war, their Office of Strategic Services (then the OSS, today's CIA), established its presence in France in July 1942, recruiting its own agents despite the fact that France officially came under the domain of SOE. The Americans had been keen to sponsor traditional military resistance that avoided political entanglement, preferring the malleable General Giraud over the irascible General de Gaulle. In January 1943, the Organisation de la résistance de l'armée (the ORA) was formed, whose members Général Verneau and Capitaine Cogny were such a help to Orion.

In February 1943, German-enforced labour laws came into effect: those young Frenchmen determined to avoid the call-up escaped the country while others went underground and hid in the countryside, in forest cabins, caves and mountain refuge huts, fed by supportive locals. Pro-Communist refugees who had escaped Franco's Spain went underground and joined up with their French compatriots and together they began to create a network of guerillas and partisans: this was the foundation for what would become known as the Maquis. Towards 1944, they numbered over 25,000 members. Despite their significant contribution to the Resistance, the Maquis were at times not taken seriously by the Allies, who often thought of them as terrorists. Their support for the Allies during the Normandy landings, however, was invaluable; they helped delay the Germans bringing in reinforcements to fight the landing troops.

Frenchmen and women also helped save the lives of thousands of Jews. In 1940, France's Jewish population measured some 330,000: of those, over 75,000 died at the hands of the Nazis and/or the Vichy government. Many of the 255,000-plus survivors avoided capture because they were hidden in homes or on farms around the country. Thousands of Jewish children were smuggled into villages and subsequently schools. Some authorities may have been simply unaware of what was happening; in other parts, people turned a blind eye. Every man and woman who helped in this way was part of the French Resistance, regardless of intent: with such actions, they risked a great deal, often their own lives.

After the Allied landings in North Africa in November 1942, the Wehrmacht marched into the Free Zone and occupied the whole of France. Préfet of Chartres, Jean Moulin, later to be described as the head of the French Resistance, was worried about the existence of so many separate and autonomous Resistance groups. He travelled to London to discuss the situation with de Gaulle, suggesting to him that all the resistance groups should be brought under de Gaulle's leadership. Moulin believed that de Gaulle needed to be recognised as leader of the whole of the French Resistance – a movement which included the Maquis, Communists and

Socialists, the Forces françaises de l'interieur, and de Gaulle's Free French army in London. Both Moulin and de Gaulle were concerned that the liberation of France might provide the Communist Party with the opportunity to take over the Resistance movement, which in turn would threaten the US, which would then impose an American provisional military government of occupation until free elections could be held. De Gaulle was determined to avoid such an outcome at all costs.

In March 1943, Moulin set up a Coordination Committee to help the Resistance organise itself on a national scale: on 27 May Le Conseil national de la Résistance (the National Resistance Council) was formed. In June 1943, Moulin was caught and tortured by the Gestapo. He died while in custody, but his plan to unite the disparate Resistance groups into a strong and powerful movement was already developing.

Andrée always claimed that she and her friends knew nothing of Jean Moulin and the National Council until well after the end of the war. She often said that during the occupation she never heard of the Resistance, nor what it represented or meant. She knew de Gaulle was in London, listened to some of his broadcasts and was personally determined to do everything she could to 'resist' and humiliate the occupying forces in her country, but the concept of the Resistance, as far as she was concerned, only came into existence after the liberation. Similarly, François Clerc told me: 'we did not know this word Résistance'. The expression 'la résistance' only came into vogue after 1944.

At the end of the war, the French authorities officially recognised approximately 270 networks as 'les réseaux de résistance de la France combattante' or Resistance groups of the Free French. Each group had to provide details of its activities, name, purposes, numbers of members, and its dates of operation. The Ministry of Defence checked this information and then created a file for each group.

I have seen the file for the Orion Group, which includes the correspondence Alain Griotteray had with the armed forces at the end of the war as part of his bid for official recognition. At that time Alain was a captain in the French army and he recorded Orion as having eighteen agents. The Ministry of Defence's file records that each agent was integrated into the army in June 1944 as the liberation of Paris was about to take place. This was most likely part of a deliberate attempt to integrate Resistance members into the French army – headed, of course, by de Gaulle – to minimise the chance of the Communists taking control of the Resistance movement and thus potentially the whole country in due course.

In what was then a heavily male-dominated society, it is unsurprising that women generally played less of a role in the Resistance movement, making up some 15 to 20 per cent of all *résistants*. Only one woman was ever recognised as the leader of a Resistance group: Marie Madeleine Fourcade, head of the réseau Alliance. Of the eighteen official agents registered as members of Orion, only two were women (Andrée Griotteray White and Margit Ehrart Hutton), though others did contribute.

After the war, 250,000 *cartes de combattants* were issued. These testified that the bearer had been an official member of a recognised Resistance group, although many fighters joined up only after the Normandy landings in June 1944. The total number of 250,000 may well have been exaggerated – with many saying they were involved in Resistance activity despite having done nothing – but de Gaulle was on a mission to revitalise and heal France, and was perhaps inclined to be generous.

Between 7 January 1944 and 31 March 1945, over 45,000 Médailles de la Résistance were awarded (15,000 posthumously). The black and red ribbon each medal hung from was a reminder of the grief France suffered and the blood spilt on her behalf during the Second World War. Despite France's humiliation and all that the people suffered during the occupation, it was perhaps through the achievements of the Resistance movement that France was able to find her honour and her pride again.

# Bibliography and Sources

I would like to express my great appreciation to Alain Gandy for his extremely useful book *La jeunesse et la Résistance: réseau Orion, 1940–1944*. Much of what he says I had already learnt about through conversations with my mother, my uncle Alain and Yves de Kermoal, but his book helped me confirm the memories of conversations which took place many years ago.

Jean-Marc Berlière's book *Les policiers français sous l'Occupation* has been a very useful source in helping me understand some of the work my mother was doing at Police Headquarters throughout the war.

My uncle's book, *1940: Qui étaient les premiers résistants?*, and his memoirs, have also helped reconfirm the conversations I had with him over the years – during which he sometimes got quite annoyed at my lack of understanding of what they had all been up to.

I am enormously grateful to Matthew Cobb for *The Resistance* and *Eleven Days in August*, both of which helped me understand better the circumstances in which my mother and her family lived during the Second World War.

Adler, Laure, *Marguerite Duras: A Life* (Phoenix, 2001).

Amoureux, Henri, *Quarante millions de pétainistes, Juin 1940–Juin 1941*, (Robert Laffont, 1977).

Beevor, Anthony and Cooper, Artemis, *Paris After The Liberation* (Hamish Hamilton, 1994).

Berlière, Jean-Marc, *Les policiers français sous l'Occupation* (Éditions Perrin, 2001).

Berr, Hélène, *Journal*, (MacLehose Press, 2009).

Bailey, Rosemary, *Love and War in the Pyrenees* (Phoenix, 2008).

Burns, Michael, *Dreyfus: A Family Affair* (Harper Collins, 1991)

Cobb, Matthew, *Eleven Days in August* (Simon & Shuster, 2013).

Cobb, Matthew, *The Resistance* (Pocket Books, 2010).

de Chambrun, René, *Pierre Laval devant l'histoire* (Éditions France-Empire, 1983).

du Jonchay, R. (dir.), *The Sorrow and the Pity* (Arrow Films, 2004).

Fenby, Jonathan, *The General: Charles de Gaulle and the France He Saved* (Simon & Shuster 2011).

Foot, M. R. D., *SOE: The Special Operations Executive 1940–46* (Pimlico, 1999).

Gandy, Alain, *La jeunesse et la Résistance: réseau Orion, 1940–1944* (Presses de la Cité, 1992).

Griotteray, Alain, *1940: La naissance de la résistance* (Fernand Lanore, 2008).

Griotteray, Alain, *1940: Qui étaient les premiers résistants?* (L'Age d'homme, 1999).

Griotteray, Alain, *Mémoires* (Éditions du Rocher, 2004).

Harris Smith, Richard, *OSS: Secret History of America's First Central Intelligence Agency* (University of California Press, 1972).

Hastings, Max, *All Hell Let Loose* (HarperPress, 2012).

Hourmilougué, André, *Liberté, Liberté* (self published, 2009).

Humbert, Agnes, *Resistance* (Bloomsbury, 2009).

Jobelot, Jean-Pierre, *Henri d'Astier de la Vigerie, 1897–1952* (NSA Bastille, 2008).

Joly, Laurent, *L'antisémitisme de bureau* (Grasset & Fasquelles, 2011).

Kladstrup, Don and Kladstrup, Petie, *Wine and War* (Hodder, 2002).

Longuet, Stéphane and Genet-Rouffiac, Nathalie, *Les réseaux de Résistance de la France combattante* (Economica, 2013).

Lormier, Dominique, *La Gestapo et les Français* (Pygmalion, 2013).

Masson, Madeleine, *Christine* (Hamish Hamilton, 1975).

Mulley, Clare, *The Spy Who Loved* (Macmillan, 2012).

Némirovsky, Irène, *Suite Française* (Denoël, 2004).

Norwich, John Julius (ed), *The Duff Cooper Diaries* (Weidenfeld & Nicolson, 2005).

Schoenbrun, David, *Soldiers of the Night* (Robert Hale, 1981).

Shakespeare, Nicholas, *Priscilla* (Harvill Secker, 2013).

Tcheky, Keryo and Nick, Cristophe (dirs.), *La résistance* (France Télévisions Distribution, 2008).

Williams, Charles, *The Last Great Frenchman* (Little Brown, 1993).

Williams, Charles, *Pétain* (Little Brown, 2005).

# Notes

1. Matthew Cobb, *The Resistance* (Pocket Books, 2010), page 18.

2. http://www.theguardian.com/century/1940-1949/Story/0,,128218,00.html

3. Cobb, *The Resistance*, page 43.

4. Cobb, *The Resistance*, page 44.

5. Cobb, *The Resistance*, page 45.

6. Alain Griotteray, *Mémoires* (Éditions du Rocher, 2004), page 32.

7. Alain Griotteray, *Qui étaient les premiers résistants?* (L'Age d'homme, 1999), page 206.

8. Griotteray, *Mémoires*, page 32.

9. Gandy, *La jeunesse et la Résistance*, page 38.

10. Cobb, *The Resistance*, page 144.

11. Alain Gandy, *La jeunesse et la Résistance: réseau Orion, 1940–1944* (Presses de la Cité, 1992), *page 88.*

12. Gandy, *La jeunesse et la Résistance*.

13. Gandy, *La jeunesse et la Résistance*, page 127.

14. Gandy, *La jeunesse et la Résistance*, page 106.

15. Griotteray, *Mémoires*, page 60.

16. Gandy, *La jeunesse et la Résistance*.

17. Gandy, *La jeunesse et la Résistance*, page 148.

18. Gandy, *La jeunesse et la Résistance*.

19. Griotteray, *Les premiérs résistants*, page 247.

20. Matthew Cobb, *Eleven Days in August*, page 319.

21. Griotteray, *Les premiérs résistants*.

22. M. R. D. Foot, *SOE: The Special Operations Executive 1940–46* (Pimlico, 1999), page 18.

23. Foot, *SOE*, page 73.

24. Foot, *SOE*, page 150.

25. Dominique Lormier, *La Gestapo et les Français* (Pygmalion, 2013).

# *Acknowledgements*

I would like to thank my husband Martin for his enormous encouragement, my son Alexander and my daughter Chantal for their continual support and interest from the conception of this project until its end, and also my close friend Jill Burton, whose good humour and technological prowess helped this book make its way to my publisher's desk.

*Andrée's War* could not have been written without the long interviews I had with François Clerc and le comte Yves de Kermoal, both members of the Orion Resistance group, who shared with me many memories of their exploits in occupied France and to whom I am greatly indebted.

I am grateful to my grandmother, my mother, my aunt and my uncle for telling me so many stories about the French Resistance from an early age, and also to Alain for the various Resistance reunions he organised between 1985 and 2000, many of which I was able to attend and where I learned so much.

I want to thank my brother, Patrick, for giving me our mother's diaries and journals, from which I have quoted liberally, and I hope our mother will forgive me for publishing what was written, at the time, as a private record of her life in Paris during the years of its occupation.

La comtesse Patricia de Kermoal has provided much support in explaining the small details of some of the issues described in the story and I have warm and lasting memories of our stay at the Domaine de Rateau with her and her husband Yves.

I am grateful to Jean Pierre Jobelot, grandson of Henri d'Astier de la Vigerie, for his tireless checking and rechecking of my version of the political events unfolding in French North Africa in 1942 and 1943, in which his grandfather played such an important part.

I thank Frau Elke Jeanrond-Premauer for her warm welcome when I stayed at the Château d'Orion and for introducing me to Madame Jean (Marguerite) Labbé, who was a source of much information (passed on to her by her mother-in-law Madame Marie Labbé) about the events in the area surrounding the château in the early 1940s.

I spent many hours with my neighbour and friend in Ramatuelle, Madame Jeanine Nouveau, who told me about life in Paris during the Second World War, including her participation in the city's exodus as the Germans arrived in the city in 1940. Jeanine's unstinting interest in my book encouraged me to ask her questions I had never dared ask my mother or my uncle.

Jean Paul Gay checked many historical points and Irina Hands explained and translated several words and German expressions used at the time.

Dr Garry Savin checked my description of the symptoms of scarlet fever and André de Clermont explained the term Louis d'or.

Clyde Kent of Eos Operating Systems Ltd helped me fix any technical difficulties I had in recording my interviews and Erica Donnellan reread the whole manuscript several times at different stages; I would like to thank her for her ongoing encouragement and support.

Sarah Burton, my tutor on the life writing course I attended at the University of Oxford department for continuing education, encouraged me to tell my story in writing. And I would also like to thank the Society of Authors for reviewing my contract.

I would like to thank the Service Historique de la Défence for sourcing copies of the information registered by Alain Griotteray and the Centre des Archives du Personnel Militaire in Pau for obtaining copies of the certificates relating to the medals awarded to several members of the Orion group. The staff of the Service des Archives of the Préfecture de Police in Paris, the Mémorial de la Shoah and of the Musée du Général Leclerc de Hautecloque et de la Libération de Paris-Musée Jean Moulin were all very helpful with my numerous enquiries.

It is difficult to know how to thank my editor Olivia Bays for helping me turn a fascinating story into such a readable, understandable and enjoyable one.

# Index

...rtout mettre un mot ce
...oi c'est plus naturel.
...uand les sentiments sont
...is sur le vif.
Peut-être demain matin
...ous reveillerons nous sous
... regime allemand. Moi je
...ange autant de gateaux
... [que] je peux pendant qu'il
... en a encore —

Well Bouton — Je vais
prendre mon allemand que
malheur de l'avoir laissé
tombé. Cela me servirait
maintenant !!!!


Ce Vendredi 14.
...ournée memorable dont je me
...uviendrai toute ma vie
...eme si elle est longue.
D'abord premier coup au cœur